The Global South after the Crisis

The Global South after the Crisis

Growth, Inequality and Development in the
Aftermath of the Great Recession

Edited by

Hasan Cömert

Assistant Professor, Middle East Technical University, Turkey

Rex A. McKenzie

Lecturer, Kingston University, UK

Edward Elgar
PUBLISHING

Cheltenham, UK • Northampton, MA, USA

Published by
Edward Elgar Publishing Limited
The Lypiatts
15 Lansdown Road
Cheltenham
Glos GL50 2JA
UK

Edward Elgar Publishing, Inc.
William Pratt House
9 Dewey Court
Northampton
Massachusetts 01060
USA

A catalogue record for this book
is available from the British Library

Library of Congress Control Number: 2016931791

This book is available electronically in the **Elgar**online
Economics subject collection
DOI 10.4337/9781783474318

ISBN 978 1 78347 430 1 (cased)
ISBN 978 1 78347 431 8 (eBook)

Typeset by Servis Filmsetting Ltd, Stockport, Cheshire
Printed and bound in Great Britain by TJ International Ltd, Padstow

Contents

Contributors

Serdal Bahçe is an Associate Professor at the Department of Public Finance of Ankara University. He obtained his BSc degree from the Department of Computer Engineering at Middle East Technical University in 1994. He completed the Master's program and PhD at the Department of Economics in the same university in 1998 and 2003 respectively.

Ahmet Benlialper is currently conducting PhD studies at Middle East Technical University (METU). He obtained his Bachelor's degree from Bilkent University, Department of Mathematics and completed an MSc at the Department of Economics at METU. Since 2013 he has also worked as a research assistant in Ipek University, Department of Economics.

Hasan Cömert is an Assistant Professor of Economics in the Department of Economics at Middle East Technical University (METU), Turkey. Cömert received his PhD from the University of Massachusetts at Amherst in 2011. His research interests include central banking, financial markets, financial flows, developing countries and the Turkish economy. Among other publications, he is the author of *Central Banks and Financial Markets: The Declining Power of US Monetary Policy* (Edward Elgar Publishing, 2013). He has contributed to different working packages in the FESSUD project as a researcher.

Mehmet Selman Çolak is a PhD student in Economics at Middle East Technical University (METU), Turkey. He holds an MSc in Economics at the same institution. He is also a former research assistant in Economics at METU. He obtained a Bachelor's degree in Economics from Bilkent University, Ankara.

Orlando Justo (PhD in Economics, New School for Social Research, New York, 2013) is an Assistant Professor in the Department of Business Management at BMCC/City University of New York. His research works and publications have focused on topics in international economics and business, particularly within Latin America and transitional economies.

Ahmet Haşim Köse is a Professor at the Department of Economics, Ankara University, Turkey. His research interests are political economy and development economics. He has published books and articles on political economy of Turkey, labor markets and income distributions. He co-authored a book with Fikret Şenses and Erinç Yeldan; *Neoliberal Globalization as New Imperialism: Case Studies on Reconstruction of the Periphery* (Nova Publishers, 2007).

Rex A. McKenzie was trained at the New School for Social Research in New York, USA. His 2006 PhD thesis was entitled 'Three essays in the political economy of the English speaking Caribbean'. He has held Lecturer, Assistant Professor and Senior Researcher posts in Economics at the University of Technology, Kingston Jamaica, Purchase College, SUNY, New York, USA and the University of Witwatersrand, Johannesburg, South Africa. He has four main research interests: political economy of development, political economy of finance, political economy of small island states and the history of economic thought.

Andre de Melo Modenesi is an Associate Professor at the Institute of Economics of the Universidade Federal do Rio de Janeiro (IE/UFRJ) and researcher at the CNPq. He holds a PhD in Economics (UFRJ), a Master's of Arts in Economics (Universidade Federal Fluminense), and Bachelor's degrees in Economics (Pontifícia Universidade Católica do Rio de Janeiro) and in Social Sciences (Universidade do Estado do Rio de Janeiro).

Rui Lyrio Modenesi is a former Under Secretary of Economic Policy of the Ministry of Finance, was Head of Department at the Brazilian Development Bank, and Associate Professor at the Fluminense Federal University. He was also Under Secretary of the Commission on Tariff Policy, Minister of Finance, and Senior Researcher at the Instituto de Política Econômica Aplicada (IPEA). He holds a Master's degree in Economics (Fundação Getúlio Vargas) and a Bachelor's degree in Economics and Law.

Shankaran Nambiar is a Senior Research Fellow at the Malaysian Institute of Economic Research. He has been a consultant for the Ministries of Finance, International Trade and Industry, and Domestic Trade and Consumer Affairs as well as for multilateral organizations such as UNECLAC, UNESCAP, ILO, ADBI and the ASEAN Secretariat. He has also been a visiting scholar with the IMF. He holds Bachelor's and Master's degrees in Economics from the Universities of Madras and Delhi, respectively. He obtained his PhD in Economics from Universiti Sains Malaysia.

Marcos Reis is an Associate Professor of Economics at the National Institute of Higher Studies (IAEN), Ecuador. He is also a senior econo-mist at the Center for Strategic Foresight (CEPROEC) at the same institution. He holds a PhD in Economics from the Federal University of Rio de Janeiro (UFRJ) and was a visiting scholar at the Institute of Latin American Studies (ILAS) at Columbia University.

Juan E. Santarcángelo is a researcher of the Consejo Nacional de Investigaciones Económicas y Técnicas (CONICET) and a professor at the Universidad Nacional de Quilmes in Buenos Aires, Argentina.

Esra Nur Uğurlu is a Master's student in International Economics in the EPOG (Economic Policies in the Age of Globalisation) program. During the program, she has been based in the Berlin School of Economics and Law and Université of Paris 13. She obtained Bachelor's degree in Economics from Middle East Technical University, Turkey.

Acknowledgements

This book would not have been possible without the support and encouragement of my wife, Duygu, my mother Satıa, my father Mustafa and my elder sister Söngül. I am very grateful to Professor Gerald Epstein and Emeritus Professor Jim Croty for their support and encouragement throughout my career. I am indebted to my colleagues at METU for providing me with a very friendly atmosphere in which to work on this book.

Hasan Cömert

I would like to thank my teachers who have over many years and at all stages furnished me with decisive frames of reference. I owe them all an intellectual debt of gratitude that can never be repaid. I would also like to thank colleagues Paul Auerbach and Gary Dymski for their general encouragement and willingness to engage with ideas from different constituencies. The publishing of this book happens to coincide with the tragic loss of Professor Sam Moyo. Sam was the Editor of the influential *International Journal of Agrarian Studies* and the Director of the African Institute of Agrarian Studies which he founded himself. My part in this book is in memory of Sam.

Rex A. McKenzie

Introduction

The world witnessed one of the worst crises in its history in 2008–9. In the advanced world the crisis was transmitted from country to country via several channels. Although many developing countries weathered the crisis well enough, the effects in the developing world were transmitted in an uneven manner. In the aftermath of the crisis when this book was conceived, there was an outpouring of papers and studies as to its effects on the advanced capitalist countries. We set out to study the crisis in the rest of the world. In this book, we focus on a selected group of countries, and investigate the implications of the recent crisis for the developing world. The book brings these individual case studies together and focuses on the general implications of the crisis in developing countries. We believe that the general findings of this book are relevant not only for a few countries but also to the global south in general. The book is entitled *The Global South after the Crisis*. The global south refers to the developing world in its entirety and includes those countries in Central and Eastern Europe formerly in the Soviet Union's sphere of influence. Geographically they lie in the North Atlantic, but their *dependency* on the world system has more in common with Latin America, Asia and Africa than any of the OECD countries. The book consists of two main parts. Part I is thematic and is made up of four chapters; Chapter 1 concentrates on the impact of the crisis on the worst affected countries. Chapter 2 details the changes in income inequality trends across a heterogeneous group of developing countries. Chapter 3 is on monetary transmission in Africa with a specific focus on the aftermath of the crisis and Chapter 4 details the policy responses and policy shifts in key areas of central banking in the developing world. Part II, Chapters 5 to 8, consists of four country case studies: Bolivia, Brazil, Malaysia and Turkey.

The general and somewhat surprising story is that in the global south, the crisis was not a crisis. Although output was lost during the period, most of the developing world continued growing (albeit at slower rates), and continued increasing its share in world output. In addition, as Bahçe and Köse show, the worsening income distribution that characterized the advanced world is largely absent in the global south context.

However, as many of the chapters in this book demonstrate, the hetero-geneity among developing countries in their ability to cope with the crisis is often disregarded. Indeed, some countries were severely affected, more so than many advanced countries. The overall evidence shows that where the crisis did take effect, the trade channel was the most important mechanism in the transmission of the crisis from advanced economies to the rest of the world. The first chapter investigating the cases of the worst affected countries supports this observation for the 15 worst affected countries. According to this chapter, the limited trade partners and the specificity of these countries' exports were the main reasons behind the intensity of the crisis in these countries. In other words, the dependency on the limited number of trade partners and the dependency on the foreign demand for a specific group of undiversified products account for the intensity of the crisis in the worst affected countries. These countries faced a very sharp contraction in their export growths since they either produced and exported manufactured goods or commodities with high income elasticity to the US or the European markets which were the epicenters of the crisis. The chapters on Turkey, Malaysia, Bolivia and African countries verify this claim. Although the crises of the 1980s and 1990s highlighted the fra-gilities of the global south with respect to financial flows, the limitations of export-led growth and reliance on commodity exports become apparent in the recent case. Malaysia is a perfect example of the countries which based their growth strategy on high exports. Nambiar argues that the export growth strategy might have reached its limit in Malaysia. For the Bolivian case Justo and Santarcángelo maintain that the movements of commod-ity prices hang over the head of Bolivia like a Damoclean sword. Bolivia's growth is very much bound up with the state of the commodity super cycle. According to the authors, the quick rebound in commodity prices meant that the Bolivian economy recovered very quickly. The crisis was short-lived but because of its dependency on commodity prices Bolivia remains susceptible to any crisis that drives down commodity prices.

During the earlier crisis, financial reversals were rare events in the developing world. In general and as expected those countries experiencing financial reversals or sudden stops were among the most affected coun-tries. What is common among these countries is, as Cömert and Ugurlu show, that they had also accumulated important vulnerabilities such as large current account deficits, domestic currency appreciation and high credit growth in the preceding period. However, as stated above, financial reversals were generally absent, even the severely affected countries were not faced with financial reversals during the crisis. Among the case studies, there is no country experiencing financial reversals. Making a detailed comparison of the financial shocks the Turkish economy experienced in the last two decades Cömert and Çolak demonstrate that the recent financial shock to the economy was short in duration and low in magnitude relative to the previous crises. The increasing liquidity in international markets and very low interest rates in advanced countries that ensued after the crisis helped to reduce the magnitude and duration of financial shock and supported fast recoveries in the global south. They argue that developing countries might not have tested during the global crisis due to the fact that the epicenter of the crisis was among the advanced countries. Given the fact that the international financial architecture and domestic structure of many developing countries have not gone through a significant transformation since 2008, developing countries may not avoid significant downturns in case of bigger shocks hitting their economies in the future. It is the uneven degree of integration of the developing countries to the world system that accounts for the uneven impact of the crisis across the developing world. Generally the countries in the global south experienced temporary slowdowns in GDP that recovered quite quickly. The countries most dependent on trade with the EU and US were the ones that suffered the most. McKenzie's review of continental Africa's experience of the crisis (Chapter 4) illustrates the point. He finds that that Africa's relatively loose integration into the world system shielded its economies from the worst vicissitudes of the downturn. As a result, although the financial and trade globalization may bring some benefits to the global south, this process seems to be making them much more vulnerable to global cycles.

We find that fiscal and monetary policy seem to have played important roles in weathering the crisis. On the one hand, as Cömert and Ugurlu document in Chapter 1, in the most affected countries there was an unwillingness or inability to initiate countercyclical policy that may have mitigated the more deleterious effects of the crisis. For example, the conditionalities imposed on those CIS countries seeking to join the EU more or less ruled out countercyclical policy responses to the crisis. The case study on Turkey (Chapter 8) shows that the Turkish government has been very hesitant in taking fiscal measures, which partially explains the severity of the crisis in this country. Indeed, Cömert and Çolak argue that Turkish government fiscal expansion was one of the lowest among comparable countries. On the other hand, the Brazilian, Bolivian and Malaysian authorities adopted significant fiscal policy measures in order to mitigate the crisis. These measures enabled them to stave off the worst effects of the crisis. Reis et al. in Chapter 6 maintain that the active fiscal intervention of the Brazilian government was one of the reasons behind the relatively good performance of the country during the crisis. Among these countries, Bolivia seems to have embarked on relatively more aggressive fiscal expansion (see Chapter 5).

With respect to monetary policy, central banking in the global south has evolved in response to the crisis. Theoretically and practically a new consensus that sees inflation targeting as one of many (and not the only) objectives seems to be emerging. For example, Reis et al. show that although the Brazilian central bank was relatively conservative in its response to the crisis at the beginning, it gradually moved away from inflation targeting and is now more concerned with other macroeconomic variables. In many developing countries, financial stability has become more important and many new instruments have been introduced alongside short term interest rates to give more flexibility to monetary policy management which now has multiple aims.

Chapter 4 on the monetary transmission mechanism in Africa looks back to the crisis in order to ask how the foremost political economy and macroeconomic trends have affected the mechanism. Because of the paucity of research in this area answers are sought in a review of the official literature on the subject. That literature is extensive and exhaustive as far as it goes. But the recent recalibration of GDP statistics by countries in Africa points to the need for a monetary policy that targets employment alongside the longstanding fixation on price stability. Benlialper and Cömert (Chapter 3) point out that the shift in emphasis in central banking in developing countries is not addressing these real concerns. The case of Brazil where the central bank now has multiple targets combined with the new consensus (described above) offers the hope and promise that we may yet develop an international financial architecture that protects us all from the destabilizing effects of monetary shocks and crisis.

In many developing countries concerns about the implications of financial flows are being raised. But at the time of writing there has not been a genuine attempt to address these problems. In the existence of massive financial flows, the effectiveness of monetary policy is likely to diminish as external finance substitutes for domestic funding, and financial flows directly affect the main macroeconomic variables such as credit growth and exchange rates. Although some countries such as Brazil have actively started using some capital control measures, the effectiveness of these measures has not yet been established. Furthermore, some countries like Turkey are still relying on very indirect methods to tackle destabilising financial flows. Overall, in the absence of a rethinking of the international financial architecture in advanced countries, countries of the global south are to a greater or lesser degree vulnerable to financial shocks coming from the advanced countries. The degree of vulnerability remains dependent upon the degree of integration into the world economy.

PART I

Growth, inequality and policy responses

1. The impacts of the 2008 global financial crisis on developing countries: the case of the 15 most affected countries[1]

Hasan Cömert and Esra Nur Uğurlu

1.1 INTRODUCTION

The financial crisis that originated in the US subprime mortgage market in 2007 to 2008 spread quickly to the rest of the world and became a global crisis affecting both real economic and financial activities in virtually all countries in the world. There has been a growing literature on the impacts of the crisis on different economies. Among these studies, the popular perception regarding developing countries is that they weathered the crisis relatively well. Although this point is widely recognized in the literature,[2] the heterogeneity among developing countries in their ability to cope with the crisis is often disregarded. In this vein, some countries experienced significant slowdowns comparable to, or even larger than, those in advanced economies. There have been some attempts to explain the heterogeneous effects of the crisis on different developing countries.[3] However, the existing literature on cross country differences is limited and fails to draw consistent conclusions. Many of them do not pay enough attention to the country selection procedures and country specific factors. Furthermore, these studies, in general, focus solely on econometric analysis. Although econometric methods may be useful for different purposes, they may also downplay the complex process of the events leading to the crisis.

In this study, we focus on 15 countries that were affected by the crisis most severely. These countries are Armenia, Botswana, Bulgaria, Croatia, Hungary, Kuwait, Latvia, Lithuania, Mexico, Moldova, Paraguay, Russia, Romania, Turkey and Ukraine. We utilize an event analysis in order to capture the dynamic process behind the relatively bad performance of these countries. Our aim is twofold: first, we explore the transmission mechanisms through which the recent global crisis affected these countries.

Second, we attempt to reveal the common characteristics of these countries that made them more vulnerable to the crisis.[4,5]

There is always some arbitrariness in selecting a set of countries on which to conduct comparable and meaningful research. Here, we attempt to overcome this problem by only focusing on relatively big countries hit hardest by the crisis in terms of GDP growth. To this end, all countries were first ranked according to the IMF specification in terms of GDP growth rates in 2009.[6] Then 15 relatively big countries with the lowest growth rates were selected. Since very small economies experience very frequent fluctuations, we excluded some very small island countries such as Grenada, Montenegro, Antigua and Barbuda, the Bahamas, Samoa, Solomon Islands, Trinidad and Tobago, St Kitts and Nevis, Madagascar and Barbados from our sample.[7] In this way, we are able to focus on countries with significant economic scale and population size.[8]

The main findings of this study are as follows. First, the overall evidence shows that the trade channel was the most important mechanism in the transmission of the crisis from advanced economies to the countries under investigation. The degree of openness, the geographical concentration and the composition of export products were important factors contributing to the deterioration of the export performances in these countries. Countries that we selected were particularly affected by the contraction in global demand because of limited trade partners and products that they export. More specifically, they faced very sharp contraction in their export growths since they either produced manufactured goods with high income elasticity, exporting them to the US or the European markets, which were the epicenters of the crisis, or they were commodity exporters. Second, the role of the financial channel varied in different countries. Some countries encountered massive financial reversals while others experienced varying degrees of financial stops. In general, as expected, the most affected countries in our set are the ones that experienced both a dramatic decline in their exports and financial reversals. Third, although the countries under investigation experienced high growth rates before the crisis, they also accumulated significant vulnerabilities in the same period, which were mainly related to the structural problems of the integration of these countries into the world economy. In this vein, many of these vulnerabilities were related to massive financial flows, which went hand in hand with exchange rate appreciation, decreasing competitiveness, domestic (especially private sector debt) and foreign indebtedness, and high current account deficits. Fourth, the majority of countries under investigation were either unwilling or constrained in their ability to conduct countercyclical monetary and fiscal policies. In terms of monetary policies, early and significant reductions in policy rates were not realized. In terms of fiscal measures, there was limited fiscal space and, in the case of the transition countries trying to join the EU, entry requirements limited the ability of these countries to take countercyclical measures. As a result, these countries could not mitigate the effects of the crisis by using expansionary policies.

The organization of the rest of the chapter is as follows. In the second section, the general performance of countries in the pre-crisis period is discussed. The third section focuses on the impact of the crisis on the 15 selected countries. The fourth section investigates the policies taken by the countries under investigation in response to the crisis. The last section concludes.

1.2 PERFORMANCES OF THE DEVELOPING COUNTRIES PRIOR TO THE GLOBAL CRISIS

After getting over the global downturn in 2001, developing countries as a group entered the new millennium in a much better economic environment than they did in the previous two decades and experienced historically high rates of growth. From 2002 until 2007, developing countries grew on average at 7.16 percent. In this sense, the overall performance of these countries was better than the advanced countries (Table 1.1).

Although almost all developing countries experienced positive GDP growth rates during this period, it masks the vastly different growth patterns of individual economies over the last several decades. For example, countries from developing Asia and the Commonwealth of Independent States (CIS)[9] experienced the largest output increase. On the other hand, growth rates were lower in Central and Eastern European countries (CEE)[10] and more volatile in Latin America, the Middle East and sub-Saharan Africa regions (Table 1.1).

Some changes in economic policies in developing countries might have played a role in the acceleration of growth in the pre-crisis period. However, the exceptional growth performance of countries was significantly related to the positive global outlook after 2001.[11] In general, the growth was fueled by a mix of four ingredients: (1) high global demand, (2) exceptional financing, (3) high commodity prices and (4) for a significant number of countries, large flows of remittances mainly resulting from the consumption and property bubbles in the advanced economies (Griffith-Jones and Ocampo, 2009). In other words, policies implemented in advanced economies created a favorable environment for all countries in trade activities, financial flows and commodity prices until the outbreak of the financial crisis.

After 2001, advanced economies started to pursue expansionary

Table 1.1   GDP growth of different groups of countries before and during the crisis (percentage change)

	1990–2001 average	2002–7 average	2008	2009
World	3.15	4.48	2.69	−0.38
Advanced Economies	2.77	2.60	0.1	−3.43
European Union	2.31	2.53	0.58	−4.41
Emerging Market and Developing Economies	3.85	7.16	5.84	3.09
Central and Eastern Europe	1.85	5.70	3.16	−3.61
Commonwealth of Independent States	−1.61	7.60	5.34	−6.44
Developing Asia	7.19	9.22	7.32	7.70
Latin America and the Caribbean	2.82	4.08	4.23	−1.22
Middle East and North Africa	4.34	6.24	5.04	2.99
Low Income	2.80	5.36	5.49	5.23
Lower Middle Income	3.41	6.69	4.48	4.99
Middle Income	3.88	6.82	5.56	3.10
Upper Middle Income	4.03	6.86	5.87	2.56
High Income	2.50	2.69	0.36	−3.56

Source: IMF, WEO, October 2013 and World Development Indicators.

monetary policies. In the US, policymakers decided to use monetary expansion in order to minimize the depth and the duration of the crisis arising from the bursting of the US high tech bubble in 2000 and the September 11 attacks of 2001. In Japan and in Europe the Central Banks brought the interest rates down to unusually low levels in order to break out of deflationary spirals. More importantly, financial innovations and many other institutional changes taking place in the US and advanced countries enabled financial firms in the center to expand their balance sheets almost limitlessly (Cömert, 2013). Given increased financial openness, financial account liberalization and ease of conducting financial activities, financial capital started to flow into emerging market countries with higher returns. In this process, due to significantly improved risk appetite, the spreads between the emerging market debt instruments and advanced countries decreased, which resulted in a sharp decline in the cost of external financing for developing countries (Akyüz, 2012). In other words, many developing countries were able to take advantage of abundant and cheap borrowing opportunities from the rest of the world.

The growth of exports and improvements in current account balances in the Global South were also significantly affected by the developments in the advanced countries. The high US consumption and corresponding current account deficits gained momentum in the 2000s as US financial institutions generated massive cheap credits. The growing external deficit of the US led to improvements in the current accounts of its trade partners, the majority of which were developing countries from the Global South.[12] In this way, the US acted as a locomotive for the rapid expansion of export growth in developing countries. Although smaller in size when compared to the US, the European Union and the UK were also running current account deficits in the pre-crisis period. Furthermore, the high growth performance of China and India together with some other BRIC countries such as Brazil generated extra demand for many raw materials and goods of other developing countries. In relation to these developments, improvements in the current account balances of developing countries were further enhanced by rises in commodity prices.[13]

Countries in the South also enjoyed a rapid growth of workers' remittances. In middle income and upper middle income countries remittances amounted to 1.93 and 1.10 percent of GDP respectively. The increase in remittances particularly in India, Mexico, Indonesia, China and Moldova brought about considerable improvements in the current account balances.

Although positive shocks from advanced economies played a major role in shaping the growth performances of many of these countries, some macroeconomic policies may also have had a positive impact on this process (Bibow, 2010). Many country governments in the South conducted macroeconomic reforms mainly aimed at reducing inflation and strengthening their public finance positions and financial markets in the beginning of the 2000s.[14] Overall, many developing countries achieved lower inflation rates, better public debt indicators and, in some cases, healthier banking systems relative to those in the 1980s and 1990s. However, interestingly, these were not independent of the positive global outlook and the massive financial flows to the emerging market countries. Domestic currency appreciation improved the debt to GDP ratio in many cases due to the fact that an important part of total debt in developing countries is denominated in foreign currencies whereas GDP is measured in local currency.[15] High financial flows going hand in hand with local currency appreciation may also improve the balance sheets of financial institutions by decreasing the value of foreign liabilities in domestic currency. Moreover, a positive global outlook stimulating high growth may increase tax revenues, which may contribute to the improvement in public balance in developing countries. Last but not least, currency appreciations related to high financial flows served as anchors to inflation in many developing countries (Benlialper and Cömert, 2013).

Overall, thanks to global outlook and some policy measures, while the Global South enjoyed high growth rates and some positive macroeconomic trends, important vulnerabilities started to be formed in this period as well. As we will discuss in the following sections, this pattern is very apparent in the countries in our set.

1.2.1   Performances of Developing Countries in 2009

The financial crisis that began in the advanced countries in 2008 spread all around the world through different channels. In this environment, the Global South could not sustain its high growth performances. However, overall, the South was affected to varying degrees by the crisis. In Table 1.2, the 15 most affected countries are listed. It is observed that growth rates in these countries fell significantly in 2009 compared to the previous years. Also, their economic performance was far lower than both the world average (−0.3 percent) and the developing economies' average (3.1 percent). In our sample, four countries experienced a more than 14 percent decline in their GDP in 2009 and the other 11 countries were faced with negative growth rates ranging from about 4 percent to 8 percent.

Table 1.2   Countries most severely affected by the global crisis

	2002–6 average	2007	2008	2009
Latvia	8.99	9.6	−3.27	−17.72
Lithuania	8.01	9.79	2.91	−14.84
Ukraine	7.44	7.6	2.3	−14.8
Armenia	13.32	13.74	6.94	−14.15
Botswana	5.18	8.68	3.90	−7.84
Russia	7.03	8.53	5.24	−7.8
Kuwait	9.74	5.99	2.48	−7.07
Croatia	4.71	5.06	2.08	−6.94
Hungary	4.20	0.11	0.89	−6.76
Romania	6.16	6.31	7.34	−6.57
Moldova	6.80	2.99	7.8	−6
Bulgaria	5.95	6.44	6.19	−5.47
Turkey	7.21	4.66	0.65	−4.82
Mexico	2.76	3.13	1.21	−4.52
Paraguay	3.83	5.422	6.35	−3.96
Developing Countries	6.86	8.701	5.87	3.11
World	4.31	5.348	2.705	−0.381

Source: IMF, WEO, October 2013.

Table 1.3   The magnitude of trade and financial shock

Countries	Trade Channel		Financial Channel		
	Export of Goods (% Growth) (average 2006–8)	Export of Goods (% Growth in 2009)	Financial Account/ GDP (average 2002–8)	Financial Account/ GDP (average 2005–8)	Financial Account/ GDP in 2009
Latvia	24.12	−22.58	13.57	20.28	−6.97
Lithuania	27.65	−31.35	7.97	12.31	−7.09
Ukraine	25.63	−41.23		7.19	−9.31
Armenia	3.87	−32.67		7.41	16.48[1]
Russia	24.99	−36.27		−0.21	−2.30
Kuwait	24.80	−37.40		−38.61	−25.17
Croatia	17.06	−25.60	9.20	11.82	10.44[2]
Hungary	20.82	−24.56	8.21	10.44	2.75
Romania	41.62	−15.81	8.53	14.8	0.84
Moldova	11.39	−21.18		14.49	0.15
Mexico	10.86	−21.21		1.94	1.74
Bulgaria	24.20	−27.21	16.92	31.01	5.46
Turkey	21.53	−22.12		7.31	1.66
Botswana	2.96	−28.47		4	1.12
Paraguay	26.04	−20.28		2.93	0.17
MI	21.18	−21.02		–	–
UMI	21.42	−21.26		–	–
Developing Countries	–	–		2.68	1.43

Notes:
1. We consider that the positive record of Armenia in its financial account is resulted from the IMF loan of $540 million. The decline in net financial account starts after 2009. (Source: interview with the prime minister of the Republic of Armenia, retrieved on June 24, 2014 from www.gov.am/en/interviews/1/item/2883/.)
2. The decline in net financial flows in Croatia started after 2009. (Net fin. Acc./GDP ratio fell to 2.94% in 2010 from its ratio of 10.44% in 2009.)

Source: IMF, WEO, October 2013 and WB, WDI.

Although all countries under investigation were hit very hard by the trade channel, the role of the financial channel varied in different countries (Table 1.3). Some countries experienced massive financial reversals; others experienced different degrees of financial sudden stops. Apart from Romania, which encountered about 15 percent in export shock, all countries in our sample experienced more than 20 percent in export shock. Although financial flows to all countries decreased, only four countries in our sample experienced unexpected financial reversals. In general, as expected, the most affected countries were the ones that experienced both a dramatic decline in their exports and financial reversals. However, our analysis in this section also supports the idea that, unlike the experiences in the 1980s and 1990s, even some of the worst affected countries in our sample did not experience financial reversals during the recent crisis.

The 15 countries can be grouped in different ways for different purposes. For example, these countries can be divided into two subgroups by focusing on commodity exporters and non-commodity exporters. They can then be grouped according to the magnitude of their trade and financial shocks. Although we will refer to these distinctions in our discussions, since the Eastern Bloc (transition countries) dominate our sample, we will divide these countries into two groups, namely 'transition countries' and 'others'.[16] In this sense, Armenia, Bulgaria, Croatia, Hungary, Latvia Lithuania, Moldova, Ukraine, Russia and Romania are in the first group of countries. These economies have historical similarities. After sharing a similar economic system for decades, they hastily moved to a market-based economic system at the beginning of the 1990s. For these countries, Russia and Europe have been very important as exports markets and sources of remittances. The second set of countries includes Kuwait, Turkey, Mexico, Botswana and Paraguay. As can easily be seen, Mexico and Turkey are relatively big upper middle income countries that have had strong ties with the epicenters (US and Europe) of the crisis. Kuwait, Botswana and Paraguay are commodity exporter countries.

1.3 TRANSITION ECONOMIES

In the years preceding the crisis, the transition economies under consideration encountered unabated capital and output growth. Latvia, Lithuania, Armenia, Ukraine and Russia grew by more than the average of developing countries. In particular, the Baltic States (Latvia and Lithuania) grew at very high rates (approximately 7.5 percent between 2002 and 2008). Romania, Moldova and Bulgaria grew at an average phase with other CIS countries.

Apart from Russia, who has had current account surpluses, these economies, from the beginning of the decade to 2008, enjoyed strong financial inflows from the rest of the world (Table 1.3). Table 1.4 demonstrates that, as a general rule, the growth of domestic credit to the private sector was higher in the CIS countries than the world averages for upper middle income. Credit growth reached more than 200 percent in Lithuania, Romania, Bulgaria and Ukraine. It was more than 100 percent for Armenia, Latvia and Russia. Even the credit growth in Croatia and

Table 1.4 Investments, consumption and credit growth

	The Growth of Domestic Credit to Private Sector (as % of GDP) from 2002 to 2007	Annual Percentage Growth of Final Consumption Expenditure		Total Investment (% of GDP)		Growth of Households' Annual Consumption Expenditure in 2009	Growth of Total Investment in 2009
		2002	2007	2002	2007		
Latvia	172	6.1	12.8	25.728	39.959	−24.08	−34
Lithuania	271	4.6	10.3	20.340	31.231	−17.82	−57
Hungary	78	6.8	−1.5	24.670	22.433	−6.55	−23
Romania	244	3.7	9.6	22.002	30.975	−23.25	
Croatia	42	6.8	6.1	26.072	34.093	−7.68	−17
Bulgaria	225	3.2	7.1	19.681	34.093		
Russia	115	7.6	16.9	20.035	25.360	−16.03	−28
Ukraine	229	4.7	13.4	20.191	28.210	−19.88	−38
Armenia	100.36	7.92	16.50	18.15	38.16	−4.5	−23
Moldova	114	7.5	10.9 (2006)	21.661	38.106		
UMI Countries	8	2.0	7.1				
MI Countries	11	2.3	7.6				
Developing Countries				24.921	29.496		
World	7	2.4	3.4	21.970	24.563		

Note: Domestic credit to private sector refers to financial resources made available to the private sector through loans, purchases of non-equity securities, trade credits and other accounts receivable that establish a claim for repayment. Some cells are left blank because the data was not available for these aggregates. Hungary experienced negative growth in 2007. For this reason, consumption data for Hungary is negative in 2007.

Source: IMF, WEO, October 2013 and WDI.

Bulgaria, which was less than 100 percent, was way beyond the world and upper middle income averages. In connection with large financial inflows and rapid credit growth, there was a rapid rise in consumption. Investment and asset prices in some countries (especially in the Baltic States) also increased. For instance, in Latvia total investment as percentage of GDP increased to approximately 40 percent of GDP from its level of 25 percent in 2002. Similarly, in Lithuania the investment to GDP ratio increased from 20 percent in 2002 to 31 percent in 2007. The growth in consumption and investment expenditures were higher in these countries than the rest of the world averages (Table 1.4).[17]

Furthermore, as described in a monthly bulletin of the ECB (July, 2010), wealth effects[18] arising from rising asset prices increased domestic demand. Combined with expansionary fiscal policies implemented by several countries such as Romania and the Baltic States, macroeconomic policy also contributed to high GDP growth rates in these countries.[19]

However, as mentioned before, the high growth took place along with an increase in monetary/financial vulnerabilities. As foreign capital continued to flow in, real appreciation of exchange rates and credit growth accelerated. As a result, consumption expenditures, some of which fed imports, increased and current account deficits worsened. The current account deficit of Bulgaria, Latvia, Moldova, Lithuania, Romania, Croatia, Armenia and Ukraine reached enormous amounts: 25.2 percent, 22.4 percent, 15.2 percent, 14.5 percent, 13.4 percent, 7.3 percent, 6.4 percent and 3.7 percent respectively (Table 1.5). In other words, these countries accumulated liabilities to be paid to the rest of the world in the future, which made them highly dependent on financial flows.[20]

The high current account deficits and dependency on financial flows were important factors, but these were not the only vulnerabilities. In many of the countries that we investigate here, total debt was denominated primarily in foreign currency (from euro to yen), making corporate and household borrowers, and hence creditor banks, vulnerable to a depreciation of the exchange rate (Berglöf et al., 2009). Another significant characteristic of the debt structure was related to the high levels of debt accumulation by the private sector. Table 1.6 demonstrates that private debt/GDP ratio increased significantly in all countries, whereas, except for Hungary, government debt/GDP ratio decreased in countries for which data are available. In other words, although these countries enjoyed improvements in their public balances, they continued to accumulate debt in different forms.

In addition to the financial flows, high commodity prices were another driver of growth in Russia, Ukraine and Armenia.[21] These countries produced a relatively narrow spectrum of industrial products compared to

Table 1.5   Inflation, real exchange rate and current account

	Inflation		REER / REER Index		CA Balance (% of GDP)	
	2002	2007	2002	2007	2002	2007
Latvia	1.95	10.1	−2.9	6.6	−6.66	−22.44
Lithuania	0.34	5.82	2.8	3	−5.15	−14.47
Hungary	5.26	7.93	84.5	100.2	−6.99	−7.27
Romania	22.5	4.83	82.3	111.6	−3.33	−13.42
Croatia	1.67	2.87	90.8	97	−7.2	−7.26
Bulgaria	5.8	7.57	75.8	91.1	−2.37	−25.2
Russia	15.78	9	65.1	91.8	8.43	5.48
Ukraine	0.75	12.8	102.3	115	7.48	−3.69
Armenia	1.071	4.55	94.18	124	−6.228	−6.401
Moldova	5.21	12.4	71	87.4	−1.19	−15.24
Kuwait	0.797	5.47			11.18	36.79
Mexico	5.037	3.97	111.4	99.12	−1.883	−1.368
Turkey	5.134	8.76			−0.269	−5.838
Botswana	8.026	7.08			3.83	15.11
Paraguay	10.51	8.13	110	126.2	9.808	5.606
Emerging Markets	7.11	7.81			−1.12	−3.73

Note: Since the REER index data was not available for Latvia and Lithuania, REER data from the Eurostat are given for these two countries. In the remaining countries, the REER index was used. Data was not available for cells that have been left blank.

Source: IMF, WEO, October 2013 for Inflation, CA deficit, Eurostat REER and REER Index.

other countries in this group. For example, Russia and Ukraine based their exports on mainly the oil and steel industries respectively. Armenia sells mainly metals and some precious minerals. Since commodity prices were rising prior to the crisis, these three countries benefited from rising prices and the concomitant rise in export revenues. As a result, Russia in particular was able to achieve current account surpluses. In fact, it was the only country with a current account surplus in this group of countries.

The situation in Moldova was slightly different to other countries in the set. The country based its growth performance prior to the crisis mainly on its exports to Russia and on remittances of workers living in Russia. The main export commodities of Moldova were agricultural products. When Russia entered into a political and economic crisis because of the Russia–Georgia war and banned Moldovan wine exports, the country faced huge difficulties. Therefore, the economic environment in Moldova had already deteriorated prior to the crisis.

Table 1.6 *Debt structure*

	Private Debt (% of GDP)		General Gov Gross Debt (% of GDP)		External Debt Stocks (% of GDP)	
	2002	2007	2002	2007	2002	2007
Latvia	51.2	123	13.6	9.1		
Lithuania	29.8	77.9	22.2	16.8		
Hungary	65.5	139.8	55.9	67	23.70	65.44
Romania	30.9	66.8	24.9	12.8	12.91	23.41
Croatia	64.2	117.3	34.7	32.8		
Bulgaria	32.8	137.3	52.4	17.2	6.95	32.50
Russia			40.30	8.511		
Ukraine			33.53	12.31	6.45	27.60
Armenia			38.105	14.249	15.09	10.84
Moldova			66.19	25.15	20.35	26.29
Kuwait			32.333	11.832		
Mexico			42.951	37.562	4.53	4.39
Turkey			74	39.907	13.43	19.60
Botswana			8.31	8.212		
Paraguay			58.445	19.325	7.38	4.13
Developing Countries			51.49	34.61		

Note: External debt stocks/GDP data is obtained by dividing 'External debt stocks, private nonguaranteed' to GDP (current USD).

Source: IMF, WEO, October 2013 General Gov. Gross Debt, Eurostat for private debt add WB for External Debt Stocks/GDP and REER Index.

To sum up, it would not be misleading to state that, although these countries were experiencing their golden age in terms of growth performance from 2002 to 2007 and 2008, important vulnerabilities, which were mainly related to the structural problems in the integration of these countries into the world economy, emerged in the same period.

1.3.1 Trade Channel

As the recession deepened in advanced countries during the second half of 2008, the economies in our sample were seriously affected by the contraction in global trade due to their high dependence on advanced country markets for their exports.

The overwhelming majority of the countries have a very high trade to GDP ratio. In this sense, the trade to GDP ratios in 12 of the 15 countries

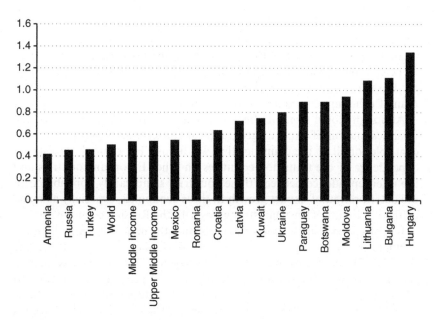

Source: WB, WDI, 2008 data was used.

Figure 1.1 Trade openness (X+IM)/GDP

were considerably higher than the middle income, upper middle income and world averages. Given the high degree of openness (Figure 1.1), the trade channel is crucial in explaining the impact of the crisis on the transition economies. In general, the trade channel played a role during the recent crisis in upper middle income countries through two mechanisms. First, the demand for goods and services plummeted in 2008. Immediately thereafter, the prices of commodities began to fall.

As the global economy entered into a recessionary period, the decline in global demand was accompanied by a drop in commodity prices. For example, after reaching a peak of US$133 per barrel in July 2008, the price of oil fell by more than 70 percent to an average of US$39 per barrel in February 2009. Similar declines were observed in the prices of metal products such as copper.[22]

The decline in global demand affected all the transition countries, whereas the decline in commodity prices mainly hit commodity exporting countries (Ukraine, Russia and Armenia). Overall, both effects implied that exporter countries sold their goods and services at lower prices. As a result, as Table 1.3 demonstrates, all countries experienced a sharp decline in the growth of exports of goods in 2009 compared to the pre-crisis period. The magnitude of the export shock the transition economies experienced varied from about 15 percent to 40 percent. As expected, commodity exporters Armenia, Russia and Ukraine were faced by a more than 30 percent decline in their exports. In other words, the trade shock hitting the Russian, Ukrainian and Armenian economies was considerably larger than of other upper middle income countries.

Although global turmoil affected all export activities regardless of the final destination of exports, geographical concentration played a significant role for all of the countries that we discuss. For example, the strong dependence of the transition countries on other European countries and the interdependence between these countries significantly contributed to the deterioration of export growth in these economies, especially as many of these economies have had strong ties with the Russian economy.

It is observed that EU countries constitute the majority share of export partners of the countries in this sample (WTO data).[23] For instance, the share of EU countries in total exports reaches 70 percent in Romania. In Ukraine and Moldova the share is below 50 percent (25 percent and 47 percent respectively, but this ratio is still quite high). However, these countries have strong trade relations with Russia, which experienced a sharp decline in its GDP. Although it is difficult to reach a conclusive verdict, the contagion effect might have been weaker if these countries had diversified trading routes prior to the crisis.

In addition to the degree of openness and geographical concentration, the composition of export products was an important factor in the deterioration of export performances in these countries. As the analysis carried out by Berkmen et al. (2009) demonstrates, the countries exporting manufactured goods to advanced countries were hit hard by the decline in demand compared to countries exporting food. Given the high income elasticity of the demand for manufactured goods, it is reasonable to conclude that the ten countries that are discussed in this section were severely affected by the crisis since industrial products constitute the majority of their exports (except for Armenia and Russia) (based on WTO data).[24]

To some extent, in some countries the degree of the importance of the trade channel was also influenced by the choice of exchange rate regimes. In general, countries may lose competitiveness in international markets if their trading partners devalue their currencies. Among the countries that we discuss in this section, Latvia and Lithuania were members of the European Union. Therefore, their currencies were pegged to the euro. Since membership of the European Union requires the adoption of the euro in due course, these countries were not allowed to devalue their currencies due to the Maastricht criteria (which define the preconditions for the adoption of the euro). Therefore, these countries faced a tradeoff between maintaining their peg and their commitment to the Union, and gaining competitiveness in international markets. In both countries national authorities decided to maintain their peg at the cost of reduced competitiveness. For example, policymakers in Latvia discredited devaluation because adherence to the euro peg was seen as the only reasonable long term strategy to secure access to international lending facilities and investment (Reinart et al., 2010). Similarly, Lithuania gave priority to a stable fixed exchange rate in order to be able to be a part of the eurozone. According to Purfield and Rosenberg (2010), the Baltic countries' real effective exchange rates appreciated against the euro while many trading partners' currencies depreciated, contributing to reduced competitiveness in international markets and further deterioration of export performances.

1.3.2 Financial Channel

According to many economists, the majority of developing countries did not encounter a financial collapse during the recent crisis relative to the crises in the 1980s and 1990s. However, some of the transition economies were among exceptions thanks to very hasty liberalization, rapid deregulation and strong linkages between their financial markets and those of European countries. In the period from 2002 to 2007 these policy initiatives contributed to the buildup of vulnerabilities that lay just below the surface. As we previously stated, the significant share of credits in these countries was denominated by foreign currencies, particularly in the CEE countries in our set. In the same vein, the loans taken in foreign currency were central to the transmission of the financial crisis into the Central and Eastern European (CEE) countries (Sprenger and Vincentz, 2010).[25] Since these countries were in the process of integration into the eurozone, they ignored the risks related to exchange rate volatility. Additionally, many firms that borrowed in foreign exchange before the crisis had foreign currency incomes coming from exports. As a result, investors and households found foreign currency loans manageable. However, the boom in financial markets came to an end with the global crisis. With the emergence of a global turmoil, borrowing in foreign currency opportunities decreased as foreign banks reduced their net assets. As asset holdings were reduced, credit to these CIS countries also dried up.[26]

The ratio of financial account balance to GDP in the transition countries can be seen in Table 1.3.[27] Accordingly, in all countries the ratio decreased compared to the pre-crisis period. However, the importance of the financial channel was more significant for Latvia, Lithuania, Ukraine and Russia. In these countries macroeconomic vulnerabilities such as high current account deficits (except for Russia) generated adverse expectations for foreign investors and high vulnerability of the domestic financial system (Griffith-Jones and Ocampo, 2009). As a result, rapid withdrawals of private financial flows occurred. For the Russian case, the Georgian–Russian war had already decreased the appetite of international investors for Russian assets. In the remaining countries, a reversal of financial flows did not occur but they faced a sudden stop and were left with no credit or liquidity.[28]

As explained before, in the transition economies financial flows also served to feed domestic demand by contributing to consumption and investment expenditures in the pre-crisis period. Therefore, when international financing opportunities were limited and the cost of external financing increased, contractions in consumption and investment took place through a decline in credit to domestic players (Table 1.4). Total investment declined by 57 percent, 41 percent, 38 percent, 34 percent, 28 percent, 23 percent, 23 percent and 17 percent in Lithuania, Moldova, Ukraine, Latvia, Russia, Hungary, Armenia and Croatia respectively.[29] Additionally, a decline in consumption contributed to the sharp decline in domestic demand.

In countries such as Latvia, Ukraine and Russia the banking sector experienced particular stress due to a lack of liquidity. Increased foreign ownership of CIS banks, in some cases, turned out to be a source of fragility as these banks withdrew lending to their subsidiaries from developing and transition countries in order to strengthen their very weak positions in developed countries (Griffith-Jones and Ocampo, 2009).[30] As a result, the balance sheets of financial institutions contracted and governments had to support the banking system with liquidity injections. For example, in Latvia, Swedish banks, which had strong connections with the Latvian banking sector, reacted to the crisis early and severely by withdrawing money from their Latvian investments. This resulted in deterioration of the balance sheet of one of the largest Latvian banks, Parex (Dudzińska, 2011). Similarly, Russia and Ukraine experienced stress in their banking sectors. In Ukraine, many banks were unable to refinance foreign loans and meet their obligations. As individual depositors tried to withdraw their money, a run on the banks developed and a banking crisis emerged (Shkura and Peitsch, 2011). In Russia the effects of the global crisis on the banking sector were much more severe, with 47 Russian banks failing after September 2008 (Fidrmuc and Süß, 2009).

In addition to export revenues and financial inflows, remittances provided another source of income from advanced economies to upper income CIS countries in the pre-crisis period. However, as advanced economies became caught up in the crisis, remittances provided a channel for the transmission of the crisis to these countries. Among the countries that

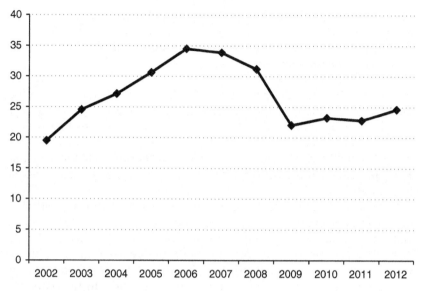

Source: WB, WDI.

Figure 1.2 Personal remittances received in Moldova (% of GDP)

we have focused on, Moldova was particularly affected by this channel. With the slowdown in the Russian economy, incomes of Moldavian immigrants in Russia fell sharply and they could not send money back to their families at home in Moldova (Figure 1.2).

1.4 OTHER COUNTRIES

As discussed above, the 15 most affected countries are dominated by the transition economies, which were affected by the trade channel and various degrees of financial flows shocks. The remaining five countries include Kuwait, Botswana, Paraguay, Mexico and Turkey. The first three countries can be considered as commodity exporters with current account surpluses. However, Mexico and Turkey are relatively big upper middle income countries with strong industrial bases with relatively mild and high current account deficits respectively. Although the majority of the countries investigated in this section experienced considerable sudden stops, as elaborated in the following sections, the trade channel can be considered the main channel through which the crisis spreads into these countries. Pre-crisis conditions in these countries were relatively better than in the first set of countries although the Turkish case demonstrates some characteristics of the transition economies such as high current account deficits. After investigating pre-crisis conditions in these countries, we will shift our focus to the transmission mechanisms.

Mexico and Turkey focused on fixing several traditional sources of fragilities in the pre-crisis period. Mainly, they gave priority to reforming their macroeconomic policy framework. Accordingly, they shifted to a flexible exchange rate system and adopted an inflation targeting regime as a framework to conduct monetary policy. Inflation rates were reduced from 17.3 and 71.28 percent (average between 1990 and 2002) to 4.32 and 12.46 percent (average between 2003 and 2008) in Mexico and Turkey respectively.

In Mexico the more stable macroeconomic environment was reflected in export performance and the availability of credit; exports of goods and services increased by approximately 10 percent between 2002 and 2008. The current account was in a moderate deficit position with an average 1.25 percent deficit between 2002 and 2008. In the pre-crisis period financial resources from abroad became more available to the economy. In relation to this, domestic credit to the private sector (as percentage of GDP) grew by 40.98 percent from 2002 to 2007 (Table 1.4). In line with increasing availability of credit, there were moderate increases in consumption and investment expenditures as well. Final consumption expenditures increased to 3.82 percent in 2007 from its negative level of 0.05 percent in 2002. As for investment expenditures, there was a slight increase in total investment to GDP ratio from 2002 to 2007. However, the level stayed at around 20 percent, which cannot be considered high enough among emerging market countries, especially compared to the Asian countries. The Mexican economy did not experience a rapid credit boom accompanied by high investment and consumption increases before the crisis. Its vulnerability lay in the fact that the Mexican economy was limited in its diversity and was highly dependent on export revenues and financial flows coming from the US. Indeed, trade with the US made up 78 percent of Mexico's total trade.

After the crisis of 2001, Turkey entered into a new economic era. As a response to the crisis of 2001, a new program under the auspices of the IMF, which included many structural reforms, was put in practice (Cömert and Çolak, 2014). For instance, new regulations for the banking system were introduced, privatization attempts were accelerated, and the Central Bank was turned into an independent body and started to implement inflation targeting policies. As a result of these reforms, Turkey managed to decrease the high inflation rates that were prevalent in the 1990s, and there was an important decline in the public debt to GDP levels after 2002.

Similar to other countries in our set, Turkey also benefited from the abundance of global liquidity in the pre-crisis period. For instance, partially thanks to high financial inflows, domestic credit to the private sector (as percentage of GDP) grew by 103.12 percent between 2002 and 2007 (Table 1.4). The bonanza of financial flows caused a considerable appreciation in the Turkish lira that worked as an implicit exchange rate peg curbing inflation and improving the balance sheets of economic agents (Benlialper and Cömert, 2013).

Although a group of academics and politicians interpreted the period after 2002 in Turkey as a prosperous period (Karagöl, 2013), several structural macroeconomic problems continued to persist. For instance, investment rates continued to stagnate at around 20 percent.[31] Although exports rapidly increased prior to the crisis, because of structural problems (such as high dependence on imports to produce export products) and the appreciation of TL, the current account deficit widened significantly. The current account deficit to GDP ratio increased from 0.26 percent in 2002 to 5.53 percent in 2008 and was 4.02 percent on average during this period. In relation to this, as will be elaborated on in the next sections, Turkey had relatively low diversification in its exports markets. Additionally, although the inflation rate was reduced after 2001, it was still relatively high given the global disinflation environment.[32] Last but not least, the unemployment rate remained at a high level, with an average rate between 2002 and 2008 of 9.25 percent despite the apparent economic growth. For this reason, a substantial number of economists, such as Telli, Voyvoda and Yeldan (2006), Yeldan and Ercan (2011), and Herr and Sonat (2013), concluded that the growth that the Turkish economy experienced after 2002 has been 'jobless growth'.

Kuwait, Botswana and Paraguay based their growth performances on high export revenues from high commodity prices. For instance, the exports of fuels and mining products constituted 94.7 percent of total exports for Kuwait. As for Botswana, the mining sector has the biggest share in GDP.[33] In Paraguay, the export sectors were divided into three main sectors, namely agricultural products (58.5 percent), fuels and mining products (31.1 percent), and manufacturing (8.8 percent) (WTO data).

From Table 1.4, we see that the increases in the domestic credit, consumption and investment expenditures in the countries under investigation in this section were much more moderate compared to the first group of countries that were severely affected by both the trade and financial channels.[34] As in the case of other countries, public debt had been decreasing. Although deteriorations were observed in some variables, such as current account balances in some countries, the magnitude of deterioration was smaller compared to the transition economies. Apart from

Turkey, none of these countries suffered from significant current account deficits.[35] Rather, as mentioned before, it was generally the limited number of export partners and high dependency on commodity prices that exacerbated the effects of external shocks in these countries. In the Turkish case a large sudden stop[36] also put significant pressure on important macroeconomic variables.

1.4.1 Trade Channel

As in the case of the transition economies, the countries that we consider in this section were affected by the trade channel through two main mechanisms: (1) the demand for their goods from advanced countries plummeted and (2) commodity prices declined.

As Table 1.3 demonstrates, it is evident that the export of goods declined significantly in 2009 compared to the pre-crisis period in five countries under investigation. It seems that the magnitude of the trade shock more or less determined the size of GDP growth reduction among these countries. Export growth declined in Kuwait, Botswana, Turkey, Mexico and Paraguay by 37.4 percent, 28.5 percent, 22.1 percent, 21.2 percent and 20.3 percent respectively. The magnitude of GDP declines was more or less in the same order: 7.8 percent (Botswana), 7.0 percent (Kuwait), 4.8 percent (Turkey), 4.5 percent (Mexico) and 3.9 percent (Paraguay).

When we look at the trade partners of these countries, it is observed that European countries and the US have the biggest share in total exports from Turkey and Mexico respectively. The share of exports to the European countries from Turkey is 63 percent[37] and the share of exports to the US from Mexico is 78 percent (WTO data). Since diversification of export partners is highly concentrated and these partners were hit hard by the crisis, a sharp contraction in exports can be easily understood.

If we look at the composition of export products from these countries, it is observed that manufactured goods constitute the majority, making up 70.8 percent and 72.7 percent of exports for Turkey and Mexico respectively. Since the elasticity of demand for manufactured products is high, it follows that demand for manufactured goods declined when the income levels in advanced countries deteriorated. For instance, the car industry, which is a very sizeable export industry in Turkey, was greatly affected by the global crisis (Sturgeon et al., 2009). Therefore, the lower external demand contributed negatively to export performance and GDP growth in the country. The lower export prices amplified the direct impact of a lower global demand and spread the global crisis specifically into commodity exporter countries.

Risks regarding high dependency on commodity prices were pronounced for commodity producer countries in many studies. For instance, Meyn and Kennan (2009) argue that Botswana was among the high risk countries since 80 percent of exports were derived from mining, and writers suggest the direct transition of declining demand and prices into decreased investment and unemployment show up as reality later on. In the same study, Kuwait was among the most dependent country exporters in terms of share of oil in total exports. Paraguay was also partially vulnerable to the changes in commodity prices. Eventually, when the commodity boom came to a halt, varying degrees of reductions in export revenues and GDP growth rates occurred in these countries depending on the degree of the importance of commodity exports and other factors including policy responses. However, as in the case of other commodity producers, these countries benefited from a fast recovery of commodity prices as well.[38]

1.4.2   Financial Channel

The transition economies experienced a significant decline in net financial flows. Moreover, in Latvia, Lithuania, Ukraine and Russia a reversal of financial flows occurred in 2009. Not surprisingly, these four countries were most affected by the crisis.

As for the countries that are discussed in this section (Turkey, Mexico, Kuwait, Botswana and Paraguay), they also experienced a decline in net financial flows. However, compared to the shock that advanced economies and the countries in the first group faced, the magnitude of the decline in financial flows was relatively small in these five countries.

Figure 1.3 demonstrates financial flows relative to GDP for Turkey, Mexico, Paraguay, Botswana and Kuwait. For Turkey net financial flows reached 7.2 percent of GDP in 2007 then declined to 1.65 percent in 2009. Although this was a significant slowdown leading to a depreciation pressure on the lira and a decline in domestic credits, Turkey did not experience a reversal of financial flows. Overall, financial capital continued to flow into Turkey but in smaller amounts. If we compare this situation with the 1994 and 2001 crises, it is obvious that the magnitude and duration of the past financial shocks were much higher in Turkey. Both in 1994 and 2001 the reversal of net financial flows occurred with magnitudes 3.26 and 7.43 percent of GDP respectively (Cömert and Çolak, 2013). When we compare the financial shock that Mexico faced in 2009 with its past crisis experiences, it is obvious that the magnitude of the decline is much smaller compared to the shocks in 1983 and 1995. Similarly, from the figures below, it is observed that Paraguay and Botswana did not face a financial flow shock in 2009. Kuwait has traditionally been a capital exporter due

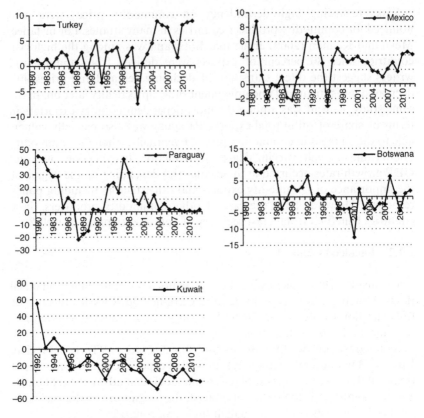

Note: Data for Kuwait before 1991 was not available.

Source: Central Bank of Republic of Turkey for Turkey and IMF, BOP Statistics and BPM5 for others.

Figure 1.3   Net financial account (% of GDP)

to its historically massive current account surpluses; this did not change much in the recent crisis.

In relation to developments in financial accounts, in general, the financial systems of the countries in this group were not under severe pressure. In the literature the resilience of the financial sectors observed in the majority of the developing countries is mainly attributed to high reserve policies (Jeanne, 2007), adoption of the flexible exchange rate regime (Berkmen et al., 2009) and to the strong balance sheet indicators in the banking sectors. However, although all these factors might have played a role, they do not completely explain the resilience of the financial sectors.

As our study shows, only a handful of countries with very poor pre-crisis macroeconomic indicators experienced financial reversals. In this sense, we believe that the financial sectors of the majority of countries in the Global South were not overtly hurt by the crisis because the amount of net financial flows to these countries did not decline significantly. Furthermore, unlike many previous crises, sudden stops or reversals did not last long after the recent crisis. As a result, as even our sample consisting of the worst performing countries during the recent crisis demonstrates, the duration and the magnitude of the financial shocks hitting these countries were relatively mild. This partially explains why financial collapse did not take place in the majority of the countries in our sample.

1.5 POLICY RESPONSES

Developing countries attempted to weather the crisis by using several policies. In terms of monetary policy responses, contrary to past crisis experiences, developing countries in general were able to conduct countercyclical policies by slashing policy interest rates and pumping liquidity to the financial markets. In past crises, governments in the Global South were forced to respond procyclically by increasing the interest rates in order to prevent capital flight, international reserve losses and currency runs. During the recent global crisis there were still risks associated with confidence and currencies. However, the slowdown in growth and widening interest rate differentials in favor of emerging market economies suggest that these economies had the incentive and leeway to cut interest rates (Moreno, 2010). Besides this, as explained above, since the financial markets in advanced countries were in total disarray, there were not many safe haven assets or financial markets, which enabled emerging market and other countries in the Global South to have some extra room for the conduct of expansionary monetary policy.[39]

Countries in the South as a group improved their fiscal positions prior to the crisis. Improved fiscal stances across the South allowed them to acquire enough fiscal space to design and implement packages to counteract the contraction in the world economy (Ceballos et al., 2013).

However, the majority of the countries we analyze in this chapter could not utilize fiscal policy and/or monetary policy relative to many other developing countries. On the one hand, the majority of the countries that we consider were limited in their fiscal responses either by limited fiscal space or by the eurozone entry requirements. On the other hand, the monetary policy responses of these countries were either ineffective and/or insufficient. In this sense, the lack of fiscal policy room and/or the will to boost economic growth and ineffective/insufficient monetary policy responses are among the reasons behind the very poor performance of the countries in our sample. As a result, these countries were not able to boost domestic consumption and investment to counter the impact of the crisis.

1.5.1   Monetary Policy Responses

Analyzing policy responses in all these countries is an extensive subject that exceeds the scope of this chapter. Therefore, in this section our primary aim is to understand whether there was an early reaction to the crisis in the form of a significant cut in policy rates. There existed heterogeneity in the ability of developing countries to undergo significant reductions in their policy rates. In Table 1.7 policy interest rates are given for certain time periods. Since the aim of the chapter is to explain the contractions in the GDP growth rates in 2009, we only considered the reductions from 2008 to the first quarter of 2009.

An early and significant reduction in policy rates did not take place in any of the countries that we consider. In Moldova and Turkey policy rates were cut by more than 10 percent; however, the reductions started when these economies were already in deep recession.

There are some attempts to explain the differences in the ability of countries to cut interest rates. In general, the exchange rate regime, inflationary outlook, fiscal situation and BOP constraints are seen as the main factors that created divergences in policy responses.[40] Akyüz (2009) points out that the Balance of Payments (BOP) constraint is an important factor in preventing significant reductions in interest rates in some developing countries. In other words, the BOP repercussions to lower interest rates might prevent some countries from implementing expansionary monetary policies due to fear of financial reversals. Furthermore, one of the obstacles to implementing an effective monetary policy would be concerns about international reserves. Many studies stress that the vulnerabilities of developing countries to rapid deterioration in capital flows diminished since many of these countries had far higher levels of foreign exchange reserves in relation to previous crises' financing needs.[41]

In Figure 1.4 the level of reserves in relation to GDP is given for countries in our set. Comparing the existing data with that of the developing countries' average,[42] it is observed that the level of reserve accumulation was lower for the majority of countries in our set, except for Bulgaria and Botswana.[43] We can conclude that the countries in our sample may not have had enough space in terms of reserve accumulation with which to cushion the impact of the crisis. Under this condition, the authorities may

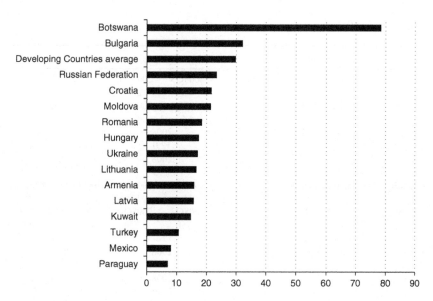

Notes:
Total reserves minus gold (current US$) data was divided by GDP (current US$), then the average between 2002 and 2008 was taken.
Developing countries' average was calculated by taking the average of the data between 2002 and 2008 for developing countries that are among the top 50 countries in terms of GDP size. These countries are: China, Nigeria, Kazakhstan, India, Malaysia, Pakistan, Thailand, Argentina, the Philippines, Indonesia, Venezuela, Colombia, Republic of Korea, Algeria, Egypt, South Africa, Chile, Poland and Brazil.

Source: WB, WDI and authors' calculations.

Figure 1.4 Total reserves (% of GDP)

have been avoiding slashing policy rates significantly because of a fear of financial reversals.

The timeliness and the magnitude of the reduction in policy rates is an important indicator that shows the approaches of various countries to the crisis. However, policy measures can be translated into recovery in economic activity if reductions in policy rates can be reflected to market interest rates and, in relation to this, to real interest rates. In Table 1.8 real interest rates between 2008 and 2011 are given. When the rates in Table 1.7 and 1.8 are compared, it is observed that, although policy rates were cut from 2008 to 2009 in all countries, real interest rates increased significantly in this period. This might be caused by two factors. First, market interest rates might be unresponsive to the policy rates. This phenomenon would be a sign of the fact that policy interest rate cuts were not translated into

Table 1.7   Policy rates

	Policy Rate				
Latvia	Overnight Interbank Rate	2008Q3	2008Q4	2009Q1	
		4.3	2.5	1.1	
Lithuania	Overnight Interbank Rate	2008Q3	2008Q4	2009Q1	
		4.6	3.6	1.0	
Ukraine	Discount Rate	2008		2009	
		12.0		11.0	12.0
Armenia	REPO Rate	2008		2009	
		7.75		7.25	7.75
Russia	Refinancing Rate	2008Q3	2008Q4	2009Q1	2009Q2
		11	13	13	11.5
Kuwait	Discount Rate	2008Q3	2008Q4	2009Q1	2009Q2
		5.750	3.750	3.750	3.000
Croatia	Lombard Rate				
Hungary	Base Rate	2008		2009	
		10		9.50	6.25
Romania	Policy Rate	2008		2009	
		10.25		9.5	8
Moldova	Key Monetary Rate	2008		2009	
		16.0		14.0	5.0
Mexico	Overnight Interbank Rate	2008		2009	
		8.25		4.50	
Bulgaria	Base Interest Rate	2008		2009	
		5.77		5.17	0.55
Turkey	Overnight rate until 2010, 1	2008		2009	
	Week REPO rate after 2010	19.50		15.50	9.0
Botswana	Bank Rate	2008		2009	
		15.0		15.0	15.0
Paraguay	14 day Interest Rate				
Euro Area	The interest rate on main	2008		2009	
	refinancing operations	2.50		1.0	
United	Federal Funds Rate	2007		2008	2009
States		4.33		0.54	0.13

Note: Since countries use different interest rates as policy variables, there is no unity of data sources. Therefore, we have searched for policy interest rates of all countries individually. For some countries, data was available quarterly. We tried to determine the data period in a way that give us as much necessary information as possible. For some countries, only yearly data was available. For these countries, data is given for 2008 (at the end of the year), 2009 and 2010 (at the beginning and end of the year). Data was not available for the cells that have been left blank.

Sources: Passport database (for overnight interbank rates, Latvia and Lithuania); IMF, IFS (refinancing rate of Russia, discount rate of Kuwait); Central Bank of Armenia (www.cba.am); National Bank of Ukraine (www.bank.gov.ua); The Central Bank of Hungary (www.mnb.hu); Banca Nationala a Romaniei (www.bnro.ro); Bulgarian National Bank (www.bnb.hg); Central Bank of Republic of Turkey (www.tcmb.gov.tr); Bank of Botswana (www.bankofbotswana.bw); IMF, International Financial Statistics (for Moldova, Mexico, Euro Area and United States).

Table 1.8   Real interest rates and inflation

	Real Interest Rate (%)				Inflation	
	2008	2009	2010	2011	2008	2009
Latvia	−2.21	17.99	12.15	−0.05	15.25	3.26
Lithuania	−1.24	12.56	3.88		11.08	4.16
Ukraine	−8.62	6.88	1.86	1.41	25.20	15.90
Armenia	42.03	15.80	10.60	12.91	9.01	3.54
Russia	−4.86	13.05	−2.95	−6.12	14.10	11.65
Kuwait	−7.10	30.89	−9.17	−13.4	6.30	4.61
Croatia	4.14	8.45	10.46	6.57	6.06	2.37
Hungary	4.65	7.21	5.28	5.58	6.06	4.21
Romania	−0.47	12.52	7.59	4.36	7.84	5.58
Moldova	10.78	17.99	4.75	6.305	12.70	0.006
Mexico	2.55	3.41	1.13	0.05	5.12	5.29
Bulgaria	2.25	6.71	8.12	5.44	11.95	2.47
Botswana	7.2	10.0	−6.3	5.2	12.62	8.10
Paraguay	15.1	25.7	18.8	6.9	10.15	2.59
Turkey					10.44	6.25

Note: Real interest rate is the lending interest rate adjusted for inflation as measured by the GDP deflator. Inflation refers to percentage change in consumer prices index. The interest rate for Lithuania for 2011 is not available.

Source: WDI and IMF, WEO 2014.

other market interest rates such as lending rates. Given the fact that the countries in our sample face a lot of challenges in terms of the interest rate channel, these results are not surprising. Second, some economies under investigation such as Latvia and Lithuania were overheating before the crisis. Therefore, sharp declines in inflation rates resulting from global contraction in demand caused real interest rates to increase. For example, inflation decreased from 14.25 percent to 3.26 percent, from 11 percent to 4 percent, from 12 percent to 0 percent and from 11.9 percent to 2.5 percent in Latvia, Lithuania, Moldavia, Bulgaria and Paraguay respectively. As a result consumption and the investment inducing effects of interest rate cuts did not work properly in these countries.

1.5.2   Fiscal Policy Responses

One of the main weaknesses of the countries under the investigation was the lack of proper fiscal response to the crisis due to limited fiscal space, among other considerations. In Figure 1.5 fiscal positions of these

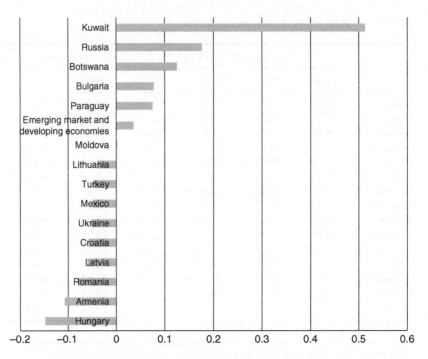

Note: Fiscal positions of the countries before the crisis are calculated as follows: (2005–8 average fiscal deficit/gdp)÷(2005–8 average government. revenue/gdp).

Source: IMF, WEO, October 2013.

Figure 1.5 Fiscal positions before the crisis

countries are shown by a very simple index. A negative value indicates that the country had fiscal deficit prior to the crisis. Therefore, the smaller the index, that is, small positive or negative numbers, the smaller the fiscal space that a country can use to respond to the crisis. From the figure it is observed that the fiscal space was highly constrained in the majority of countries.[44] In countries where the majority of the government revenue was constituted by high commodity prices (Kuwait, Russia, Botswana and Paraguay), the situation was different.

They seemed to have enough fiscal space. However, overall, the majority of the countries were not prepared for the crisis in terms of fiscal space. In Table 1.9 fiscal developments after the crisis are demonstrated. It is observed that, in the majority of countries, the growth of total government expenditure was lower than the developing countries' average. Interestingly, only Paraguay, who had more fiscal space relative to others,

Table 1.9   Government expenditures

	Growth of General Government Total Expenditure (as % of GDP)		General Government Final Consumption Expenditure (annual % growth)	
	2008	2009	2008	2009
Latvia	20.86	2.14	1.53	−9.15
Lithuania	7.32	18.06	7.34	−1.88
Ukraine	8.23	2.36	1.1	−2.4
Armenia	−0.82	28.40	−1.85	−1.22
Russia	3.61	20.57	3.4	−0.6
Kuwait	34.20	4.42		
Croatia	−3.30	6.36	−0.24	0.44
Hungary	−2.76	4.47	1.07	−0.63
Romania	4.59	3.98	6.84	9.49
Moldova	−2.35	8.90	11.64	−2.86
Mexico	12.29	6.12	3.03	2.24
Bulgaria	0.66	2.86	−0.98	−6.48
Turkey	2.71	11.84	1.74	7.77
Botswana	30.94	8.57	4.98	2.96
Paraguay	−6.91	27.03	3.5	13.67
Emerging Markets	5.28	5.17		
UMI			5.67	6.81
MI			6.59	7.55
Advanced Economies	4.79	10.14		
Euro Area	2.55	8.63	2.323302	2.583143

Note: General government final consumption expenditure (general government consumption) includes all government current expenditures for purchases of goods and services (including compensation of employees). It also includes most expenditure on national defense and security, but excludes government military expenditures that are part of government capital formation. Some data for some countries and country groups are not available.

Source: WB, WDI and IMF, WEO.

seemed to utilize considerable expansionary fiscal policies. This may explain a mild GDP decline in Paraguay relative to other countries in our set. Beside this, Romania and Turkey also were engaged in some expansionary policies though Turkish fiscal expansion was initiated relatively late (Cömert and Çolak, 2014).

Five of the six CEE countries (Bulgaria, Hungary, Latvia, Lithuania and Romania) in our set were already members of the European Union prior to the crisis and were also candidate countries for the eurozone.[45] According to the Maastricht criteria, which define eurozone entry criteria, the public deficits were not expected to exceed 3 percent. Therefore, these countries faced a tradeoff between their commitment to the euro and taking countercyclical measures. As a result, these countries had to adopt fiscal consolidation and applied procyclical fiscal policies during and after the crisis. Moreover, the IMF and EU financial support programs, coming with several conditions, prevented some from implementing expansionary fiscal policies. For example, in Latvia, Hungary and Romania the requirements of the IMF and EU financial support programs imposed strict financial consolidation through wide ranging revenue and expenditure measures from 2009 onward (ECB report, July 2010). Similarly, Bulgaria and Lithuania also adopted comprehensive fiscal measures in order to prevent rapid budget deterioration. As a result these countries could not use fiscal policy to tackle the impact of the crisis and experienced large GDP declines.

1.6 CONCLUSION

The 2008 global crisis that originated in the US had a pronounced effect throughout the world. The global economy contracted by 2.15 percent in 2009. Although developing countries as a group weathered the crisis relatively well, some countries experienced significant contraction in their GDP growth rates. In this chapter we have analyzed the impact of the crisis on the 15 countries that recorded the lowest GDP growth rates in 2009.

Understanding the dynamic process of the crisis is not an easy task due to the heterogeneous nature of pre-crisis conditions and the importance of different channels during the crisis in different countries. However, it is still possible to discern general patterns. The overall evidence shows that the trade channel was the most important mechanism in the transmission of the crisis from advanced economies to the countries in our sample. Fluctuations in commodity prices and a limited number of export markets, together with high income elasticity of exports goods, played important roles in this channel. This implies that export-led growth strategies have their own limitations and are very sensitive to cycles in Western countries.

The role of the financial channel varied in different countries. Some countries encountered massive financial reversals while others experienced different degrees of financial stops. In general, as expected, the most affected countries in our set are the ones that experienced both a dramatic decline in their exports and financial reversals. Although almost all these countries experienced spectacular growth performances from 2002 to 2008, they also accumulated significant vulnerabilities, which were mainly related to the structural problems in the integration of these countries to the world economy, during the same time period. In this sense, massive financial flows prior to the crises were responsible for the accumulation of considerable vulnerabilities among the countries in our set. As the increasing recent emphasis on macro prudential policies and the adverse effects of portfolio and other flows to developing countries implies, developing countries should take necessary steps against volatile flows, which are the sources of increasing vulnerabilities in developing countries. Furthermore, those countries that were unwilling or unable to conduct considerable countercyclical fiscal and monetary policies were among the most affected ones. Our study suggests that all countries should work on timely and proper fiscal and monetary responses instead of being relatively inactive in the face of global shocks.

Overall, our analysis demonstrates that how an economy is integrated to the world economy is a crucial factor to understanding why some countries were affected more than others by the crisis. Economies that experienced very hasty trade and financial flows integration without much institutional capacity accumulated especially huge vulnerabilities during the 'great moderation'. Furthermore, those countries with more reliance on certain export markets and commodity exports are very vulnerable to the cycles in advanced countries. Therefore, our analysis implies that developing countries would be less exposed to external shocks by choosing a strategic integration to the world economy rather than embracing a fully-fledged neo-liberal agenda.

NOTES

1. The names of the authors are in alphabetical order by author's last name. This does not necessarily reflect the relative contribution of the authors.
2. For example: Ceballos et al. (2013); Eichengreen (2010); Cömert and Çolak (2014).
3. For instance, the IMF working paper (2009) written by Berkmen et al. (2009), using cross country regressions, tries to explain the differences in the impacts across developing countries. They utilize growth forecast revisions for this purpose. They primarily associate the decline in revisions to financial linkages and, contrary to our findings, they attach secondary importance to the trade channel. In another study, focusing on policy responses and recovery period, Didier, Hevia and Schmukler (2011) explore the cross country incidence of the crisis for 183 countries. Similarly, Rose and Spiegel (2009) conduct an econometric analysis on a cross section of 85 countries to measure the crisis incidence. Contrary to common perceptions, they do not find strong evidence that associates international linkages with the incidence of the crisis. However, these studies don't pay enough attention to country specific factors that may not be easily captured by panel data econometrics.
4. It should be noted that a complete cross country analysis would only be possible if the countries that were least affected are also analyzed and comparisons between the least and the most affected ones are made. However, that discussion is beyond the scope of

this chapter. We are considering comparing the least and the worst affected countries as a further research agenda.

5. Apart from some regional studies, there are not many studies focusing on a set of worst affected countries. Many existing studies focus on Central and Eastern European Countries. Berglöf et al. (2009), Kattel (2010), Sprenger and Vincent (2010), ECB Bulletin (July 2010), Aslund (2011) and Bartlett and Prica (2012) discuss the effects of the crisis on Central and Eastern European countries.

6. As a selection criterion, even if we use the difference in the average GDP growth of countries from 2002 to 2008 and GDP growth in 2009, the countries in our set remain mostly intact.

7. We have eliminated the UAE from the analysis because trade and financial account data were unavailable for this country.

8. Since our main focus is on economic factors, the role of other factors such as the existence of political crises in the growth performance of these countries was also investigated. Among the selected countries only Russia went through a political crisis (Russian–Georgian War in 2008). Therefore, we mentioned the effect of this war on Russia and other countries in the region such as Ukraine and Moldova in our discussion. With regard to the effects of natural problems, the effect of drought at the start of the crisis in Paraguay was considered as well, since it is a country highly dependent on agricultural exports, particularly soybeans.

9. CIS, a group of alliance countries, refers to former Soviet Republics excluding Baltic States Estonia, Latvia and Lithuania. Formally, these CIS countries are: Armenia, Azerbaijan, Belarus, Georgia, Kazakhstan, Kyrgyzstan, Moldova, Russian Federation, Tajikistan, Turkmenistan, Ukraine and Uzbekistan. Georgia left the group after the Russian–Georgian War of 2008.

10. CEE refers to a group of countries including Albania, Bulgaria, Croatia, the Czech Republic, Hungary, Poland, Romania, the Slovak Republic, Slovenia, Estonia, Latvia and Lithuania. Among these countries, six of them (Bulgaria, Croatia, Hungary, Latvia, Lithuania and Romania) are in our set.

11. Although it has recently become much more obvious that a positive global outlook was a driving force behind the overall positive performance of developing countries from 2002 to 2008, many economists and institutions including the IMF argued that the performance of the developing countries in this period was the outcome of the improvements in their policies and institutional structures. For instance, the IMF October 2008 World Economic Outlook widely stresses sound policy choices in developing countries, which enabled them to achieve lower fiscal deficits, inflation levels and historically high levels of international reserves.

12. Countries with the highest shares in the US imports are as follows: China (19 percent), EU (16.7 percent), Canada (14 percent), Mexico (12 percent) and Japan (6.4 percent). In other words, developing countries have a share of more than 50 percent in the US's total imports.

13. In the period 2002 to 2008, out of 106 developing countries, 42 countries had surpluses, 52 countries had almost current account balance and the rest had considerable deficits in their current accounts.

14. Many of these countries took measures to strengthen their financial markets as well.

15. An appreciation of domestic currency would decrease the debt to GDP ratio by causing an increase in GDP converted in foreign currency.

16. A region based classification is possible as well. Transition economies and Turkey can be investigated in terms of their proximity to Europe. Mexico, Paraguay, Botswana and Kuwait can be put into the category 'others'.

17. Rapid credit expansion also caused real estate bubbles in some countries that are analyzed in this chapter. For instance, housing bubbles in Baltic States are widely discussed in the literature. According to a study by Krusinskas (2012), three Baltic States (Latvia, Lithuania and Estonia), two of which are discussed in this chapter (Latvia and Lithuania), experienced housing bubbles as housing prices rose out of proportion

with the income of these countries' residents. For other countries that we investigated, there are some debates on whether they experienced a housing bubble or not. For most countries, house price data is unavailable or only became available for the years following the global crisis. Therefore, given the scope of this chapter and ongoing debates in literature, we cannot firmly assert the existence of housing bubbles in the countries that we analyze. However, existing literature helps us to conclude that increases in house prices were observed prior to the crisis in many countries. For further discussion, we can suggest the following studies:

Manookian and Tolosa (2011), 'Armenia's housing boom bust cycle', retrieved from https://www.imf.org/external/country/arm/rr/2011/112811.pdf on August 18, 2014.

Abotalaf (2011), 'Kuwait economic report', retrieved from http://www.capstandards.com/CSR_KuwaitEconomicReport_Feb2011.pdf on August 18, 2014.

Crowe, Dell'Ariccia, Igan and Rabanal (2012), 'Policies for macrofinancial stability: managing real estate booms and boosts', retrieved from https://www.imf.org/external/np/seminars/eng/2012/fincrises/pdf/ch12.pdf on March 1, 2016.

18. Wealth effect refers to the change in consumption expenditures that accompanies a change in perceived wealth. For example, when asset prices rise, agents feel that the value of their portfolio rises and they feel more comfortable and secure about their wealth, leading them to consume more out of their wealth.

19. High GDP growth trend based on financial inflows and increased consumption is emphasized for these countries by many others. For example the ECB report in July 2010 argues that, in the years preceding the crisis, Eastern European countries grew rapidly at unsustainable rates. In this sense, Dudzińska (2011) associates high growth rates observed in Latvia between 2004 and 2007 mainly to substantial inflows of foreign capital, which stimulated domestic demand. Similarly, Stoiciu (2012) maintains that the growth in Romania in the pre-crisis period is mainly related to the boom in the domestic consumption of durable goods, which also induced a large current account deficit.

20. The effects of financial inflows in creating higher levels of external indebtedness can be summarized as follows. Accordingly, large financial inflows resulted in rapid credit growth, which fed consumption expenditures and put upward pressures on asset prices. As rises in asset prices created excess demand pressures, their effects were translated into high inflation and appreciated REERs. As a result, in the countries under investigation and in many other upper middle income countries, there was decreasing competitiveness in international markets and, relatedly, higher Current Account deficits.

21. In the Russian case financial flows did not reach the levels of other transition countries. However, since the Russian economy has been giving current account surpluses, positive financial flows put significant extra pressure on domestic currency and credit expansion in this country.

22. The decline in commodity prices can also be seen from commodity price indexes. For example, the crude oil price index fell from 181.87 in 2008 to 115.787 in 2009. Similar declines were observed for the metals price index (169.03, 2008 to 136.53 in 2009) and the agricultural raw material price index (113.367, 2008 to 93.929 in 2009).

23. This is related, to a large extent, to geographical proximity and economic integration provided by the European Union.

24. The shares of the manufacturing sector (which is an important subset of industrial products) in total exports are given as: Bulgaria (48.9 percent), Croatia (61.3 percent), Hungary (83.7 percent), Latvia (57.3 percent), Lithuania (54.2 percent), Romania (77.7 percent), Armenia (27.2 percent), Moldova (54 percent), Ukraine (57.4 percent) and Russia (19.3 percent) (Source: WTO).

25. The main motive behind the high share of foreign currency credits was lower interest rates that paid for these credits relative to domestic currency denominated credits.

26. This has created significant stress in these countries since they ran up dangerously large current account deficits (except for Russia) and took on substantial international debt (Boorman, 2009). In other words, as our study demonstrated, the countries with large

current account deficits were disproportionately hit by the crisis as foreign investors deleveraged and capital flows dried up.

27. Although the analysis of the financial channel is highly complex since there are various types of financial instruments and several ways in which financial intermediaries like international banks or global bond markets operate, the general picture of the financial channel can be seen by focusing on the developments in the financial account. There are different approaches about which indicator would best describe the impact of financial flows on economies. Borio and Disyatat (2011) argue that gross flows are much more important indicators for this purpose. However, as Cömert and Düzçay (2014) argue, although gross flows would be a much more meaningful indicator for developed countries, net flows are still crucial to understanding the pressure on exchange rates, which are the most important factors for asset prices and reserves in developing countries. Moreover, the difference between net flows and gross flows are not very significant in many developing countries. Therefore, we will focus on net financial flows in our discussion on developing countries whereas gross flows will be emphasized more in our discussion on the advanced economies. The trends in gross and net private flows will be discussed in some cases for the purpose of highlighting different risk perceptions of private players in different periods.

28. The decline in financial flows into Croatia started after 2009. Although the magnitude of the decline seems low from the figure, a sharp decline of financial flows occurred in Croatia after 2009. The net financial account to GDP ratio fell to 2.94 percent in 2010 from its ratio of 10.44 percent in 2009.

29. An ECB bulletin (2010) also highlights similar points.

30. Financial institutions in advanced countries found themselves in a very bad situation when asset prices lost their values and the interbank lending market froze. Therefore, these institutions stopped lending (sudden stop). And some of them started to call back their lending or withdrew funds from their subsidiaries in developing countries to strengthen their balance sheets in their headquarters (financial reversal).

31. This shows that the Turkish economy did not devote enough resources to investment in machinery or technology, which play important roles in terms of productivity, capacity utilization and sustainable growth paths in developing countries.

32. For instance, a study by Benlialper et al. (2015) demonstrates that Turkey had the second highest average inflation rate between 2002 and 2007 compared to 25 developing countries with similar GDP size and economic structure.

33. The mining sector accounted for 34.7 percent of GDP in 2011. Source: http://www.afdb. org/fileadmin/uploads/afdb/Documents/Publications/Bostwana%20Full%20PDF%20 Country%20Note.pdf retrieved on June 20, 2015.

34. Even though the credit growth in Turkey can be considered moderate relative to that in countries such as Latvia, Lithuania, Romania, Bulgaria and Ukraine, on average, the credit growth in this country was higher than that in other upper middle income countries.

35. Botswana, Kuwait and Paraguay had large current account surpluses whereas Mexico's balance was slightly negative.

36. Sudden stop means a slowdown in financial inflows to a country rather than a reversal of financial flows.

37. When we consider the European Union instead of Europe, the exports from Turkey to the European Union were 39 percent.

38. The recent downturns in commodity prices after 2012 have adversely affected many commodity exporters.

39. For the details of this discussion see Cömert and Çolak (2014).

40. For instance, the ECB report (July 2010) links the limited ability of CEE countries to reduce interest rates to inflationary pressures, risks about financial stability associated with exchange rate depreciations, the share of outstanding foreign currency loans to the private sector and to high government debt ratios.

41. See, for example: *How Did Emerging Markets Cope in the Crisis?* (Gray et al., 2010).

42. Detailed information about calculating this average is given in the note under the figure.
43. The high level of reserves in Botswana is a result of high mining revenues registered under reserves.
44. It was also lower than the developing countries' average.
45. Latvia, Lithuania and Hungary joined the European Union in 2004. Romania and Bulgaria became members in 2007.

REFERENCES

Abotalaf, A. (2011), 'Kuwait Economic Report', *Capital Standards*, retrieved from http://www.capstandards.com/CSR_KuwaitEconomicReport_Feb2011.pdf on August 18, 2014.

Akyüz, Y. (2009), 'Policy response to the global financial crisis: key issues for developing countries', Research Paper, No. 24, South Centre.

Akyüz, Y. (2012), 'The staggering rise of the south?', Background Paper, No. 1, South Centre.

Aslund, A. (2011), 'Lessons from the East European financial crisis, 2008–2010', *Peterson Institute for International Economics*, Washington, DC.

Bartlett, W. and I. Prica (2012), 'The variable impact of the global economic crisis in South East Europe', LSEE Research on South Eastern Europe.

Benlialper, A. and H. Cömert (2013), 'Implicit asymmetric exchange rate peg under inflation targeting regimes: the case of Turkey', ERC Working Papers in Economics, No. 13/8, Economic Research Center, METU.

Benlialper, A., H. Cömert and G. Düzçay (2015), '2002 Sonrası Türkiye Ekonomisinin Performansı: Karşılaştırmalı Bir Analiz', ERC Working Papers in Economics, No. 15/4, Economic Research Center, METU.

Berglöf, E., Y. Korniyenko, A. Plekhanov and J. Zettelmeyer (2009), 'Understanding the crisis in emerging Europe', Working Paper, No. 49, European Bank for Reconstruction and Development.

Berkmen, P., G. Gelos, R. Rennhack and J.P. Walsh (2009), 'The global financial crisis: explaining cross country differences in the output impact', IMF Working Paper.

Bibow, J. (2010), 'Global imbalances, the US dollar, and how the crisis at the core of global finance spread to 'self-insuring' emerging market economies', Working Paper, No. 591, The Levy Economics Institute.

Boorman, J. (2009), 'The impact of the financial crisis on emerging market economies: the transmission mechanism, policy response and the lessons', Global Meeting of the Emerging Markets Forum 2009, Mumbai.

Borio, C. and P. Disyatat (2011), 'Global imbalances and the financial crisis: link or no link?', BIS Working Paper Series, No. 346, Bank for International Settlements.

Ceballos, F., T. Didier, C. Hevia and S. Schmukler (2013), 'Policy responses to the global financial crisis: what did emerging economies do differently?', Working Paper, No. 2013-002, The Central Reserve Bank of Peru.

Cömert, H. (2013), *Central Banks and Financial Markets: The Declining Power of US Monetary Policy*, Cheltenham, UK and Northampton, MA, USA: Edward Elgar Publishing.

Cömert, H. and S. Çolak (2013), 'Gelişmekte olan ülkelerdeki kriz sırası ve sonrasınndaki trendleri açıklamakta 'güvenli liman faktörü' ve finansal şokların boyutunun önemi: Türkiye örneği', ERC Working Papers in Economics, No. 13/09, Economic Research Center, METU.

Cömert, H. and S. Çolak (2014), 'The impacts of the global crisis on the Turkish economy and policy responses', ERC Working Papers in Economics, No. 14/17, Economic Research Center, METU.

Cömert, H. and G. Düzçay (2014), 'Küresel dengesizlikler ve kriz tartışması ışığında Cari denge ve sermaye hesabını anlamak', ERC Working Papers in Economics, No. 14/16, Economic Research Center, METU.

Crowe, C., G. Dell'Ariccia, D. Igan and P. Rabanal (2012), 'Policies for macro-financial stability: managing real estate booms and boosts', International Monetary Fund.

Didier, T., C. Hevia and S.L. Schmukler (2011), 'How resilient were emerging economies to the global crisis?', Policy Research Working Paper, No. 5637, The World Bank.

Dudzińska, K. (2011), 'Latvia: the economic crisis and (im)possible changes?', Lithuanian Foreign Policy Review, No. 26.

Eichengreen, B. (2010), 'Lessons of the crisis for emerging markets', *International Economics and Economic Policy*, 7 (1), 49–62.

European Central Bank Monthly Bulletin, July 2010, Frankfurt: European Central Bank.

Fidrmuc, J. and P.J. Süß (2009), 'The outbreak of the Russian financial crisis', Ludwig-Maximilians-Universität München.

Gray, G., B. Joshi, P. Kehayova, R. Llaudes, G. Presciuttini, M. Saenz and M. Chivakul (2010), 'How did emerging markets cope in the crisis?', Washington, DC: International Monetary Fund.

Griffith-Jones, S. and J.A. Ocampo (2009), 'The financial crisis and its impacts on developing countries', Working Paper, International Policy Centre for Inclusive Growth, No. 53.

Herr, H. and Z.M. Sonat (2013), 'Neoliberal unshared growth regime of Turkey in the post-2001 period', Global Labour University Working Paper, No. 19.

IMF (2011), World Economic Outlook 2011, IMF.

Jeanne, O. (2007), 'International reserves in emerging market countries: too much of a good thing?', Brookings Papers on Economic Activity, 1–55.

Karagöl, E.T. (2013), 'The Turkish economy during the Justice and Development Party decade', *Insight Turkey*, 15 (4), 115–129.

Katte, R. (2010), 'Financial and economic crisis in Eastern Europe', prepared for the conference on finance in Muttukadu, India.

Krusinskas, R. (2012), 'Research on housing bubbles in the capitals of the Baltic and Central Europe', *Economics and Management*, 17 (2), 480–485.

Manookian, A. and G. Tolosa (2011), 'Armenia's housing boom-bust cycle', retrieved from www.imf.org/external/country/arm/rr/2011/112811.pdf on August 18, 2014.

Meyn, M. and J. Kennan (2009), 'The implications of the global financial crisis for developing countries' export volumes and values', Overseas Development Institute.

Moreno, R. (2010), 'Central Bank instruments to deal with the effects of the crisis on emerging market economies', BIS Papers, No. 54.

Purfield, C. and C.B. Rosenberg (2010), 'Adjustment under a currency peg:

Estonia, Latvia and Lithuania during the global financial crisis 2008–09', IMF Working Paper.

Reinart, T., Z. Svetlosakova, A. Karaisl and P. Bednarczyk (2010), 'International and domestic financial responses in Latvia and Ukraine, 2008–2010', retrieved from www.mitchellorenstein.com/wp-content/uploads/2012/07/UKRAINELATVIA TRIPREPORT.pdf in August 2015.

Rose, A.K. and M.M. Spiegel (2009), 'Cross country causes and consequences of the 2008 crisis: international linkages and American exposure', NBER Working Paper Series.

Shkura, I. and B. Peitsch (2011), 'Assessing Ukrainian banking performance before and after the crisis', *Journal of Entrepreneurship, Management and Innovation*, 7, 29–42.

Sprenger, E. and V. Vincentz (2010), 'Financial crisis in Central and Eastern Europe', Osteuropa Institut.

Stoiciu, V. (2012), 'Austerity and structural reforms in Romania', Freidrich Ebert Stiftung.

Sturgeon, J.T., O. Memedovic, J.V. Biesebroeck and G. Gereffi (2009), 'Globalisation of the automotive industry: main features and trends', *International Journal of Technological Learning, Innovation and Development*, 2 (1–2), 7–24.

Telli, Ç., E. Voyvoda and E. Yeldan (2006), 'Modeling general equilibrium for socially responsible macroeconomics: seeking for the alternatives to fight jobless growth in Turkey', Middle East Technical University Studies in Development, 33 (2), 255–293.

Yeldan, E. and H. Ercan (2011), 'Growth, employment policies and economic linkages: Turkey', International Labour Organization.

2. A tale of two worlds? Income distribution and the global crisis: observations from the North/South nexus

Serdal Bahçe and Ahmet Haşim Köse

2.1 INTRODUCTION

The disastrous outcomes of neo-liberal economic programs followed by most of the world since the beginning of the 1980s have called forth a growing literature on income distribution.[1] The rationale behind these programs perceives the distribution of income as a result of a market pricing mechanism. In this sense, the conventional wisdom had been inclined to abstain from any analysis of income distribution. However, the aggravated impoverishment observed in Africa, Asia and Latin America, and the uneven development in the advanced world at the end of the 1990s has reinvigorated this long forgotten issue. The initial response to this pressing problem was a mere replication of the basic premises of the neo-liberal economic programs. The World Bank's highly acknowledged reports about poverty promulgated a thesis indicating that mass poverty is due to the inaccessibility of the market dynamics (World Bank, 1990, 2001). In this context the cure is obvious; economic and financial support targeting the impoverished masses will enhance their access to the market dynamics and improve their physical and mental capacity. This improvement will eventually raise their employability. These steps should also be supported by proper market friendly reforms. After the proclamation of this diagnosis, widespread international and national poverty mitigation schemes were put into operation. Nevertheless, more recent empirical research has revealed highly disturbing facts; studies show that the working classes make up the majority of the stock of the poor (BLS, 2010; Eurofund, 2010). This suggests that participating in market processes does not provide a protective belt against impoverishment. Naturally, this brings about a reinvigorated interest in the distribution of income. This renewed interest has also been fed by the growing literature concerning the effects of capitalist crises.

The moment of a capitalist crisis is a particular instance in which structural tendencies become highly crystallized and easily observed. Capitalism has a tendency to extend beyond the boundaries of inequalities, and this tendency, in itself, operates in a highly uneven manner. In this context, the repercussions of a capitalist crisis have been distributed unequally both at national and international levels. The global crisis, which erupted in the center of the system, undoubtedly had strong contagion effects, which swept across the capitalist world economy through capital and trade linkages. However, it is important to note that, as indicated, these effects were distributed and felt unequally. Besides this, even though it was assumed to be global, this does not mean that all the constituent parts faced contraction in output and employment. Under full capital mobility, some countries/regions exploited the capital reversal in crisis prone countries/regions. Therefore, some countries have exhibited a completely different story. Again the detection of these countries necessitates a well-grounded income distribution analysis. This analysis should extend beyond the mere measurement of relative income shares.

The effects of any crisis upon income distribution in all dimensions are likely to be temporary since the distribution of income has been determined by structural and permanent factors. However, this does not mean that these effects deserve less analytical effort and can be overlooked. First of all, these effects disclose the different ways of integration to the world economy. Second, the analysis of these effects may reveal the most vulnerable entities. Third, such an analysis also allows for the identification of the structural determinants.

One basic concern about the income distribution analysis is methodology. The most commonly used methodologies, namely size distribution of income and functional income distribution analyses, have serious deficiencies. The size distribution of income distribution divides the whole population into fixed income brackets and then looks for the income share of each segment. This approach prioritizes the income earned over all social and economic attributes. The underlying economic and social processes are totally neglected. Therefore, size distribution of income distribution is quite useless in detecting the roots of any change in income distribution. On the other hand, functional income distribution analysis, which focuses on the shares of factor incomes, is likely to promise more, at least in analyzing the cause of any change in income distribution. Besides this merit, there is one basic shortcoming of this line of analysis: it dehumanizes production relations and reduces all to a mere interplay of income shares. Moreover, it fails to discriminate among the social identities of factor income earners emanating from production relations.

Besides all shortcomings and merits, each methodology provides important information about the change in income distribution. In this study we will provide the results of our analysis employing both methodologies. The object of the analysis is the global capitalist economy. The time under scrutiny is the crisis period, the years 2008 and 2009, even though we will briefly outline the developments just prior to the crisis in order to provide a short historical background.[2] It is very obvious that since our topic is too large to fit in a book chapter we will be forced to be highly selective and categorical about the facts and trends. In a scientific analysis each categorization and periodization has inevitably resulted in too broad categories in which dissimilar items or temporalities are grouped together. Nevertheless, any analysis, most particularly one that is to be conducted at a global level, will run the risk of being trapped in highly inclusive generalizations. This study is no exception.

This study will, at last, show that the latest global capitalist crisis proceeded very unevenly and most of the countries in the Global South were not affected to the same extent as the developed capitalist world. Moreover, the trend of a decreasing share of developed capitalist countries in world income began prior to the crisis and continued during the crisis. The Global South's wage share showed a steep incline during the crisis, and most of this incline was due to the contraction of output. Finally, this study shows that the advanced countries and the countries in the Global South exhibited different and antithetical trends during the crisis. In the South, most of the countries increased their output, albeit at a lower rate compared to the pre-crisis period, and income distribution improved for most of these countries. On the other hand, most of the developed countries experienced a decline in output and worsening income distribution. The detailed evidence will be given below.

Section 2.2 will mainly focus on the income shares of country groups categorized according to the World Bank definition. Section 2.3 will provide an analysis based on the global Gini coefficient. In this part, a simple Gini decomposition technique will be employed to decompose the change in the global Gini coefficient into 'within' group and 'between' group components. Then, in Section 2.4 we proceed to the functional income distribution and focus mainly on the movement of the global wage share. Up to this point, the framework for the analysis is global and highly generalized. However, it is well known that global capitalism has been reproducing itself in an environment founded upon an eternal contradiction between homogenization and differentiation. Unevenness is the structural tendency of capitalism. In order to facilitate the analysis of this structural tendency during the global crisis, our analysis moves from the safe terrain constructed of simplified generalizations to the challenging soil of the analysis of the effects of the crisis upon countries/country groups. Section 2.5, therefore, reveals the effects of the crisis upon the income distribution within countries and among country groups by using both size distribution and functional distribution analyses. We also present supplementary observations – in order to assess the channels through which the contagion effects of the crisis have permeated into national economies.

2.2 INCOME DISTRIBUTION AND CRISIS ON A GLOBAL SCALE

Prior to the crisis that erupted in the USA toward the end of 2007 the capitalist world, according to Krugman (2009), had been living in a mood of drowsiness.[3] The leading economists of the developed capitalist world heralded the end of depression economics and joyfully advised the removal of the topic of business cycles from curricula. This environment was very similar to the optimistic mood of the early 1970s just before the recession of the capitalist world economy. However, this environment was razed to the ground with the eruption of crisis. All the macroeconomic indicators turned downwards, especially for the developed capitalist world. Figure 2.1 shows the change in growth rates for the major country groups.

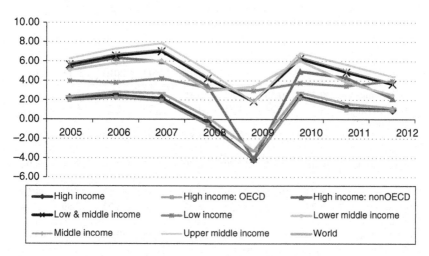

Source: World Development Indicators, World Bank.

Figure 2.1 The annual growth rates in world economy, 2005 to 2012

As Figure 2.1 shows, the growth rate of OECD countries dropped below zero in 2008 and, as a result, the growth rate of the whole world economy was sluggish during the same year. The main change came in 2009. In this year the growth rate of OECD countries in particular and high income countries in general dropped to nearly −4.1 percent. Because of the dominance of these countries in the total world income, the world economy grew by −3.25 percent in this year. On the other hand, low and middle income countries achieved positive growth, albeit at a relatively lower rate. In 2010 all the country groups displayed positive growth. Indeed, it seemed that all the groups returned to their pre-crisis growth paths. Nevertheless, 2011 and 2012 brought an end to this illusion. Without any exception, the growth rates of all the groups began to decrease in 2011. The prospects for the future in 2012 seemed bleak.

The differing growth rates, given above, resulted in a change in the shares in world income. Table 2.1 shows the share of each country group in total world income. As Table 2.1 indicates, since 2005 there has been a significant alteration in the distribution of world income among different country groups. The share of High Income Countries declined from 80.64 percent in 2005 to 74.98 percent in 2012. The trend of the decreasing share of High Income Countries seemed to start before the crisis. The rate of decrease increased slightly in 2009 and 2010. The major beneficiary from this trend was the middle income country group. Between 2005 and 2012 the combined share of the countries in this group rose by more than

Table 2.1   The share of country groups in world income, 2005 to 2012 (%)

	2005	2006	2007	2008	2009	2010	2011	2012
Low income	0.52	0.53	0.54	0.56	0.60	0.61	0.63	0.66
Lower middle income	4.40	4.54	4.71	4.85	5.20	5.39	5.53	5.62
Low and middle income	19.36	20.09	20.95	21.81	22.98	23.79	24.58	25.21
Upper middle income	14.45	15.02	15.70	16.39	17.17	17.78	18.41	18.94
Middle income	18.84	19.56	20.40	21.24	22.37	23.17	23.94	24.55
High income: nonOECD	5.27	5.42	5.57	5.73	5.66	5.77	5.89	5.94
High income: OECD	75.37	74.51	73.52	72.53	71.45	70.58	69.71	69.07
High income	80.64	79.92	79.08	78.24	77.09	76.33	75.58	74.98

Source: World Development Indicators, World Bank.

5 percent. Overall, the global crisis had a very low repercussion upon the world income distribution at first sight.

The analysis up to now views each country as a single entity and does not consider the relative size of each one. For a more accurate analysis of world income distribution one should also take the relative population size into consideration. In order to achieve this we employ a standard Gini decomposition technique. We benefit from a user written Stata module, *ginidesc*. This method allows the use of populations of countries as weights. It decomposes the overall Gini into three: (1) between, (2) within and (3) overlap components. The first refers to the distance between average incomes of groups and the second one designates the dispersion within a group. The last component is a residual and incorporates the part of the Gini that can be accrued to neither the 'between' nor the 'within' components. For this analysis we use the World Bank classification of countries (which was also used above). In this classification countries are categorized according to per capita real GNI of the year 2012 under the headings high, higher middle, lower middle and low income countries. Table 2.2 presents the results.

There are two panels in Table 2.2. Panel A shows the change in overall Gini and its components for the set of countries, including China and India. Panel B, on the other hand, gives the figures for the list of countries excluding China and India. The number of countries in the list is given between the two panels. The change in this column is due to the varying data availability for each year.

In Panel A there is an observable secular decline of Gini between 2000 and 2012, except for the year 2005.[4] The global crisis seemed to have no effect upon this tendency. Obviously, this trend is dominated by the parallel decline in the 'between' component. Between 2000 and 2012 this component declined by nearly 20 percent. In the same period only a slight decrease was observed for the 'within' component. For the overall Gini the rate of decline between the beginning and the end of the period is about 10 percent. This table provides very optimistic outcomes for a prospective analysis. However, these results are biased because of the overwhelming weight of India and China. For this reason, we remove China and India from the list and look for the movement of Gini without these countries.

As Panel B in Table 2.2 indicates, the exclusion of China and India raises the Gini coefficient by more than 10 points. The gap between the two Gini coefficients widens toward the end of the period. In 2000 the gap between the two Ginis was 12.6 points. The gap increased to 16.9 points at the end of the period. China and India, as the alleged new factories of the world, have increased their share in world income since the beginning of the 1990s. Both of them are grouped under middle income countries with China in the higher and India in the lower stratum of the group. Their

Table 2.2   The decomposition of world Gini, 2000 to 2012

	A. Gini with China and India				No. of Countries	B. Gini without China and India			
	Between	Overlap	Within	Total		Between	Overlap	Within	Total
2000	51.5	5.0	11.6	68.1	139	60.5	0.9	19.3	80.7
2001	51.0	5.2	11.6	67.8	141	60.8	0.8	19.1	80.8
2002	50.3	5.4	11.6	67.3	142	61	0.8	18.9	80.7
2003	49.5	5.8	11.6	66.9	143	61.3	0.8	18.7	80.8
2004	48.9	6.0	11.6	66.5	145	61.4	0.8	18.5	80.8
2005	48.1	6.8	11.9	66.8	183	61.9	0.9	18.6	81.4
2006	47.0	6.9	11.7	65.6	144	61.6	0.9	18.2	80.7
2007	45.5	7.6	11.6	64.7	142	61.3	0.9	18.2	80.3
2008	45.3	7.4	11.2	63.8	139	62.1	0.8	16.9	79.8
2009	43.4	8.5	11.3	63.2	136	61.9	0.8	16.9	79.6
2010	42.4	9	11.3	62.6	133	61.5	0.9	17	79.3
2011	41.6	9.3	11.2	62.1	124	61.2	0.9	16.9	79.0
2012	40.8	9.3	11.2	61.3	103	60.7	0.8	16.7	78.2

Note: For the sake of simplicity, all the values are multiplied by 100. 'Total' (the Gini coefficient of the corresponding year) is the sum of the 'Between', 'Within' and 'Overlap' components.

Source: Author's calculation based on various data sources explained in Appendix 1.

combined population was nearly 2.6 billion in 2012, which constitutes 37 percent of the world population. Since their income share has been increasing and this increase has been taking place mainly at the expense of the share of high income countries, inclusion of these countries will certainly reduce the Gini coefficient.

Panel B in Table 2.2 above provides interesting observations. The Gini without China and India dropped by only 3 percent between 2000 and 2012, while the Gini with China and India decreased by nearly 10 percent in the same period. Up to 2006, the former did not show any sign of decline. Rather, it increased. For the former, the dominant contribution came from the decline in the 'within' component; this is a stark contrast to the dominancy of the change in the 'between' component of the Gini with China and India included, since, as mentioned earlier, the 'between' component declined by nearly 20 percent with China and India. On the other hand, the 'between' component without China and India increased between 2000 and 2008 (with the exception of a slight decline in 2006 and 2007) then decreased nearly to its 2000 level in 2012. These figures point to the fact that the equalization of the world income distribution between country groups has no basis without China and India. China and India, in this period, have been assuming vital roles and generating an illusion of equalization of world income distribution. The global crisis of 2007 to 2009, even though erupting mainly in the center, was unlikely to channel the income from the developed to developing world.

However, there is one important shortcoming of the size distribution of household income analysis; household income does not cover undistributed profits of capitalist firms. This inevitably results in the underestimation of the incomes of stock holder families and individuals. For this reason, all the Gini coefficients are biased downwards. Moreover, the extent of underestimation directly increases with the share of undistributed profits.

Functional income distribution analysis overcomes this problem by benefiting from national accounts or sectoral aggregated data. For the effects of the global crisis upon the global economy in general, and upon the Global South in particular, this analysis should be complemented with a functional income distribution analysis at both global and national levels. However, as with the size distribution analysis, there is a significant data problem. Functional income distribution data for the Global South does not cover a long time span. Moreover, data for many countries is missing. In addition, there is a dangerous tendency observed in countries in the Global South. Many countries have stopped providing functional income distribution data.[5] In order to tackle this problem authors benefit mainly from the UN database for functional income distribution. In addition to this, many researchers compile data from national statistical sources. For the developed North, the AMECO database is the main data source.

In this analysis we will focus on wage share as the basic indicator of functional income distribution. However, there is still a deficiency in our analysis. The GDP at income approach data for many countries also covers a mixed income component. As indicated above, a part of the income from self-employment is wage income. However, measuring this part and isolating it from the profit component imposes some strictly limiting assumptions. A commonly employed method is to use the average wage rate of a particular group for the measurement of the 'wage' component of the income from self-employment. However, this method does not extricate us from confusion and gives rise to serious doubts. It inevitably brings about the question: which group and which wage? The benchmark group and wage should differ across countries. Since we will employ data from more than 100 countries and the selection of group and wage for each country requires country specific sociological and economic information, we will focus only on the wages of employees.

First of all, a brief sketch of the development of the wage share across the world economy should be given. Figure 2.2 gives the change in global wage share between 1960 and 2010. For reference, the annual growth rate

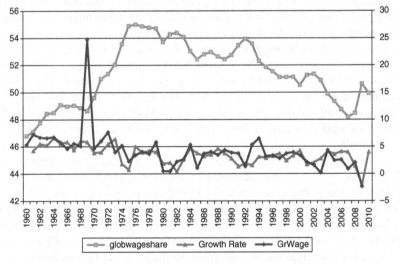

Note: globwageshare (% of world GDP) left axis; Growth Rate (Real World GDP growth, %) and GrWage (total world real wage growth, %) right axis.

Source: Author's calculation based on various data sources explained in Appendix 1.

Figure 2.2   The global wage share, 1960 to 2010

of the global economy is also given on the right vertical axis. Some reservations about the figure should be underlined. First, the data for the period 1960 to 1980 comes mainly from the developed capitalist countries. The data for the Global South begins mainly after 1980. Second, the wage shares for each country[6] are multiplied by respective GDPs at constant US$ (2005=100) in order to attain the total real wage of the country. Then the sum of national total real wages is divided by world real GDP, which is deflated in the same manner. There might be other means of estimation and we do not think that our method is the best one. For example, GDP at Purchasing Power Parity (PPP) might be a reasonable option. Nevertheless, each method has its own shortcomings.

As Figure 2.2 indicates, the global wage share rose steeply between 1960 and 1978. Since data for this period is from developed countries, this rise is the result of Keynesian macroeconomic policies in the 1960s and industrial unrest as a result of the global capitalist crisis of the 1970s. Thereafter a long run tendential decline has ensued. In our model the wage share displayed a sudden increase globally after the eruption of the global crisis in 2007. This is unexpected since the growth rate of global GDP was negative during the crisis and wage share is taken to be a variable that adjusts with a lag. In addition, for the long run tendency, the correlation between the wage share and real GDP growth is negative. We estimated the correlation coefficient as −0.4. This means that the wage share is likely to increase while the real GDP growth rate declines. We interpret these unexpected results cautiously and, because the denominator in the wage share equation is real GDP, it substantiates our initial assumption that between 1960 and 1978 real GDP grew at a slower rate.

For the analysis of the effects of the crisis, the time span should be shortened and the analysis should be conducted for different country groups. Figure 2.3 shows the wage share of different country groups for the period 2000 to 2011. As Figure 2.3 shows, the wage share declined between 2000 and 2008. The rate of decrease was highest for the upper middle income group. As a subgroup to middle income countries, China and India had the largest decrease in the middle income group.

On the other hand, during the crisis the wage share increased for all groups except for the less developed countries (Figure 2.3). The reasons for this increase can be found at the national level.

2.3   INCOME DISTRIBUTION OF COUNTRIES DURING THE CRISIS

The world capitalist system has been founded upon the network of nation states. The hierarchical bidirectional and multidirectional

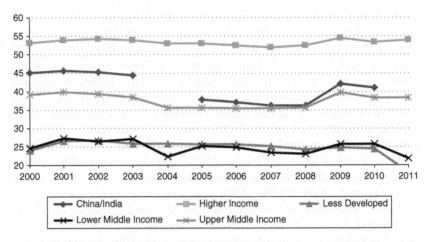

Source: Author's calculation based on various data sources explained in Appendix 1.

Figure 2.3   The change in wage share of different country groups (%)

flows of power operate in line with the structure of global capitalist production relations. However, capitalist production relations, at the last resort, have an inescapable tendency to personalize production relations. In this respect, inequality on a global scale is the direct outcome of the inequalities institutionalized at the national level. Therefore, such an analysis should be extended to cover an analysis of inequality at a national level.

In order to evaluate income distribution at country level, we utilize both size distribution and functional distribution analyses. However, this step also requires the extension of the boundaries of the analysis to incorporate the evaluation of change in our three critical indicators:

1.   The GDP growth rate;
2.   The employment growth rate; and
3.   The real wage growth rate.

In addition, the analysis must tell us something about the actual components of GDP. Therefore our model has to be able to compute and record three important ratios:

1.   The change in the current account balance/GDP;
2.   The change in gross fixed capital formation/GDP; and
3.   The change in final consumption/GDP ratios.

The entire functional income distribution analysis benefits from two simple identities:

1. Growth rate of wage share = Growth rate of total real wage − Growth rate of real GDP.
2. Growth rate of total real wage = Growth rate of real wage per employee + Growth rate of employment.

These identities tell us that the change in wage share is determined by our three critical growth rates: (1) GDP, (2) real wage per employee, and (3) the growth rate of employment. Moreover, we use the change in the Gini coefficient of each country during the crisis as an additional criterion. Since the wage share is a proxy only displaying the share of the working class, the study of the relative income shares of other classes necessitates a general income distribution indicator like the Gini coefficient (even though it has the shortcomings mentioned above).

These four indictors are used to construct a map of the effects of the global crisis upon income distribution. For this mapping, the direction of change during the crisis is more vital than the magnitude of the change. For the direction of the change in these indicators, we subtract the average of the values of the particular indicator for the period 2005 to 2007 from that of the period 2008 to 2009, then determine the direction of change.[7]

The data comes from multiple sources and we know that this has generated serious comparability problems. However, due to incompleteness of data from a unique data source, we have to use multiple sources. The data sources are briefly outlined in Appendix 1. Our dataset consists of 113 countries in three groups:

1. G10 (comprising the core North countries);
2. Other developed countries and emerging market economies (incorporating noncore North and emerging South); and finally
3. Periphery.

Table 2.3 gives the direction of change in our critical indicators and some of the secondary indicators for G10.[8] The table shows that, except for Switzerland, G10 countries did not fare well during the crisis. Even Switzerland was not immune to the deterioration in income distribution. The UK and Sweden displayed deterioration in all four critical indicators. Except for the real wage per employee, the USA also performed badly in income distribution, GDP growth and employment growth. Ten out of eleven had to face a contraction in real GDP while eight of them also experienced a deterioration in income distribution. There are four countries that experienced a reduction in employment, and the real wage per employee decreased in six countries. The most interesting observation is that even though unemployment increased in the USA, the real wage per employee seemed to increase. This might be due to the reflexive strategy of employers, which dictates laying off the less skilled and lower earning employees first. The impact of the crisis environment could be observed in the change in relative shares of investment and final consumption in national income. Without any exception, all the countries in the list faced a relative decline in the share of investment while the share of final consumption increased with the exception of Italy. The last column shows the change in the share of public expenditures in GDP. Except for Switzerland, all the countries increased the share of public expenditure. The increase in the share of final consumption and the share of public expenditure should both be seen as the results of policy steps taken to mitigate the effects of crisis. Both were used to augment (or at least to limit the rate of decrease in the case of some countries) national demand. From Table 2.3, we can infer that in the run up to the crisis the UK, the USA, Sweden and Japan were the most fragile and susceptible to the vagaries of world capitalism.

Table 2.4 shows 38 countries from the noncore North and emerging market industrial South. There are 38 countries in the list. Using the change in income distribution and GDP growth as criteria, the table is divided into four sub-panels. Countries in the first group experienced deteriorating income distribution and a contraction of output during the crisis. This group mainly covers noncore North and transition countries. The second group of nine countries, on the other hand, shows evidence of deteriorating income distribution while output grew. The third group of nine includes a group of countries that generally recorded marginally positive performance across all critical indicators (with the exception of Colombia, China and Venezuela) except our critical employment/unemployment ratio indicator. The fourth group of countries includes those countries with negative growth but a positive change in income distribution.

As a matter of fact, the growth rate naturally delimits two main groups in the list: contracting and growing countries. Most of the noncore North and transition countries are found in the first group while the alleged new factories of the capitalist world are in the second. Again, we should find some prime examples that could be used to effectively portray the repercussions of the crisis. Iceland, Lithuania, Latvia, Spain, Denmark, Finland, Hungary and Ukraine are the most important candidates since in at least three of the four indicators they displayed a bad performance. On the other hand, the second and third panels, which include the countries that had positive growth rates during the crisis, prove the unevenness of the global capitalist crisis. There are 18 countries in these sub-panels and wage

Table 2.3 *Performance of G10 during the global crisis*

	Income Distribution	Growth of GDP	Growth of Employment	Growth of Real Wage per Employee	Change in Gross Capital Formation (% of GDP)	Current Acc. (% of GDP)	Change in Final Consumption Expenditure, etc. (% of GDP)	Change in Public Expense (% of GDP)
USA	–	–	–	+	–5.5	–5.4	2.3	5.0
UK	–	–	–	–	–3.6	–2.8	1.3	5.9
Sweden	–	–	–	–	–2.4	8.4	1.8	0.6
France	–	–	+	–	–2.0	–0.7	1.3	2.8
Canada	–	–	+	–	–1.9	1.4	3.5	1.6
Germany	–	–	+	+	–1.8	6.3	0.7	4.9
Netherlands	–	–	+	+	–1.4	7.8	0.9	5.7
Switzerland	–	+	+	+	–3.1	12.2	–1.2	–0.2
Belgium	+	–	+	+	–2.6	1.8	2.6	3.0
Italy	+	–	+	–	–2.8	–2.2	1.7	4.8
Japan	+	–	–	–	–3.0	4.1	2.5	3.6

Note: '–' indicates deterioration, '+' signifies improvement. For income distribution a negative sign points to an increase in the Gini coefficient for the period 2008 to 2009 relative to the period 2005 to 2007.

Source: Author's calculation based on various data sources explained in Appendix 1.

Table 2.4 *Performance of developed and emerging market economies during the global crisis*

	Income Distribution	Growth	Wage Employment	Real Wage per Employee	Change in Gross Capital Formation (% of GDP)	Curr. Acc. (% GDP)	Change in Final Consumption Expenditure, etc. (% of GDP)	Change in Public Expense (% of GDP)
Iceland	–	–	–	–	–17.1	–18.6	–4.9	8.1
Lithuania	–	–	–	–	–16.4	–10.8	4.8	10.7
Latvia	–	–	–	–	–17.9	–19.1	1.4	7.1
Spain	–	–	–	+	–7.1	–8.8	1.7	5.7
Denmark	–	–	–	+	–6.4	2.9	2.6	8.5
Finland	–	–	–	+	–3.5	5.0	3.6	4.8
Greece	–	–	+	+	–5.7	–11.2	4.3	8.5
Luxembourg	–	–	+	+	–4.4	10.7	1.1	6.4
Austria	–	–	+	+	–1.7	2.8	0.6	0.6
Russia	–	–	+	+	–2.8	8.6	2.9	10.3
Indonesia	–	+	+	+	5.6	1.8	–1.2	–1.4
Korea	–	+	+	+	–3.3	1.9	1.4	1.7
Thailand	–	+	+	+	–7.5	1.0	0.6	2.9
South Africa	–	+	+	+	–0.1	–5.2	–1.4	3.5
Israel	–	+	+	–	–2.0	3.6	–0.6	–3.1
Australia	–	+	+	–	0.2	–6.2	–1.6	1.5
Bulgaria	–	+	–	+	–1.9	–18.8	–5	–0.3
Romania	–	+	–	+	–1.5	–10.8	–3.9	19.6

Country								
Pakistan	−	+	+	−	−1.5	−4.6	3.8	1.5
Malaysia	+	+	+	+	−5.0	15.1	3.1	3.8
Argentina	+	+	+	+	−2.1	3.1	1.5	..
Chile	+	+	+	+	−1.6	3.4	4.5	4.9
Poland	+	+	+	+	−1.2	−4.2	−0.4	0.3
India	+	+	+	+	0.2	−1.0	2.1	1.6
Brazil	+	+	+	+	0.7	1.0	0.5	−0.3
Colombia	+	−	+	+	0.6	−2.0	−1.4	..
China	+	−	+	+	6.0	8.2	−2.6	..
Venezuela	+	−	+	+	−1.0	12.9	10.0	..
New Zealand	+	+	−	+	−5.1	−7.0	1.9	15.0
Norway	+	+	−	+	−1.2	15.2	1.0	4.1
Taiwan	+	+	−	+	..	15.3	..	..
Turkey	+	+	−	−	−6.2	−6.3	1.1	..
Mexico	+	+	−	−	−0.1	−0.1	−0.2	..
Estonia	+	−	−	+	−18.3	−18.3	3.3	9.5
Ireland	+	−	−	+	−12.0	−4.1	6.3	13.4
Portugal	+	−	−	+	−2.9	−10.4	1.5	4.1
Ukraine	+	−	−	−	−7.6	−7.1	4.5	4.8
Hungary	+	−	−	−	−5.7	−5.8	−0.4	2.7

Source: Author's calculation based on various data sources explained in Appendix 1.

employment increased in 12 of them. Moreover, real wage per employee dropped in only two of them. These two exceptions, Israel and Australia, belong to the noncore North. In this list, only six countries (Indonesia, Australia, Brazil, Colombia, China and India) increased their share of gross investment in GDP. Since these countries also increased their real GDP during the crisis, this points to the fact that these countries also succeeded in increasing investment in magnitude. Twelve out of 37 countries in the list decreased their share of final consumption during the crisis. The table provides interesting facts. For example, four out of six countries listed above that increased their share of gross fixed capital formation in GDP during the crisis decreased their share of final consumption in GDP. This directly contradicts the general pattern displayed by most of the countries whose data is used here. This indicates that these countries reacted to the contagion effects of the global crisis with an investment driven regime.

Up to now, we have not focused on the magnitude of change but rather on the direction of change. However, some regularity can be seen in the figures indicating change. For example, the decrease in the share of investment in GDP was much higher for the first sub-panel, which includes the countries exhibiting the worst performance. With reference to the last column, dependence on the increase in the share of public expense seems to be a more viable alternative for northern cone and transition countries. Even though positive, the increase in the share of public expense in the southern cone countries was comparably lower.[9] It seems that it is very hard to detect a deterministic relation between performance during the crisis and current account balance.

Table 2.5 provides observations for the remaining 45 countries. We label this group as 'periphery', although we know that some of the included countries may prove to be a challenge to this label. Even though this categorization does not seem convincing, it will ease the analytical workload.

In Table 2.5, only eight countries had to endure a decrease in real GDP; five of them are transition countries (Georgia, Slovenia, Armenia, Czech Republic and Croatia). Four of them also experienced deterioration in income distribution and seven showed evidence of declining wage employment. Of the remaining 35 countries that displayed positive growth during the crisis, 13 countries had more unequal post-crisis income distribution. These countries, with few exceptions, increased wage employment during the crisis. The last 22 countries, with the exceptions of Moldova and Serbia, decreased inequality in income distribution and achieved positive growth rates for GDP and wage employment. When the change in real wage per employee is also taken into account, 13 out of these last 22 countries showed a positive performance for all the indicators.

Sixteen countries above also increased the share of gross investment in

Table 2.5 *Performance of periphery during the global crisis*

	Income Distribution	Growth	Wage Employment	Real Wage per Employee	Change in Gross Capital Formation (% of GDP)	Curr. Acc. Balance (% GDP)	Change in Final Consumption Expenditure, etc. (% of GDP)	Change in Public Expense (% of GDP)
Georgia	–	–	–	+	-19.1	-15.2	14.2	10.8
Croatia	–	–	–	–	-6.6	-6.4	-0.1	2.4
Slovenia	–	–	–	+	-6.8	-2.7	2.1	4.2
Armenia	–	–	+	–	-0.1	-3.1	6.8	6.4
Czech Rep.	+	–	–	+	-4.2	-2.5	1.2	2.3
Puerto Rico	+	–	–	+	-3.6	..	0.6	..
El Salvador	+	–	–	–	-3	-4.6	0.7	3.9
Hong Kong	+	–	–	+	0.3	12.5	2.5	1.5
Azerbaijan	–	+	+	+	-12	15.4	2.5	..
Malta	–	+	+	+	-4.9	-7.6	0.9	-54.6
Mauritius	–	+	+	+	-3.7	-6.6	3.3	..
Uganda	–	+	+	+	0.1	-3.3	-4	-2.7
Tanzania	–	+	+	+	1.5	-8.5	-2.1	..
Albania	–	+	+	+	2.8	-8.3	-3.3	..
Macedonia	–	+	+	+	3.7	-3.5	1.8	1.3
Kyrgyz Republic	–	+	+	+	5.7	-5.9	-4.2	7.5
Costa Rica	–	+	–	+	-8.9	-5.2	2.3	..
Vietnam	–	+	+	–	1.2	-3.4	4.5	..
Nigeria	–	+	+	–	4.4	24.8	2.6	0.6
Slovak Republic	–	+	–	+	-8.3	-5.7	2.8	3.9
Ethiopia	–	+	–	–	-0.7	-9.7	-0.7	1.5
Honduras	+	+	+	+	-9.3	-5.3	4.5	2.9
Jordan	+	+	+	+	-4.6	-15.4	-7.8	-4

Table 2.5 (continued)

	Income Distribution	Growth	Wage Employment	Real Wage per Employee	Change in Gross Capital Formation (% of GDP)	Curr. Acc. Balance (% GDP)	Change in Final Consumption Expenditure, etc. (% of GDP)	Change in Public Expense (% of GDP)
Cyprus	+	+	+	+	−3.7	−7.0	4.1	−28.6
Bhutan	+	+	+	+	−3.1	4.0	7.0	4.1
Dominican Rep.	+	+	+	+	−3.1	−3.4	4.7	1.1
Sri Lanka	+	+	+	+	−2.6	−4.1	1.6	0.5
Bangladesh	+	+	+	+	−0.2	1.0	1.5	1.6
Uruguay	+	+	+	+	0.8	−0.9	−0.8	3.9
Tunisia	+	+	+	+	1.9	−1.7	−0.9	1.7
Peru	+	+	+	+	2.0	2.0	0.1	0.2
Ecuador	+	+	+	+	3.4	2.9	−2.6	..
Panama	+	+	+	+	4.9	−5.4	−10.2	..
Belarus	+	+	+	+	5.7	−3.0	0.4	..
Nicaragua	+	+	+	−	−6.4	−13.8	−1.6	1.3
Kazakhstan	+	+	+	−	−4.5	−4.1	−0.4	..
Paraguay	+	+	+	−	−2.6	2.1	6.2	2.5
Egypt	+	+	+	−	0.0	1.7	1.7	0.3
Tajikistan	+	+	+	−	1.9	−5.0	7.8	..
Bolivia	+	+	+	−	2.5	10.1	−1.0	..
Singapore	+	+	+	−	3.9	24.1	0.6	1.7
Moldova	+	+	−	+	−10.8	−11.4	1.8	6.8
Serbia	+	+	−	+	−2.7	−5.9	−0.9	2.1

Source: Author's calculation based on various data sources explained in Appendix 1.

GDP during the crisis. Out of a total of 43 countries, only 16 countries showed a decrease in final consumption. Of these 43 countries, 11 countries showed a current account surplus during the crisis with only one experiencing negative growth. There are two main clusters of countries in the sample of these 11 countries: petroleum/natural gas exporters and Latin American countries. All the rest show a current account deficit. In the countries whose data are available, only two peripheral European countries, Cyprus and Malta, decreased their share of public expense in GDP.[10]

2.4   MAPPING AT LAST

Now we can begin mapping the effects of the global crisis. In this mapping, as mentioned above, the selection of criteria for the definition of demarcation lines among regions that qualitatively and quantitatively differed in performance during the crisis is vital. We had four main indicators, as listed above: (1) the change in the Gini coefficient as a signifier of deterioration/improvement in income distribution, (2) the growth rate of GDP, (3) the direction of change in wage employment, and (4) the direction of change in real wage per employee. For mapping purposes, we use three of our four critical indicators. Since the real wage per employee depends upon several important factors and since our analysis neglects many of these factors, we leave the change in real wage per employee aside.[11]

We define our mapping vector as a sequence of critical indicators. Our vector is made up of direction of change in income distribution, direction of change in GDP and direction of change in wage employment. These three indicators define eight mutually exclusive regions around the world. Since the entities in the vector denote the direction of change, each region is assigned a unique three digit combination of '−' (signifying decrease/deterioration) and '+' (implying increase/improvement), as in Table 2.6.

As Table 2.6 shows, the global capitalist system can be divided into two parts with reference to the direction of change in our three indicators. The line of demarcation was drawn by the growth rate. The first half of the table covers the slow growing or stagnant countries. Not accidentally, this group corresponds to the core of the North. More generally, the group can be deconstructed into four subgroups: (1) core developed countries, (2) noncore developed countries, (3) nearly fully articulated transition countries and (4) the Turkey/Mexico bloc. The third group consists of the transition countries that completed the full scale articulation into global capitalism. The fourth group, which includes only two countries, seems to be an anomaly at first. However, this should not surprise us. Mexico, under the banner of NAFTA, has turned into a mere extension of the

Table 2.6   Vector of repercussions of the global crisis

−, −, −	+, +, +	+, +, −
United States	Malaysia	Colombia
United Kingdom	Argentina	China
Sweden	Chile	Venezuela
Iceland	Poland	Moldova
Lithuania	India	Serbia
Latvia	Brazil	**−, +, −**
Spain	Honduras	Bulgaria
Denmark	Jordan	Romania
Finland	Cyprus	Pakistan
Georgia	Bhutan	Costa Rica
Croatia	Dominican Republic	Slovak Republic
Slovenia	Sri Lanka	Ethiopia
−, −, +	Bangladesh	
France	Uruguay	
Canada	Tunisia	
Germany	Peru	
Netherlands	Ecuador	
Greece	Panama	
Luxembourg	Belarus	
Austria	Nicaragua	
Russian Federation	Kazakhstan	
Armenia	Paraguay	
+, −, −	Egypt	
Japan	Tajikistan	
Estonia	Bolivia	
Ireland	Singapore	
Portugal	**−, +, +**	
Ukraine	Switzerland	
Hungary	Indonesia	
Czech Republic	Korea	
Puerto Rico	Thailand	
El Salvador	South Africa	
Hong Kong	Israel	
+, −, +	Australia	
Belgium	Azerbaijan	
Italy	Malta	
New Zealand	Mauritius	
Norway	Uganda	
Taiwan	Tanzania	
Turkey	Albania	
Mexico	Macedonia	
	Kyrgyz Republic	
	Vietnam	
	Nigeria	

Source: Author's calculation based on various data sources explained in Appendix 1.

North American economy. In this environment, any crisis that ravages the economy of their northern neighbor naturally has severe effects upon Mexico's economy. Turkey, on the other hand, has been the country that signed the highest number of standby agreements with the IMF and has been fervently implementing orthodox macroeconomic policies since 1980.

The second half of the table includes the countries that grew during the crisis. Most importantly this group covers countries from Latin America, Africa and East Asia/South East Asia. Even though this group seems to be a coherent group, there are some out of line entities in the group, like some transition countries, and Israel and Australia. Leaving aside the transition countries in the group, Australia and Israel have shared a common virtue or property with the other members in the group; geographically they belong to the southern part of the capitalist world.

For mapping purposes it is obvious that this list is insufficient. In order to complete the list (or at least to increase its inclusiveness), we have to overcome missing data problems. For example, the most important problem in our dataset is that many countries do not have the Gini coefficient data for the crisis period. Moreover, for some countries we are unable to obtain data for the change in wage employment. For the first group, we crudely assume that the change in the wage share might be accepted as a good proxy for the change in overall income distribution. This is a highly restrictive assumption; nevertheless, there are good reasons to assume that the equality of income distribution improves with the increase in wage share in the countries in question (the countries lacking the Gini coefficient data).[12] For the second group of countries, for which we do not have data for wage employment, we assume that the direction of change in the wage employment is the same as that of total employment. Therefore, we take the change in total employment as the main indicator for these countries.[13]

From this, we obtain a more comprehensive list of the countries. As mentioned, for our three main indicators there are eight main groups of countries, and the world map is constructed using our vector space in which each country is assigned to one of the eight regions.

Figure 2.4 (the resulting map) shows that this was the tale of two worlds. The dotted countries experience negative growth rates. The sizes of the dots depend upon the direction of change in the other two critical indicators (the Gini coefficient and the level of wage employment). The black/gray colored countries, on the other hand, increased their GDP during the global crisis. Black colored ones displayed positive performance in all the indicators. The color markers are arranged so as to reflect our vector of three indicators. The first one is the Gini coefficient (which takes the values of 'Deterior.' or 'Improv.'), the second one signifies the GDP growth and the last one is reserved for the direction of the change in wage employment.

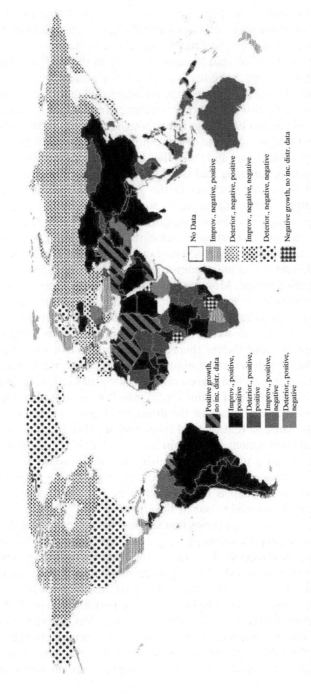

Legend (map):

Positive growth, no inc. distr. data
Improv., positive, positive
Deterior., positive, positive
Improv., positive, negative
Deterior., positive, negative

No Data
Improv., negative, positive
Deterior., negative, positive
Improv., negative, negative
Deterior., negative, negative
Negative growth, no inc. distr. data

Note: China's official statistics showed a very low rate of decrease in the wage employment. However, as many authors warn, these statistics should be evaluated cautiously. For this reason we assume that China was in the '+, +, +' region.

Source: Author's calculation based on various data sources explained in Appendix 1.

Figure 2.4 The North/South divide during the global crisis

The map proves that there are two mutually exclusive regions depending upon the experiences during the crisis.[14] That is to say, the North has one crisis story while the South has a totally different one.[15]

The map, as mentioned, exhibits two tangible regions in which the countries were clustered with reference to similar crisis experiences. However, it will be a great falsification if one assumes that each group is a homogenous entity. First of all, each group is too large to construct such a homogenous structure. Second, besides growth rates of GDP, and with reference to other indicators, performance was not consistent within the North or South groups. The map gives us two differing stories based upon three indicators. We should go beyond the information provided by the map in order to determine whether the division exhibited by the map has more dimensions or not.

Table 2A.1 in Appendix 2 provides additional information that shows these two groups display divergent paths when other indicators are included. The list covers the countries that do not have missing data in three indicators.[16]

Table 2A.1 shows that the countries in each group have tended to have different crisis experiences. The second column gives the relative wage share of each country, and the North and South in total world population. For the average of the period 2005 to 2009, the population share of the North was 19.5 percent while that of the South was nearly 65 percent. These numbers point to the fact that the last crisis initially hit nearly 20 percent of the world population. In this sense, it seems hard to characterize it as global. The last column gives the change of the share of each country, and the North and the South, in total world GDP. According to this column, the share of the North declined by 4.62 points. On the other hand, the group of countries categorized as a part of the South gained 4.03 points at the same time. However, at the end of 2009, the countries in the North together produced nearly 70 percent of world GDP while the share of the South hardly exceeded 25 percent. Out of 39 countries in the North, 16 countries experienced reductions in their share of the world GDP. However, this last group includes all the G5 countries in the system, like the USA, the UK, Germany, France, Japan and Italy. The combined shares of these G5 countries declined by 4.66 percent. These statistics underline the unevenness of the effects of the crisis within and across groups. The same pattern can be observed in the South, where only two countries, South Korea and South Africa, experienced reductions in their share of world GDP. The combined shares of Brazil, China and India increased by 3.06 points. Moreover, China alone increased its share by 2.35 points. The South is characterized by very uneven performance, as is the North.

The share in total world industrial value added contributes a little more to the picture. The North lost 7.55 percent of its share during the crisis. This decrease was due to the fall in the industrial output instead of the decrease in capacity. This might be best understood from the change in unemployment rates. Twenty-five out of 39 countries experienced an increasing unemployment rate. On the other hand, the South gained 5.7 percent of total industrial value added, and the change in the share of final consumption was more moderate (compared to the change in the share in world GDP) for both of the regions. The change for the North was 3.55 percent while it was 3.07 percent for the South. These figures point to the fact that the North did not cut back its final demand at the same rate of the reduction in its share in the world GDP. Conversely, the South did not increase its share at the same rate as the increase of its share in the world GDP. These patterns can also be observed at the country level. For the South, the countries that increased their share in world consumption at a rate more than that of the increase in their share of GDP were India, Egypt, Malaysia, Sri Lanka, Cyprus, South Korea (by decreasing their share of consumption at a rate less than the rate of reduction of the share of the GDP), Venezuela, Pakistan and Ethiopia. This might be a precaution against crisis conditions; the countries in the North avoided an excessive cut in final demand.

These last figures indicate that even variations in policies designed to alleviate the repercussions of the global crisis indicate two distinct directions. However, this brings a question to the foreground: are these groupings temporary or do they have more structural determinations? In order to answer this question, both a theoretical and an empirical investigation are needed. For the former, there has been a huge and still growing literature. Our study has more modest aims. Nevertheless, in the following section we will refer to some issues in this literature. For the latter, we will provide some pre-crisis data in order to give at least an empirical answer.

2.5   IS THIS REALLY 'A TALE OF TWO WORLDS'? LOOKING BEYOND THE MAP

The map provided is only an empirical construction in which theoretical preconceptions played no role. In this respect, it seems very accidental to observe two distinct regions, each of which performed very differently during the crisis. Moreover, the responses to the crisis also alter among the regions. The North seems to bear the burden of the crisis while the South was likely to benefit from the crisis. In this framework, some authors argue that the crisis in the North has generated unexpected but exciting opportunities for the South. Furthermore, when we focus on the economic category North/South seems to coincide with the geographical North/South.[17]

At last we come to a geographical and economic map that defines a coherent South to a great degree, at least for the episode of the global crisis.

At this juncture two questions beg an answer. First, it is clear from the map that the gray/black colored countries fared well during the crisis, however, did this performance emerge spontaneously under the crisis conditions or does it have pre-crisis antecedents? For an answer we have to look at the development of some of our critical indicators before the crisis. The first one is the growth rate of GDP and share of world GDP. Table 2.1 and Figure 2.1 above portray the development of these two indicators.

Figure 2.5 shows the share of total world GDP of the North and South. For reference, the share of Brazil/India/China/Australia (as the major element in the South) is also added to the figure. As Figure 2.1 indicates, the shrinking of the share of the North began earlier than the crisis. Particularly, in 2004, the share of the North began to decline at faster rates. On the other hand, conversely, the share of the South began to increase in the same period. Therefore, the global crisis seems to have had no effect upon the paths of the shares. On the other hand, it might have affected the magnitude of change.[18] From 2004, for example, the share of the North

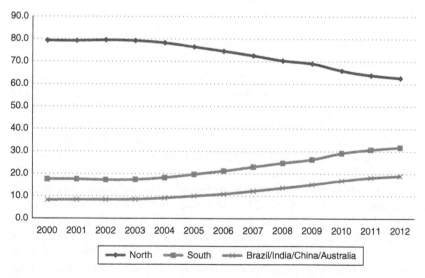

Source: Author's calculation based on World Development Indicators, World Bank.

Figure 2.5   The development of the shares in world income (%)

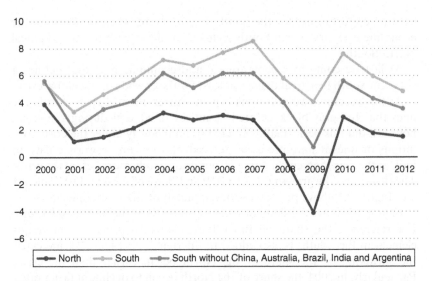

Source: Author's calculation based on World Development Indicators, World Bank.

Figure 2.6   The growth rates of the North and the South (%)

declined by nearly 2 percent each year until the global crisis. In 2009, the magnitude of the reduction in the share fell to nearly 1 percent and, most interestingly, in 2010 it was nearly 3 percent. It seems that it was not the crisis but rather recovery that strengthened the tendency.

The combined share of Brazil, India, China and Australia in total world output also increased steeply after 2004. In 2004 their combined share was 9.2 percent while it was 19.1 percent in 2012. This indicates that much of the increase of the share of the South comes from the increase in the shares of these four countries. This proves that some countries in the South have been the engine of the increasing share of the region in the world economy.

Figure 2.6 shows the growth rates of these two regions for the period 2000 to 2012. The growth rate of each region is estimated by using the GDP shares in respective regions as weights. The difference between performances is very striking. The gap between growth rates widened up to 2007, then both growth rates slowed, but that of the North slowed to below zero. There is a third line showing the growth rate of the South without China, India, Brazil, Australia and Argentina. As Figure 2.6 shows, it lies just in the middle of the other two lines. The difference between the South proper and the South without the major players like China shows the relative contribution of these five countries. Especially in 2009, the year in which the crisis was at its most intense, the difference between the two was

3.43; without China, India, Brazil, Argentina and Australia the growth rate fell to nearly zero.

Figure 2.6 shows that the trend that altered the income shares of the North and the South began much earlier than the 2007 crisis. The trend continued during the crisis and in the post-crisis period. The growth rates of the North, the South proper and narrow South (without China, India, Australia, Brazil and Argentina) rose steeply in 2010 then began to decline. Will these trends continue? Although the current developments cast some doubt about the performance of many countries in the Global South, the performance of the North is not promising either. This means that the share of the North will likely continue to decline while the share of the South will increase. This possibility generates an optimistic vision for the future of the South.

2.6 IS THERE REALLY 'AN OPTIMISTIC FUTURE' FOR THE SOUTH? LOOKING BEYOND THE FACTS AND FLOWS

In this final section we will first outline our basic findings and then, taking some trends that we have not referred to before into consideration, we will question the realism of the impression of the optimistic future.

In this study we mainly utilized three different classifications of countries. The first one is borrowed from the corpus of the World Bank, which divides the countries into groups depending upon their GNP per capita brackets. In this respect, as many other studies indicate, the shares of the low and middle income country groups in total world production have increased since the beginning of the period. The global crisis seems to have generated no break in this trend. The growth rates of the high income countries fell below zero during the crisis. On the other hand, at the same time, the growth rates of low and middle income groups (despite a substantial reduction) were positive during the crisis. Then, using this classification, we conduct a Gini decomposition analysis. The world Gini declined between 2002 and 2012. The rate of decrease was more than 10 percent. The decomposition of the change in the Gini into 'between' and 'within' components reveals a highly annoying fact for the South. The results of this analysis indicate that inclusion or exclusion of China and India in middle income countries significantly changes the results. With these countries included, the results make us believe that the income distribution between countries had a tendency to become more equal during the 2000s. However, when China and India are excluded, the results show that the distribution of world income improved by only 2 points (the Gini without

China/India was 80.7 in 2000 while it was 78.2 in 2012). With China/India included, the main factor behind the drop in the Gini was the improvement in the 'between' component. When these countries are excluded, the results show that the 'between' component did not change. On the other hand, the low rate of decrease in the Gini component is the result of the decrease in the 'within' component. Therefore, even if there has been an improvement in world income distribution, China and India have been the main benefactors. As in the past, capitalism has been reproducing itself in a very uneven manner.

Next, in order to overcome the deficiencies of the size distribution analysis, functional income distribution analysis is employed. The wage share is used as the basic indicator in this analysis to detect the improvement or deterioration in income distribution. Our long run analysis shows that the global wage share increased until the end of the 1970s, then began its steep decline until the last global crisis. During the global crisis the wage share increased suddenly. The wage shares for the groups in the World Bank categorization exhibited the same pattern without any exception.

In the next step, the income distribution analysis is conducted at country level. At this stage, the results of both income distribution analyses are used. The growth rate of the wage share is decomposed into the growth rate of total real wage payments and the GDP. Then the growth rate of total real wage payment is deconstructed into the growth rate of real wage per employee and the growth rate of the wage employment. We now have four main indicators to be used in the assessment of the performance of the countries during the crisis: the change in Gini coefficient, the growth rates of the GDP, wage employment and the real wage per employee. Even though the last one is reported, it is dropped from our mapping analysis due to several reasons. At last, we have three main indicators to construct our map of performances. Due to data unavailability, we have to make some strict and very limiting assumptions. We group countries with respect to our three main indicators; this step dictates the partitioning of the capitalist world into eight regions. It is important to note that the most important indicator is the growth rate of the GDP. When we finally construct our map it is not surprising that two distinct regions emerge over the map: fast growing and slow growing regions. Indeed, the unexpected fact is the fast growing and slow growing regions over the map are nearly the same regions defined as the South and North during the Cold War. Some additional indicators also support this division. Moreover, a simple retrospective and prospective evaluation of data also proves that the division over the map is not a one time, accidental or temporary event. The trends that create this division began much earlier and will possibly endure in the future. The future seems bright for the South.[19] Is that so?

In 2009, despite the fact that its share had been decreasing, the North still produced 56 percent of the world's industrial value added. Moreover, most of the international capital flows have continued to circulate among the countries in the North. In addition to this, the North continued to be the major importer in the world, capturing the highest share of both imports and exports. Northern countries are still the major importers for the exports from other northern countries. In this sense, the North is the *patria* for capital in its money and commodity form. Since its share is decreasing rapidly in world industrial value added, it will be very hard to put forward the same argument for the production front of capital in the very near future.[20]

On the other hand, the South has 60 percent of the total labor force. Moreover, in stark contrast to the countries in the North, the majority of countries in the South are forced to give current account surpluses (which means that they consume less than they produce) and accumulate huge sums of foreign exchange in their reserves. They have channeled these reserves to the deficit countries of the North, which means that the countries in the South are forced to finance the consumption in the North. In addition to this, the South has been working longer hours for lower wages. The allegedly bright future impression created by our map certainly owes too much to these facts.

In conclusion, it should be stated that this is not a 'tale of two worlds', but rather the tale of one unified world seemingly divided into two worlds by capital accumulation. The crisis erupted in the North, in the core of money and commodity capital. In this respect, the 'global'ness of the crisis can be questioned. However, the capital circuit, even though spatially dispersed, is a totality that transmits the crisis at one of its moments to its other moments. This transmission, inescapably, also means a spatial transmission. When the crisis comes to the South that will certainly be a global crisis.

NOTES

1. There are plenty of studies providing evidence for this trend. See ILO (2014), OECD (2011), UNCTAD (2012). For a discussion on the revival of interest in world income distribution in the 1990s see Bourguignon and Morrisson (2002).
2. Since the crisis, there has been a growing literature about the effects of the crisis upon income distribution both at national and international levels (de Beer, 2012; Habib et al., 2010; Morrison and Furtin, 2011; Stockhammer, 2012).
3. For a detailed humorous exposition of this mood see Krugman (2009).
4. Milanovic, benefiting from many data sources and using a Purchasing Power Parity approach, estimated the World Gini for the period 1950 to 2010 under three different conceptualizations. According to his estimates, the development of the World Gini

exhibits a totally different path for each of the three inequality concepts for the period 1950 to 2000. However, they all show a similar trend after 2000. They all displayed a decreasing pattern (Milanovic, 2012, p. 12).

5.   For example, Argentina and Turkey (the countries that provide vital stylized facts about the outcomes of neo-liberal experiences) stopped proving functional income distribution data. The National Statistical Institute of Argentina stopped providing this information in 2007. The GDP at income approach data was finished at 2006 for Turkey.

6.   The list of the countries and the corresponding data coverage is given in the Appendices.

7.   For the classification of countries, an ad hoc classification is used, and this classification is an amalgam of the IMF classification and a more radical one, which categorizes the countries under the headings of 'core' and 'periphery'.

8.   G10 countries refer to the countries participating in the agreement on General Arrangements to Borrow. After the participation of Switzerland in the agreement, although the number of countries signed the agreement reached 11, the group is still called G10.

9.   However, some of the countries in the Global South also initiated fiscal stimulus packages during the crisis. For example, China implemented a US$586 billion fiscal stimulus package for the years 2009 and 2010 (Yang and Huizenga, 2010, p.133; Yongding, 2010). Many African countries followed the same pattern during the crisis (Osakwe, 2010).

10. This might be due to the decisions taken at the EU level which imposed public expenditure cuts upon member countries.

11. These factors include the degree of unionization, the degree of fragmentation of labor force, the strength of corporatist relations between capital and labor, and many other important sociological factors. Since the affecting factors constitute a non-short list, it is very hard to arrive at clear cut categories depending on the real wage per employee. Therefore, it is excluded from our mapping exercise.

12. This list includes Bosnia Herzegovina, Bahrain, Cameroon, Cape Verde, Jamaica, Kenya, Morocco, Mozambique, Namibia, Niger, Oman, Saudi Arabia, Sudan and Tunisia.

13. These countries are Afghanistan, Angola, Benin, Botswana, Cameroon, Cape Verde, Central African Republic, Democratic Republic of Congo, Gabon, Gambia, Ghana, Laos, Lesotho, Madagascar, Malawi, Mali, Mauritania, Nepal, Republic of Congo, Rwanda, Senegal, Sierra Leone, Swaziland, Togo and Zambia.

14. Although there seems to be two distinct groups coinciding with two regions, there are some irregularities displayed by the map. These irregularities may raise questions about the degree of coincidence between the economic South and the geographical South. For example, there are some transition countries in Eastern Europe whose performances were very akin to that of the ones located in the South. Moreover, there are four countries in Africa that share the same experience with the countries in the North. These countries are Botswana, Equatorial Guinea, Gabon and Zimbabwe. New Zealand, on the other hand, is very far from the North, but with the performance and historical/sociological background, this country deserves to be located in the North. In the South, two countries, Australia and Israel, again with respect to economic and political relations, are supposed to belong to the economic/political North. However, their performance during the crisis implies that they adapted to the conditions of their geographical location.

15. At first sight, this map also generates a similar impression to that given by the great historians of the 1929 crisis.

16. The observations showing the change are estimated as the difference between the average value of the period 2008 to 2009 and 2005 to 2007.

17. The North/South dichotomy was conceptualized after the Second World War. This dichotomy was used to draw a demarcation line dividing the rich capitalist and socialist northern countries from the countries in the South trapped in extreme poverty (Therien, 1999). Later on, this dichotomy is used to implement new international initiatives (like the Brandt Commission Report) that transcend the ideological split between capitalism

and socialism, and define a polarized world between wealth and poverty. Since the beginning of the 1990s, this conceptualization has been used less and less frequently. One reason for this is the fact that scholars and international organizations have been realizing that the South is not as much of a homogenous body as perceived. It seems that some countries in the South have been on the verge of breaking the chains. These countries are joyfully categorized under several headings like 'middle income countries', 'emerging market economies' or simply 'developing countries'. These headings, especially the last one, are designed to efface the bad memories that paved the way for pessimistic conceptualizations like 'the development of underdevelopment'.

18. Ortiz and Cummings (2011) show that the distribution of income among countries has been improving since 1990.

19. As the major promoter of poverty mitigation programs around the world, UNDP seems very enthusiastic about the performance of the 'South' (UNDP, 2013).

20. Capitalism is a socioeconomic system in which success can hardly be accrued to regions or locations. The destinies of Detroit, Manchester, Bristol or any other success story of early capitalism could provide enough evidence to support this argument. Even though the episode of mercantilism or the import substituting industrialization era can create the illusion that the extended reproduction of capital itself has a space dimension, which might indicate that capital accumulation has been a spatially constrained process, the long run evidence contradicts this assertion. Historically, capital accumulation does not have spatial limits. Moreover, the totality of the capital accumulation process can be divided into complementary moments and these moments can be spatially distributed over a vast domain. Money capital, financial capital, commodity capital and productive capital even though organically constructing a totality may concentrate in different regions, countries and sectors. In addition to this, each moment can easily shift to another region, country or sector. Therefore, regional or national success stories should be evaluated cautiously. Indeed, the history of capitalism suggests that all regional or national miracles have been temporary.

REFERENCES

de Beer, P. (2012), 'The impact of the crisis on earnings and income distribution in the EU', European Trade Union Institute, Working Paper No. 2012.01.

BLS [Bureau of Labor Statistics] (2010), 'A Profile of the Working Poor', Washington DC: BLS, retrieved from www.bls.gov/cps/cpswp2010.pdf, on May 19, 2014.

Bourguignon, F. and C. Morrisson (2002), 'Income inequality among world citizens: 1820–1992', *American Economic Review*, 92 (4), 727–744.

Eurofund (2010), *Working Poor in Europe*, Dublin: Eurofund.

Habib, B., A. Narayan, S. Olivieri and C. Sanchez (2010), 'The impact of the financial crisis on poverty and income distribution: insights from simulations in selected countries', *World Bank Economic Premise*, 7, March.

ILO (2014), *Global Employment Trends 2014*, Geneva: ILO.

Krugman, P. (2009), 'How did economists get it wrong?', *New York Times*, September 2.

Libreati, P. (2013), 'The world distribution of income and its inequality: 1970–2009', *Review of Income and Wealth*, 61 (2), 248–273.

Milanovic, B. (2012), 'Global inequality recalculated and updated: the effect of new PPP estimates on global inequality and 2005 estimates', *Journal of Economic Inequality*, 10 (1), 1–18.

Morrison, C. and F. Furtin (2011), 'Internal income inequality and global inequality', Fondation pour les études et recherches sur le développement international (FERDI), Working Paper No. 26.

OECD (2011), *Divided We Stand: Why Inequality Keeps Rising*, Paris: OECD.

OECD (2013), 'Crisis squeezes income and puts pressure on inequality and poverty: new results from the OECD Income Database', retrieved from www.oecd.org/els/soc/OECD2013-Inequality-and-Poverty-8p.pdf, on May 20, 2014.

Ortiz, I. and M. Cummins (2011), 'Global inequality beyond the bottom billion: a rapid review of income distribution in 141 countries', UNICEF Social and Economic Policy Working Paper.

Osakwe, P.N. (2010), 'Africa and the global financial and economic crisis: impacts, responses and opportunities', in S. Dullien, D.J. Kotte, A. Màrquez and J. Priewe (eds), *The Financial and Economic Crisis of 2008–2009 and Developing Countries*, Berlin: United Nations and Hochschule für Technik und Wirtschaft Berlin, 203–222.

Stockhammer, E. (2012), 'Financialization, income distribution and the crisis', *Investigación Económica*, LXXI (279), 39–70.

Therien, J.P. (1999), 'Beyond the North–South divide: the two tales of world poverty', *Third World Quarterly*, 20 (4), 723–742.

UNCTAD (2012), *Trade and Development Report, 2012 – An Overview*, Geneva: UNCTAD.

UNDP (2013), *Human Development Report 2013 – The Rise of the South: Human Progress in a Diverse World*, New York: UNDP.

World Bank (1990), *World Development Report 1990: Poverty*, New York: World Bank/Oxford University Press.

World Bank (2001), *World Development Report 2000/2001: Attacking Poverty*, New York: World Bank.

Yang, L. and C. Huizenga (2010), 'China's economy in the global economic crisis: impact and policy responses', in S. Dullien, D.J. Kotte, A. Màrquez and J. Priewe (eds), *The Financial and Economic Crisis of 2008–2009 and Developing Countries*, Berlin: United Nations and Hochschule für Technik und Wirtschaft Berlin, 119–147.

Yongding, Y. (2010), *The Impact of the Global Financial Crisis on the Chinese Economy and China's Policy Responses*, Third World Network, Global Economy Series no. 25.

APPENDIX 1: DATA SOURCES

Gini coefficients: The Gini coefficients for the European Union Countries and OECD members are obtained from Eurostat. The Gini coefficients for Latin American countries are from the website of SEDLAC (Socio-Economic Database for Latin America and the Caribbean). For most of the remaining countries, the SWIID (Standardized World Income Inequality Database) is the main source for the Gini coefficients. For some countries, national statistical institutions provide the data for the Gini coefficients.

Income: Real GDP and GDP growth rate data is from the World Bank's World Development Indicators.

Wage employment: The number of employees data is gathered from multiple sources. Data for developed countries is obtained from ILO ILOSTAT. However, the data for the countries in the South for the crisis period is missing in this database. In order to increase data availability, national statistical databases are used (if data is available). For the countries for which data is still missing, as mentioned above, we use total employment data obtained from World Development Indicators.

Wage share: The wage share data is obtained as a ratio to GDP. The source for the OECD members is AMECO (Annual Macro-Economic database) of the European Commission. For most of the remaining countries, the source for the wage share data is UNSTAT of United Nations Statistics Division. National statistical institutions are used to obtain some of the countries' data.

Real wage per employee: The growth rate of the real wage per employee is estimated as the sum of the growth rate of the wage share and the growth rate of GDP minus the growth rate of wage employment.

Other data: Gross fixed capital formation, final consumption current account balance, unemployment rate, the share of public expense and industrial value added data is obtained from World Development Indicators.

APPENDIX 2: ADDITIONAL TABLES

Table 2A.1 Various indicators of North and South

Country Name	Population Shares (Average of 2005–9)	Change in Average Unemployment Rate	Change in the Share of Final Consumption	Change in the Share of Industrial Value Added	Change in GDP Share
–, –, –					
United States	4.530	2.73	-2.55	-3.42	-2.93
United Kingdom	0.922	1.40	-1.02	-0.88	-0.95
Spain	0.678	8.84	0.08	-0.05	0.04
Sweden	0.138	0.32	-0.05	-0.11	-0.07
Denmark	0.082	0.53	0.01	-0.03	-0.01
Finland	0.080	-0.35	0.02	-0.04	0.00
Croatia	0.067	-2.35	0.01	0.01	0.01
Slovenia	0.030	-0.62	0.01	0.00	0.01
Lithuania	0.049	3.68	0.01	0.00	0.01
Latvia	0.033	5.02	0.01	0.01	0.01
Iceland	0.005	2.47	-0.01	-0.01	-0.01
Georgia	0.066	3.13	0.01	0.00	0.00
–, –, +					
Germany	1.237	-2.40	-0.10	-0.34	-0.14
France	0.962	-0.32	0.02	-0.13	-0.04
Canada	0.495	0.87	-0.06	-1.37	-0.15
Russian Federation	2.141	0.52	0.41	0.34	0.39
Netherlands	0.247	-0.83	0.02	0.03	0.01
Austria	0.125	0.17	0.01	-0.01	0.00

Greece	0.168	-0.40	0.05	-0.03	0.02
Luxembourg	0.007	0.67	0.00	-0.01	0.00
Armenia	0.045	-3.25	0.01	0.00	0.00
+, -, -					
Japan	1.921	0.37	-0.25	-0.90	-0.49
Ireland	0.066	4.57	0.00	-0.09	-0.04
Portugal	0.159	0.78	0.00	-0.02	-0.01
Hong Kong SAR, China	0.104	-0.40	-0.01	-0.02	-0.02
Czech Republic	0.155	-1.22	0.05	0.06	0.05
Hungary	0.151	1.53	0.00	-0.01	0.00
Ukraine	0.700	0.80	0.04	0.00	0.03
Puerto Rico	0.057	2.18	-0.01	-0.01	-0.01
El Salvador	0.092	-0.10	0.00	0.00	0.00
Estonia	0.020	3.48	0.00	0.00	0.00
+, -, +					
Italy	0.893	0.38	-0.06	-0.19	-0.12
Mexico	1.708	0.98	-0.25	-0.30	-0.23
Turkey	1.045	2.13	0.04	-0.01	0.03
Belgium	0.160	-0.58	0.03	-0.03	0.00
Norway	0.071	-0.60	0.01	0.01	0.01
New Zealand	0.064	1.35	-0.02	-0.03	-0.03
Taiwan					
North	**19.474**		**-3.55**	**-7.55**	**-4.62**
+, +, +					
Brazil	2.856	-0.90	0.57	0.39	0.53
India	17.432	-0.15	0.21	0.18	0.17
Poland	0.574	-6.05	0.10	0.12	0.10
Argentina	0.592	-1.53	0.10	0.06	0.10

Table 2A.1 (continued)

Country Name	Population Shares (Average of 2005–9)	Change in Average Unemployment Rate	Change in the Share of Final Consumption	Change in the Share of Industrial Value Added	Change in GDP Share
Malaysia	0.403	0.17	0.04	0.02	0.03
Chile	0.251	1.15	0.01	-0.04	0.00
Singapore	0.069	0.18	0.02	-0.01	0.02
Egypt, Arab Rep.	1.117	-1.18	0.09	0.11	0.08
Peru	0.426	-0.32	0.03	0.04	0.03
Kazakhstan	0.234	-1.13	0.03	0.08	0.05
Bangladesh	2.202	0.43	0.02	0.02	0.02
Ecuador	0.215	0.28	0.01	0.02	0.01
Belarus	0.144	-0.27	0.02	0.03	0.02
Dominican Republic	0.145	-2.15	0.01	0.01	0.00
Tunisia	0.154	0.25	0.00	0.01	0.00
Sri Lanka	0.302	-1.18	0.02	0.01	0.01
Uruguay	0.050	-2.12	0.01	0.01	0.01
Cyprus	0.016	-0.07	0.01	-0.01	0.00
Panama	0.053	-2.20	0.00	0.00	0.00
Jordan	0.085	-1.20	0.01	0.01	0.01
Bolivia	0.146	-2.15	0.01	0.01	0.01
Paraguay	0.092	0.02	0.01	0.01	0.01
Honduras	0.108	-0.20	0.00	0.00	0.00
Nicaragua	0.084	1.15	0.00	0.00	0.00
Tajikistan	0.107	-0.03	0.00	0.00	0.00
Bhutan	0.010	0.60	0.00	0.00	0.00

−, +, +					
Korea, Rep.	0.732	−0.03	−0.34	−0.51	−0.40
Australia	0.316	−1.47	0.10	0.20	0.14
Switzerland	0.114	−0.25	0.03	0.04	0.05
Indonesia	3.475	−2.05	0.13	0.32	0.16
South Africa	0.736	0.30	−0.07	−0.04	−0.06
Thailand	0.993	0.12	0.03	0.05	0.03
Israel	0.108	−1.43	0.05	0.00	0.05
Nigeria	2.217		0.04	0.01	0.04
Vietnam	1.267		0.04	0.05	0.04
Azerbaijan	0.130	−0.67	0.02	0.07	0.03
Tanzania	0.620	−0.43	0.00	0.00	0.01
Uganda	0.463	1.52	0.00	0.00	0.00
Albania	0.048	0.60	0.00	0.00	0.00
Mauritius	0.019	−1.82	0.00	0.00	0.00
Macedonia, FYR	0.032	−3.07	0.00	0.00	0.00
Malta	0.006	−0.45	0.00	0.00	0.00
China	19.821	0.43	1.29	3.99	2.35
Kyrgyz Republic	0.079	0.10	0.00	0.00	0.00

Table 2A.1 (continued)

Country Name	Population Shares (Average of 2005–9)	Change in Average Unemployment Rate	Change in the Share of Final Consumption	Change in the Share of Industrial Value Added	Change in GDP Share
+, +, −					
Venezuela, RB	0.416		0.20	0.21	0.17
Colombia	0.669	1.33	0.05	0.09	0.06
Serbia	0.111	−4.80	0.01	0.01	0.01
Moldova	0.054	−1.40	0.00	0.00	0.00
−, +, −					
Pakistan	2.467		0.03	0.01	0.02
Romania	0.314		0.04	0.08	0.05
Slovak Republic	0.081	−2.65	0.02	0.02	0.01
Bulgaria	0.114	−6.28	0.01	0.02	0.02
Costa Rica	0.067	−5.73	0.01	0.00	0.00
Ethiopia	1.211		0.02	0.00	0.01
South	**64.907**		**3.07**	**5.70**	**4.03**

Source: Author's calculation based on various data sources explained in Appendix 1.

Table 2A.2 The change in our main indicators during the crisis

Country	Avg. Gini (2005–7)	Avg. Gini (2008–9)	Average GDP Growth Rate (2008–9)	Average Wage Employment Growth (2008–9)	Average Wage Share Growth (2008–9)
Afghanistan	36.1	36.7	12.3		
Albania	32.8	34.1	5.5	8.4	12.1
Angola	48.2	40.8	8.1		
Argentina	47.2	45.6	3.8	0.4	9.7
Armenia	32.4	33.6	–3.6	6.2	0.4
Australia	31.4	33.6	2.7	1.9	–0.9
Austria	25.8	26.0	–1.2	0.8	2.6
Azerbaijan	25.0	31.3	10.1	5.1	7.9
Bangladesh	32.1	31.8	6.0	3.7	5.6
Belarus	26.8	26.7	5.2	1.3	1.3
Belgium	27.1	27.0	–0.9	0.5	2.4
Benin	50.1	46.9	3.8		–1.5
Bhutan	46.9	43.1	5.7	3.8	1.1
Bolivia	56.0	50.4	4.8	12.6	1.9
Botswana	50.3	51.5			
Brazil	56.2	54.6	2.4	2.7	2.7
Bulgaria	33.3	34.7	0.3	–0.3	5.6
Burkina Faso	41.7	37.8	4.4		–4.2
Cambodia	52.8	50.1	3.4	3.4	
Canada	31.9	32.1	–1.0	3.3	1.9
Central African Republic	49.1	52.7	6.4		
Chile	47.6	47.4	1.1	1.3	7.5
China	49.0	47.5	9.4	–0.1	8.7

Table 2A.2 (continued)

Country	Avg. Gini (2005–7)	Avg. Gini (2008–9)	Average GDP Growth Rate (2008–9)	Average Wage Employment Growth (2008–9)	Average Wage Share Growth (2008–9)
Colombia	51.9	50.2	2.6	-2.3	1.3
Costa Rica	49.1	49.5	0.9	-0.3	3.8
Cote d'Ivoire	40.7	39.7	3.0	2.5	
Croatia	28.8	28.9	-2.4	-0.1	1.9
Cyprus	29.3	29.3	1.0	1.1	1.8
Czech Republic	25.3	24.9	-0.7	-0.8	0.5
Denmark	24.5	26.0	-3.2	-1.4	3.4
Dominican Republic	50.9	48.9	4.4	0.2	-3.4
Ecuador	53.4	49.6	3.5	0.5	5.8
Egypt	31.7	30.9	5.9	2.8	-3.9
El Salvador	43.2	42.9	-0.9	-7.2	-6.8
Estonia	33.3	31.2	-9.1	-4.2	5.6
Ethiopia	30.2	31.8	9.8	-8.7	-42.0
Fiji	33.4	31.4	-0.1	-8.1	
Finland	26.1	26.1	-4.1	-1.5	5.2
France	27.0	29.9	-1.6	0.2	1.7
Georgia	43.6	47.4	-0.7	-2.0	23.2
Germany	28.6	29.7	-2.0	0.4	3.1
Greece	32.0	32.6	-1.7	0.1	2.3
Honduras	56.7	53.6	0.9	1.2	1.2
Hong Kong	48.1	46.3	-0.2	-0.2	2.5
Hungary	29.5	25.0	-3.0	-2.0	-0.4
Iceland	27.2	28.5	-2.7	-1.7	-9.1

India	50.0	49.8	6.2	1.0	4.1
Indonesia	45.7	47.2	5.3	1.3	37.2
Ireland	31.6	29.4	-4.3	-4.4	5.2
Israel	37.2	37.6	2.9	2.4	-2.3
Italy	32.2	31.3	-3.3	0.1	2.5
Japan	30.0	30.0	-3.3	-1.4	1.7
Jordan	46.8	45.5	6.4	4.0	2.7
Kazakhstan	32.7	29.4	2.3	4.0	-0.8
Korea, Republic of	30.9	31.4	1.3	1.1	0.3
Kyrgyz Republic	35.8	36.1	5.6	4.9	3.4
Lao	46.7	47.4	7.7		
Latvia	37.2	37.5	-11.1	-7.6	-0.2
Lesotho	51.5	52.5			4.9
Lithuania	34.4	35.0	-5.9	-3.3	2.3
Luxembourg	27.6	28.5	-3.1	3.0	8.3
Macedonia	38.8	41.2	2.0	3.3	6.4
Madagascar	44.1	43.1	1.5		
Malawi	38.7	40.6	8.7		
Malaysia	45.7	45.3	1.7	1.9	3.0
Mali	35.9	33.1	4.7		
Malta	26.9	27.1	0.9	1.0	1.3
Mauritania	37.5	37.5	1.1		
Mauritius	20.3	23.1	4.3	2.4	1.2
Mexico	45.8	44.9	-1.7	0.8	1.9
Moldova	37.9	36.0	0.9	-0.1	7.8
Mongolia	50.6	51.1	3.8	8.1	19.3
Montenegro	30.3	29.9	0.6	2.7	
Nepal	52.8	46.9	5.3		-2.8

Table 2A.2 (continued)

Country	Avg. Gini (2005–7)	Avg. Gini (2008–9)	Average GDP Growth Rate (2008–9)	Average Wage Employment Growth (2008–9)	Average Wage Share Growth (2008–9)
Netherlands	27.0	27.4	-0.9	0.5	3.1
New Zealand	31.4	30.9	-0.1	0.0	1.9
Nicaragua	45.9	42.9	0.9	1.2	-0.6
Nigeria	42.2	43.4	6.6	2.9	-11.0
Norway	26.5	24.6	-0.8	1.2	4.9
Pakistan	44.2	51.8	2.3	-1.3	-2.8
Panama	53.8	52.4	7.0	0.1	0.4
Paraguay	52.9	50.3	1.2	2.8	1.1
Peru	49.4	46.6	5.3	3.9	0.5
Philippines	51.1	50.4	2.7	3.9	-0.4
Poland	32.8	31.7	3.4	2.8	1.9
Portugal	37.3	35.6	-1.5	-0.9	2.0
Puerto Rico	42.3	42.2	-1.9	-3.0	0.4
Romania	35.4	35.5	0.5	-1.0	2.2
Russian Federation	41.9	43.4	-1.3	0.4	6.2
Rwanda	47.5	47.5	8.7		
Senegal	37.3	37.2	3.1		-2.4
Serbia	30.2	28.7	0.2	-4.1	-1.4
Sierra Leone	40.0	37.2	4.3		17.1
Singapore	45.0	44.6	0.5	4.4	3.5
Slovak Republic	25.2	25.6	0.4	-1.5	2.9
Slovenia	22.9	23.2	-2.2	-0.7	3.3

South Africa	58.5	59.4	1.0	1.1	1.4
Spain	31.9	32.5	-1.5	-3.3	2.3
Sri Lanka	50.1	46.1	4.7	1.5	1.4
Swaziland	46.5	48.2	1.8		
Sweden	23.7	24.4	-2.8	-0.8	1.2
Switzerland	30.3	30.9	0.1	2.0	2.5
Taiwan	30.2	29.8	-0.5	1.0	3.4
Tajikistan	32.1	31.5	5.8	1.6	-10.9
Tanzania	35.0	36.0	6.7	1.0	4.1
Thailand	49.4	50.0	0.1	1.3	2.9
Togo	33.4	35.2	2.9		-6.9
Tunisia	37.1	35.7	3.8	2.1	9.0
Turkey	43.2	40.0	-2.1	1.0	0.8
Uganda	39.8	40.7	8.0	16.0	9.0
Ukraine	28.0	26.8	-6.3	-0.8	0.6
United Kingdom	32.6	33.2	-3.0	-0.7	1.8
United States	46.7	46.7	-1.5	-2.0	2.5
Uruguay	47.5	46.3	4.7	4.0	13.8
Venezuela	39.2	36.8	1.0	-3.9	4.4
Viet Nam	41.8	42.3	5.5	24.7	8.8
Zambia	53.4	54.3	6.0		

Source: Author's calculation based on various data sources explained in Appendix 1.

3. Central banking in developing countries after the crisis: what has changed?

Ahmet Benlialper and Hasan Cömert

3.1 INTRODUCTION

During the period before the crisis, a new consensus, which was supposed to be applicable in both advanced countries and developing countries, had emerged. According to this new neo-liberal consensus, inflation targeting[1] was perceived as the most appropriate form of monetary policy regime. Under inflation targeting regimes, short term interest rates are considered as the main policy tool by which the announced inflation targets could be met. Since, in the new consensus, in general, stabilization of inflation and output was associated with financial stability, setting policy interest rates in line with inflation targets was considered sufficient for both price and financial stability. Yet the consensus was to be dissolved as the crisis ran its course.

The recent crisis revealed the inapplicability of this 'divine coincidence'[2] approach. Thus central banks have been forced to reconsider their policy regimes and inflation targeting regimes have lost their shine. Existing inflation targeting regimes, in turn, were transformed into more complex monetary policy regimes in which financial stability concerns have gained importance. As a result, many policy tools have been added to the arsenal of central banking in order to achieve multiple goals. Although this trend was first observed in advanced countries, central banks in developing countries followed their counterparts with some lags.

The aim of this chapter is to assess how the theory and practices of central banking have evolved in developing countries in response to the crisis of 2008–9. Our findings suggest that the recent experiences of both advanced countries and developing countries during and after the global economic crisis have exposed the problems within mainstream monetary theory. In response to the crisis, mainstream thinking has been revised considerably. In line with this, there is also a shift in central banking practices in the developing world. As a result, central banks now have multiple goals and multiple tools in developing countries as well. Yet this shift is insufficient to trigger a major change in understanding and implementing monetary policy. Especially, in the absence of a rethinking of the international financial architecture and comprehending the specific natures of the transmission mechanisms in the developing world, developing countries are not satisfactorily capable of implementing effective monetary policy and are still heavily exposed to external shocks.

The outline of the chapter is as follows. Section 3.2 briefly describes the mainstream approach to central banking between 2002 and 2008. Section 3.3 focuses on the main trends and shifts in central banking in developing countries after the crisis. Section 3.4 explores whether these new policies will pass the test of time, and Section 3.5 concludes.

3.2 CENTRAL BANKING IN DEVELOPING COUNTRIES BEFORE THE CRISIS

In the two decades that led up to the crisis six major pillars of the new consensus emerged within mainstream theory. These are (1) the divine coincidence approach, (2) adoption of short term interest rate as the sole policy instrument, (3) emphasis on very low inflation, (4) adoption of flexible exchange rates, (5) transparency, and (6) central bank independence.

The divine coincidence approach implies that targeting inflation was considered sufficient to achieve stability in financial markets.[3] According to this approach, first, the central bank was assumed to have no informational advantage compared to economic agents involved in financial transactions. In case a bubble forms, 'rational' economic agents would act accordingly and the bubble would burst (Hahm et al., 2011). It was assumed that the macroeconomic outcomes of financial distress would be limited and it was believed that monetary authorities had the necessary tools to put financial markets in order in case of a downturn. The justification for inaction on the financial front was fed by the argument that intervening in financial markets may make the situation worse given that it is not easy to distinguish between what is a change in *fundamentals* from what is not. Moreover, a proactive stance would blur the public perception of the intentions of the central bank and thereby erode its credibility.

Thus, mainstream macroeconomic thinking adopted a 'benign neglect' approach in order to deal with fluctuations in financial markets. In effect this meant that monetary policy should not react to developments in the financial sector. As became apparent, it was however mandated with cleaning up in the event of a crisis. A natural repercussion of this approach was the delegation of microprudential measures for financial stability issues. Henceforth, monetary policy was expected to focus solely on price stability and institution level measures would do the job in the financial sphere.

The second tenet of the mainstream thinking was the adoption of one instrument for monetary policy, short term interest rates. Short term interest rates were considered sufficient for the management of price and output stability (Woodford, 2002). Short term interest rates were assumed to influence the prices and quantities of financial assets and the expectations of financial market players in a predictable way. It followed that the central bank would affect aggregate demand and, thereby, output and inflation through its use of short term rates.[4]

The third tenet of the new consensus was the emphasis on very low inflation in the pursuit of high and stable economic growth. It was generally assumed that, beyond a level (generally 2–3 percent), inflation deteriorates growth by creating an unstable and unpredictable environment.

The fourth principle was related to the appropriate exchange rate policy. Exchange rates were not to be used for policy purposes but, instead, should freely float. The underlying argument behind the popularity of flexible exchange rate regimes was the notorious trilemma, namely that in the presence of free capital mobility, fixed exchange rates preclude an independent monetary policy. Moreover, since one of the main principles of inflation targeting was based on transparency, a hands off approach with respect to exchange rates was deemed indispensable in order not to confuse the public's perceptions of the central bank's intentions. The case for flexible exchange rates was also promoted by currency crises that occurred before the 2000s in many countries such as Mexico, the Far East countries, Brazil and Russia.

The fifth principle is related to transparency of the central bank with respect to its actions. Central banks were encouraged to make their objectives public and give more details about their implementation of monetary policy. In the inflation targeting framework, this would lead to clarity in public perception about the intentions of the central bank, thereby increasing the effectiveness of monetary policy through shaping expectations and contributing to the central bank's credibility. Lastly, central banks were assumed to have instrument independence, implying that they implement monetary policy in order to achieve their aims (mandated by law) independent from political pressures.

In the two decades leading up to the crisis these were the ideas that made up the conventional wisdom as regards central banking around the world. When the crisis erupted, there were 20 developing countries in the process of implementing inflation targeting.[5] In line with the orthodox view, monetary authorities in inflation targeting developing countries tried to achieve low levels of inflation. This was supposed to simultaneously generate financial stability and contribute to high growth. As a result, as the new consensus before the crisis suggested, interventions regarding the financial sector remained mainly on the micro level. Pursuing low inflation through only short term interest rates, however, at best, would mean neglecting the differences in the sources of inflation in the advanced countries and the developing world. Developing countries, traditionally, are more subject to external shocks through their impact on exchange rates, commodity prices, volume of trade and external finance. In fact, in many developing countries, commodity prices and exchange rates explain much of the variance in inflation.[6] Hence, controlling inflation through affecting aggregate demand seems irrelevant. Moreover, the relation between interest rates and aggregate demand is a much more controversial one in the case of developing countries given a much weaker monetary transmission mechanism.[7]

Given the bottlenecks in their monetary transmission mechanism, sticky prices in non-tradeable goods and adverse impact of rising commodity prices, central banks in developing countries used movements in the exchange rate to their best interest although they officially declared that they had a flexible exchange rate regime. This practice can be considered as a key difference between the mainstream framework and its implementation in developing countries. The emphasis on inflation rendered such a policy stance essential on the part of central banks in inflation targeting developing countries.[8] In general, they tolerated appreciation of their currency thereby easing inflationary pressures coming from elsewhere while fighting against depreciation pressures.[9] The availability of international liquidity in this period helped the appreciation of domestic currencies. In most cases, monetary authorities welcomed this trend and made interventions only with the aim of accumulating reserves rather than containing appreciation.

Overall, the monetary policy management experience of major developing countries prior to the crisis was praised on the basis of reduction in inflation levels, relatively stable output and inflation, high levels of economic growth and the absence of significant financial turmoil (see Table 3.1). In this respect they outreached even their 'golden age' records. Nevertheless, in many ways, they were all tied to the favorable environment in the world economy.

Exceptional growth performance was strongly related to increasing world trade and foreign capital inflows. The expanding demand of the advanced countries for the goods produced in the developing world, combined with the emergence of China as an important source of demand for primary goods and intermediate goods, resulted in a surge in exports. The impact of expanding international trade on growth opportunities in the developing countries was also apparent in the rise of commodity prices by

Table 3.1   Average GDP growth and end of period inflation in consumer prices of major developing countries[10]

Countries	1980–2001		2002–8	
	GDP Growth	Inflation	GDP Growth	Inflation
Brazil	2.38	522.64(125.91*)	3.98	6.95
Chile	5.25	14.76	4.37	3.92
Colombia	3.12	21.07	4.8	5.95
Czech. Rep	2.29**	6.01	4.54	2.49
Hungary	1.96**	19.42	3.24	5.24
India	5.6	8.59	7.4	5.60
Indonesia	5.49	11.9	5.41	8.89
Korea	7.56	6.35	4.67	3.23
Malaysia	6.39	3.51	5.72	2.58
Mexico	2.9	41.99	2.63	4.65
Peru	1.79	654.25(55.17*)	6.58	2.96
Philippines	2.5	11.1	5.16	4.73
Poland	3.62	44.04	4.43	2.33
South Africa	1.96	11.24	4.46	6.37
Thailand	6.03	3.77	5.15	2.75
Turkey	3.72	68.87	5.92	13.33

Notes:
* Hyperinflation episodes are excluded.
** Data starts from 1992.

Source: World Bank (World Development Indicators) and IMF (World Economic Outlook Database, October 2014).

which the terms of trade of many developing countries were ameliorated.[11] Moreover, this period also witnessed an increase in external finance that contributed to increasing investment and consumption in the developing world. The fact that a serious financial collapse did not occur was associated with the aforementioned pro-growth nature of international demand and the persistence of capital flows into the major developing countries. In fact, even though the current account deficit increased in many countries (except Asian developing countries and oil exporting countries), thanks to the robust capital inflows, they were able to increase foreign exchange reserves to be used in case of a sudden reversal.[12]

Moderate levels of inflation ensued largely from the disinflationary impact of the integration of some of the major developing countries into world markets (most notably China) and the appreciation of domestic currencies (Figure 3.1) fed by ever increasing levels of capital inflows (a trend that eased inflationary pressures coming from the domestic economy).[13]

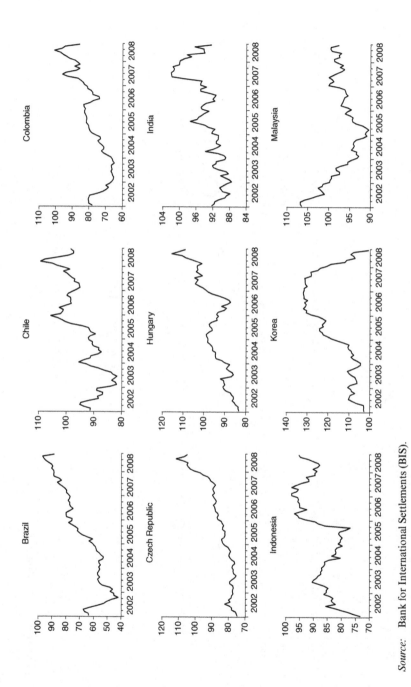

Source: Bank for International Settlements (BIS).

Figure 3.1 *Real effective exchange rates of selected countries, 2010=100*[14]

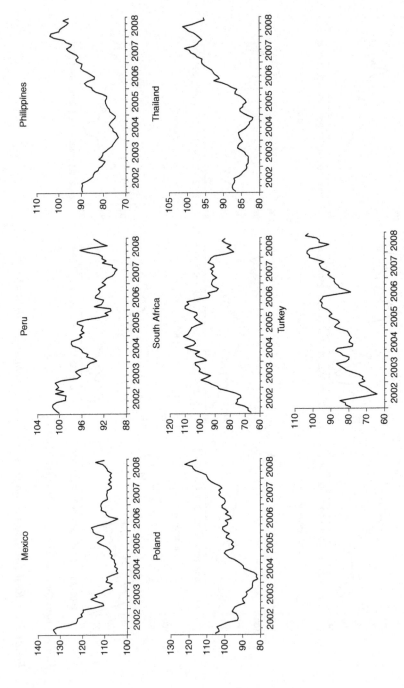

Figure 3.1 (continued)

Given the relatively high growth and appreciation of domestic currencies, many of the major developing countries also experienced improvements in their total debt to GDP ratio.

Thus, it is more likely that the 'great moderation' for developing countries was related more to the developments in the course of international trade and finance than to improvements in policy design. Although the impact of policy changes contributed to the success, its role is overemphasized in the relevant literature. This argument is validated by the events following the crisis. After the crisis, many countries were confronted with major deficiencies of their economies, which did not surface in good times. Financial stability concerns came to the forefront as international liquidity dried up and exchange rates depreciated. Most of the economies in the sample witnessed economic contractions due to the reversals in international trade and finance.[15]

In the years following the crisis, mainstream thinking revised itself, and both advanced countries and developing countries introduced more complex monetary policy regimes in which financial concerns came to the forefront. In the following section we explore what has changed in both a theoretical and a practical sense in the conduct of monetary policy in the post-crisis period.

3.3 THE POLICY SHIFT IN CENTRAL BANKING AFTER THE CRISIS

3.3.1 Changes in the Orthodox View of Monetary Policy

The main precepts of the pre-crisis framework of monetary policy have been described above. In the aftermath of the crisis, the first three principles of the mainstream approach mentioned above came under criticism. Regarding the first tenet, the pioneers of mainstream thinking and advocates of inflation targeting admitted that stable inflation does not necessarily stabilize asset prices and financial markets.[16] This was also supported by other arguments regarding the importance of a watchful eye on financial markets. First, the idea that the macroeconomic outcomes of financial stability would be limited was no longer tenable given the severity of the crisis. Second, the costs of 'cleaning up afterwards' came to be recognized as quite high, as the impact of the unprecedentedly aggressive interest rate policy response on economic activity remained limited.[17] Third, it is now ever increasingly voiced that central banks should 'lean against the wind' regardless of whether it is possible to identify a bubble or not. Trichet (2009) claims that central banks can use information about monetary and credit conditions as early warning indicators. These indicators are not perfect and may be misleading in some cases, but informational problems are always at the heart of policy decisions. The case with the asset prices is no exception in that regard (Trichet, 2009). On the other hand, some other authors distinguish between credit driven bubbles and equity type or 'irrational exuberance bubbles' (Hahm et al., 2011; Blinder, 2010; Mishkin, 2013). These authors suggest that monetary authorities should lean against the wind in case of credit driven bubbles, which can be easily detected by analyzing credit conditions, whereas they should clean up afterwards in case of an equity type bubble.

The acceptance of the invalidity of the previous approach paved the way for a more careful stance with respect to financial markets. Early on, the orthodox framework neglected the possibility of system wide risk arising from swollen balance sheets. Yet the crisis revealed the threats created by the procyclical nature of the financial system, in the sense that the relationship between credit growth, asset prices and low risk premia is quite intricate, and they support each other in economic booms. Hence, in good times, the level of risk appears to be low and individual financial institutions seem robust. However, as Borio and Shim (2007) point out, it is more plausible to consider that risk increases in booms and creates imbalances. At some point in the cycle risks materialize, reversing financial agents' risk taking behavior, triggering deleveraging and, consequently, financial turmoil in the form of huge stocks of accumulated debt. Beyond the procyclical component, the financial system is also exposed to cross sectional risks if financial institutions are highly interconnected and exposed to the same shocks. Hence, in light of the crisis, it was understood that institution level prudential measures are inadequate to ensure an orderly financial market given the procyclicality and interdependence inherent in the financial system.

Given the vital role that financial stability plays in the health of the whole economy, central banks have emerged as the natural candidates to take part in ensuring a robust financial system. The new role attached to central banks is at odds with the past experience in which central banks were operating in a narrow area. However, with the impact of the crisis, it is now widely recognized (remembered) that central banks (along with other regulatory agencies) should also be in charge of providing a smooth functioning of financial markets,[18] although the controversy over how this can be arranged is ongoing.

The arguments against attaching supervisory duties to central banks focus on the policy dilemmas that can arise due to possible conflicting priorities of bank supervision and monetary policy. They may require policy stances in opposite and contradictory directions. Moreover, it is argued that central banks may lose their transparency and thereby credibility if they engage in supervisory functions. On the other hand, proponents of the inclusion of central banks in financial supervision contend that central banks can balance these two competing objectives better than any other agent (Blinder, 2010). Another advantage of central banks is that they have a vast information network regarding financial institutions. Moreover, delegation of the task to central banks can also ease the coordination of policies regarding financial stability and price stability. It is now widely recognized that interest rate policy affects financial stability and measures to promote the soundness of the financial system affect macroeconomic conditions (through affecting credit growth, for instance), which may necessitate a change in policy interest rates in order to have the desired macroeconomic outcomes.[19] It is plausible to leave this problem to central banks, who can then find an optimum policy solution by taking into account the related interactions (Eichengreen et al., 2011).

The second tenet of the previous framework was related to the appropriate policy instruments of central banks. As previously mentioned, central banks are now seen as entities that can play a role in ensuring the stability of the financial system. To this end, policy suggestions are generally classified as 'macroprudential', implying that they target systemic risk and are implemented throughout the financial system rather than targeting individual institutions (FSB, IMF and BIS, 2011). We will analyze these measures in detail in the next subsection.[20]

Regarding the relation between interest rate policy and macroprudential policies, there is now an emerging consensus over the coordinated implementation of both interest rate policy and macroprudential policy in pursuit of both price and financial stability (Eichengreen et al., 2011; IMF, 2013b). However, the debate still continues as to the role of interest rate policy in responding to financial developments. Although it is now recognized that interest rate policy may be used where macroprudential tools remain insufficient[21] or when there are side effects of macroprudential policy, the main tendency is to leave financial concerns to macroprudential policy.[22]

The third tenet, obsession with a very low level of inflation, also came under criticism thanks to the events following the crisis. A very low inflation target (around 2 percent) is challenged on the grounds that this may restrict the capability of monetary policy in bad times given the 'zero-lower-bound problem' in nominal interest rates. If inflation is allowed to take higher values, then real interest rates could decline significantly, leaving a greater scope for the monetary policy in order to achieve recovery.

The fifth tenet, transparency of central banking, was also undermined to some extent.[23] In the new era, central banks found merit in creating some level of uncertainty in order to preserve stability in financial markets. The reason follows from the observation that a highly predictable environment may create fragilities. The mechanism is now widely known as the 'risk taking channel'. Low interest rates and a stable economy may create optimistic expectations with respect to the course of the economy and thus may prompt economic agents (particularly financial institutions) to take more risk through 'search for yield' activity and thereby to increase leverage, all eventually leading to an unsustainable expansion of credit and asset bubbles to be concluded with an overall collapse.

Mainstream thinking still lacks a different framework for the economies of developing countries (in general) which have been characterized quite differently than those of advanced countries. Hence, the practice in developing countries has mostly followed, although with a lag, mostly what is happening in advanced countries. The new development as in the advanced countries is the inclusion of financial concerns in designing monetary policy. And here lies the distinction between the mainstream design of monetary policy and its implementation in developing countries. With few exceptions, the new mainstream design, which is mainly created for advanced countries, does not emphasize the importance of cross border flows on financial stability. Nevertheless, these flows are at the heart of financial stability concerns in developing countries. Thus, many developing countries have taken measures in order to safeguard their economy against the potential detrimental spillovers of what is happening in the international economy. In the next section, to shed more light on new policies in developing countries we will present a brief discussion about the stance of monetary policy in the major developing countries in the aftermath of the crisis.

3.3.2 The Shift in Central Banking in the Major Developing Countries

The immediate response of monetary authorities in many of the major developing countries to the crisis lagged behind advanced countries. Many developing countries did not adjust policy interest rates until the beginning of 2009, as can be seen from Figure 3.2. For instance, the central bank of Brazil kept the SELIC (policy interest rate) at 13.75 until the end of January 2009. The reluctance to decrease policy interest rates was directly related to excessive focus on inflation. On the eve of the crisis, central banks in many of the major developing countries were trying to avoid overheating and sought to control inflationary pressures ensuing from hikes in commodity prices. Moreover, with the advent of the crisis, currencies in many of the important developing countries experienced

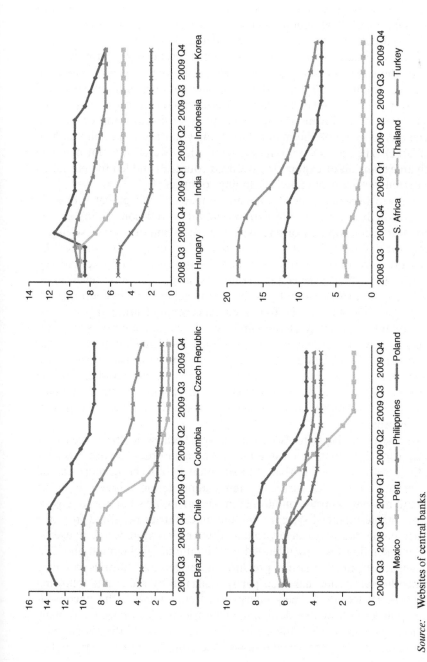

Source: Websites of central banks.

Figure 3.2   Policy interest rates of selected countries between August 2008 and December 2009 (%)

depreciations, further exacerbating inflationary outlook. In an extreme case, the central bank of Uruguay raised interest rates consecutively until the beginning of 2009, arguing that this was needed to ensure the compatibility of inflation with the target (Cespedes et al., 2012).

In the aftermath of the crisis, some of the recent trends have reversed due to the expansionary monetary policy followed by central banks in advanced countries. The abundance of international liquidity in a low interest rate environment increased external financing opportunities for domestic banks and firms, leading to credit expansion and appreciation of currencies in many of the major developing countries (especially in 2010 and 2011). The increase in domestic demand, however, was not matched with an expansion of exports to advanced countries and led to deteriorating current accounts in many developing countries.[24]

Having experienced the detrimental impact of the global economic crisis through drying of international liquidity and contracting export markets, the developing world realized the crucial importance of strengthening their financial systems in a world economy characterized by especially huge uncertainties regarding the future path of international finance. Accordingly, developing countries, in general, have given more importance to prudential policies as to financial markets in contrast with the practice before the crisis. To that end, a common feature of post-crisis central banking in many of the important developing countries is a cautious stance with respect to credit growth that could give rise to the formation of bubbles in certain types of assets. In line with this, when capital inflows have soared, putting pressure on exchange rates and expanding available liquidity to be used as loans, central banks have used many policy tools to monitor financial markets, leaving behind the one instrument approach.

The use of multiple tools was necessary, because in the presence of strong capital inflows, increasing interest rates in order to curb excessive credit growth could exacerbate the situation by attracting more capital and paving the way for further currency appreciation. These new measures did not only aim to contain the impact of inflows but also to ensure a more stable financial system. Developing countries benefited from the change in the international environment in which a more watchful eye on cross border flows is now tolerated by the international community.[25] In this sense, we can say that the pressure on developing countries to follow the neo-liberal agenda has been partly weakened by the events following the crisis. Hence, in the new international environment, the unconventional policies followed by developing countries are legitimized and many developing countries used this new policy space to shield their economies from inherently unstable capital flows. Accordingly, the monetary policy

Table 3.2   *Current account balance as a percent of GDP in selected countries*

Country	2008	2009	2010	2011	2012
Brazil	−1.7	−1.5	−2.21	−2.12	−2.41
Chile	−1.84	2.05	1.48	−1.31	−3.52
Colombia	−2.81	−2.17	−3.11	−2.92	−3.29
Czech Rep.	−2.12	−2.46	−3.83	−2.83	−2.41
Hungary	−7.21	−0.15	1.1	0.88	1.68
India	−2.53	−1.92	−3.19	−3.34	−4.97
Indonesia	0.02	1.97	0.73	0.2	−2.74
Korea	0.34	3.93	2.9	2.34	3.84
Malaysia	16.85	15.72	10.91	11.58	6.11
Mexico	−1.78	−0.86	−0.31	−1.02	−1.2
Peru	−4.11	−0.56	−2.4	−1.85	−3.5
Philippines	2.09	5.56	4.47	3.11	2.85
Poland	−6.6	−3.98	−5.12	−5	−3.73
South Africa	−7.36	−4	−2.79	−3.41	−6.26
Thailand	0.81	8.3	3.12	1.2	−0.39
Turkey	−5.54	−1.98	−6.22	−9.69	−6.05

Source: World Bank (World Development Indicators).

framework of central banks has widened, which signifies a departure from the inflation targeting regimes.[26]

We classify the policy measures used by central banks in the new era in the following way.[27] First, central banks used various instruments in order to affect capital flows. While arguing for capital flow management, central banks generally refer to problems associated with appreciation pressures, currency mismatches, and co-movement of credit growth and capital inflows. Moreover, they claim that in the new era capital flows are driven by global conditions, which, when they deteriorate, could lead to a reversal and bring associated dangers with it.[28] The new measures are generally aimed at discouraging short term speculative investment thereby lengthening the maturity of capital inflows and curbing appreciation of domestic currencies.

Second, authorities strived to contain foreign exchange exposures of financial institutions, which can culminate in a full-fledged financial crisis in the case of a sudden reversal. Third, in the new era there is an emphasis on the potential threats created by excessive credit growth. Hence, central banks (along with regulatory agencies in many cases) imposed measures in order to affect credit growth and improve credit quality. Last, measures to strengthen banks' capital base were widely implemented to provide buffers to be used in downturns, thereby avoiding financial collapse.

In what follows in this section we briefly summarize some prominent examples of these new policies[29] (Table 3.3). With regards to capital flow management (CFM),[30] some countries imposed tax on foreign investment. For instance, Thailand imposed a withholding tax of 15 percent on interest and capital gains of non-residents in the bond market in 2010. Korea, on the other hand, revived the tax on bond investments (14 percent for interest earnings and 20 percent for trade earnings) in January 2011. Brazil imposed a financial transaction tax of 6 percent on non-residents' fixed income portfolio investment as of October 2010. Some other countries (Thailand and the Philippines) have taken measures to liberalize capital outflows, which are considered to dampen the impact of inflows. Indonesia applied minimum holding periods on debt instruments of the central bank (initially for one month in June 2010 and six months after May 2011). Indonesia also put limits on short term foreign exchange borrowing of banks (as 30 percent of their capital) in January 2011. This measure also aims to reduce the foreign exchange exposure of domestic banks.

Another measure used in Indonesia and in some Latin American countries is the implementation of differentiated reserve requirements in foreign exchange deposits. In Indonesia, reserve requirements in foreign currency deposits increased from 1 percent to 5 percent in March 2011 and to 8 percent in June 2011. Peru differentiated reserve requirements in terms of residency and also applied different reserve requirements for domestic and foreign currency by applying 60 percent of reserve requirements to external liabilities whose maturity was less than two years. On the other hand, Brazil put an unremunerated reserve requirement of 60 percent on short positions of banks in the foreign exchange spot market as of January 2011.

Korea, having experienced currency and maturity mismatches prior to the global crisis, implemented other measures in order to mitigate vulnerabilities of domestic banks arising from short term external borrowing. The Korean authorities imposed a levy on banks' noncore foreign currency liabilities in June 2010 that increase with shorter maturities. Moreover, they put ceilings on banks' foreign exchange derivative positions in October 2010 and tightened this policy as of July 2011.

The last policy response in coping with capital flows was through short term interest rates. Central banks of many developing countries declared that interest rate policy should be used in order to manipulate aggregate demand and control inflation whereas financial stability concerns are left to macroprudential regulations. Although the impact of monetary policy on financial stability is now recognized by policymakers,[31] the main

Table 3.3   Some macroprudential tools used in some major developing countries

Measures for capital flows	Measures to contain foreign exchange exposures
Tax on foreign investment: Brazil (2010): financial transaction tax of 6% on non-residents' fixed income portfolio investment Thailand (2010): withholding tax of 15 percent on interest and capital gains of non-residents in the bond market Korea (2011): tax on bond investments *Liberalization of capital outflows:* Indonesia, Thailand	*Limitations on foreign currency lending:* Poland (2010): lending ceiling for foreign exchange mortgage lending *Limitations to net open positions:* Philippines (2010): exposure limits on currency mismatches Mexico: ceilings on foreign currency liabilities of banks
Minimum holding periods: Indonesia (2011): on debt instruments of central bank *Limits on short term foreign exchange borrowing of banks:* Indonesia (2011) *Differentiated reserve requirements:* Indonesia (2011): Increase in RR for foreign currency deposits Peru: 60% RR to external liabilities the maturity of which is less than 2 years Brazil (2011): Unremunerated RR of 60% on short positions of banks in foreign exchange spot market *Levy on noncore foreign liabilities:* Korea (2010)	*Reserve option mechanism:* Turkey Measures to affect credit growth and quality *LTV & DTI ratios:* Malaysia (2011), Indonesia (2012), India, Poland (2010), Turkey (2010), Korea *Countercyclical use of reserve requirements:* Malaysia, Peru, Philippines, India, Indonesia, Brazil, Turkey
Ceilings on banks' foreign exchange derivative positions: Korea (2011) *Policy interest rates:* Malaysia, Turkey	Measures to strengthen the capital base *Capital buffers and capital surcharges:* India, Brazil, Turkey, Philippines, Peru *Loan loss provisions:* Chile, Mexico, Peru, Colombia, India, Turkey

Source: Authors' compilation from different sources.

tendency in developing countries is to use interest rate policy mainly to affect inflation and output. However, some country cases distinguish themselves from others by giving a role to interest rate policy in the management of financial fragilities. The Malaysian central bank for instance emphasized that leaving policy rates at a low level could lead to financial imbalances and excessive credit growth in the economic environment of 2010. As a result, the bank argued that monetary policy should be adjusted preemptively in order to contain financial imbalances.[32]

The Turkish example, on the other hand, appears to be in contrast with the experience of the other major developing countries in that the Turkish central bank developed a new policy framework in 2010 giving a major role to interest rate policy in the management of capital flows.[33] The framework incorporated an asymmetric interest rate corridor, where the upper and lower bounds are adjusted in line with the amount of international liquidity. When capital inflows are strong, the lower bound of the corridor was decreased and the short term rate was allowed to deviate from the policy rate creating uncertainty around short term yields, thereby discouraging short term inflows. When inflows began to reverse as of August 2011, however, the Turkish central bank widened the interest rate corridor by raising the upper bound of the corridor in order to attract foreign capital.[34]

A second set of policy measures aims to contain foreign exchange exposure of economic agents. One of the measures designed to deal with this concern is the limitation on foreign currency lending. For instance, Poland introduced a lending ceiling for foreign exchange mortgage lending (50 percent out of the total mortgage). Moreover, the authorities assigned differentiated risk weights for zloty loans and foreign currency loans. In Turkey, authorities banned banks from lending to consumers in foreign currency in June 2009. Another new policy tool was the setting of limitations on the net open positions of financial institutions. Prominent examples are the Philippines, which imposed exposure limits on currency mismatches in 2010 and Mexico, which put ceilings on the foreign currency liability of banks. Moreover, a novel policy was devised by the Turkish central bank: a reserve option mechanism (ROM). ROM allows banks to hold some portion of reserve requirements in foreign currency or gold. When capital inflows soar, banks are expected to use the ROM facility more, thereby restraining the appreciation trend of the domestic currency and building up of foreign exchange reserves that can be used in downturns. In the case of outflows, on the other hand, banks in need of foreign exchange could convert foreign currency denominated reserve requirements into domestic currency. In this way, the ROM facility was presented by some authors as 'a market friendly automatic stabilizer' that moderates the impact of fluctuations in capital flows on the exchange rate and financial system.[35]

The third set of policies aims to shape credit growth and improve credit quality. The most typical examples are the implementation of maximum Loan to Value (LTV) and Debt to Income (DTI) ratios and intensive use of reserve requirements. Some countries also resort to other measures. For instance, Turkish authorities declared a credit growth target of 25 percent for 2011 (15 percent for the following years) and guided banks to achieve this target. Peru's approach was much more direct; in 2010 it introduced limits on non-performing loans in 2010.

LTV and DTI measures have been implemented by many developing countries. These measures are designed mostly to regulate loans in the residential property market. There are various forms of LTV in operation. For instance, the Czech Republic imposed LTV ratio limits differentiated by the value of property, attaching higher risk weights for higher LTV loans. Malaysia put a maximum limit of 70 percent LTV ratio for the third residential property purchase in 2011. Indonesia imposed LTV ratios for purchases in automotive and residential property beginning after March 2012. India introduced for the first time a limit of 80 percent LTV ratio for residential real estate loans. Poland differentiated LTV measures based on the maturity of the loan and imposed caps on DTI ratios for loans to consumers in 2010. Turkey differentiated LTV ratios for mortgages and commercial real estate loans (75 percent for mortgages, 50 percent for commercial real estate loans) in December of 2010. Lastly, Korea, having experienced two house price booms in its recent history, implemented limits for LTV and DTI ratios in a countercyclical manner if the property was in a speculative zone.

The aftermath of the crisis witnessed the widespread use of reserve requirements.[36] Many developing countries including Malaysia, Peru, the Philippines, India, Indonesia, Turkey and Brazil have used reserve requirements as a 'speed limit' by adjusting them in a countercyclical way to increase lending rates and thereby curb credit growth in the presence of strong capital inflows. In the case of mounting risk perception, they decreased reserve requirements to supply additional liquidity to the banking system in order to avoid credit shrinkage. The most notable cases of countercyclical implementation of reserve requirements in this respect are Turkey and Brazil. Turkey, having decreased their interest rates in order to restrain capital inflows, struggled with the adverse impact of this policy stance (excessive credit growth) via hikes in reserve requirements. The Turkish central bank also differentiated reserve requirements from December 2010 on the basis of both maturity and leverage by requiring more reserve requirements for shorter maturities and for more leveraged banks. Besides using reserve requirements countercyclically to combat the credit cycle, Brazilian authorities also aimed to direct liquidity to small financial institutions by exempting large institutions of reserve requirements if they provided liquidity for other financial agents.

The last group of measures is related to the desire to strengthen the capital base of financial institutions. During upswings, the likelihood of future losses increases as credit is extended to a broad base including more risky activities. In good times, banks' capital ratios appear robust whereas they can quickly deteriorate in downturns as the quality of credit diminishes. Countercyclical measures may provide buffers preemptively, which could be used to strengthen banks' balance sheets when circumstances change. Moreover, imposing countercyclical measures can also restrain financial institutions from extending credit excessively in the upswing. Some examples of countries using capital buffers countercyclically and capital surcharges for banks involving risky activities are the Philippines, India, Turkey, Peru and Brazil.

The Philippines imposed capital surcharges for systemically important banks in order to combat the moral hazard problem. Turkey introduced a target capital adequacy ratio of 12 percent for banks and required a higher ratio for banks which were subject to maturity mismatches. Moreover, in August 2011, the Banking Regulation and Supervision Agency imposed capital surcharges for those banks with strategic foreign shareholders. The Peruvian authorities required banks to build up an additional capital buffer, which rises when credit growth is strong and decreases when credit shrinks. Brazil imposed differentiated capital adequacy ratios for different types of credit and maturity in 2010 and 2011. As of December 2010, banks were subject to higher capital requirements for extending credit to consumers.

Many countries also required banks to build up loan loss provisions in order to ensure the maintenance of credit in case of an increase in nonperforming loans. India introduced a provisioning coverage ratio of 70 percent of gross nonperforming loans in December 2009. In Turkey in June 2011, provisions for consumer loans (excluding vehicle and housing) were increased for banks, with consumer loan to total loan ratio exceeding 20 percent and for banks with nonperforming loan ratios for consumer loans exceeding 8 percent. Chile and Mexico implemented a differentiated loan loss provisioning system depending on the risk level of banks' loans. Peru and Colombia, on the other hand, implemented a provisioning scheme in a countercyclical way and accumulated provisioning when credit growth was strong.

Some of these measures had been implemented before the crisis as well. For instance, Korea (2001), Thailand (2003), Malaysia (1995) and the

Philippines (1997) introduced LTV and DTI ratios long before the crisis. India used reserve requirements before the crisis as a policy tool. Colombia resorted to similar measures for capital flows in order to curb excessive credit growth. This is also true for some of the other measures described above.[37] What is new is that after the crisis the implementation of these measures gained the ascendancy, spread to many other countries and the macroprudential policy framework was organized much more systematically. The procyclical nature of the financial system is now widely accepted and there is a growing case for the idea that central banks should lean against the wind.[38] There is also more emphasis on systemic risks rather than soundness of individual institutions. Another new feature is that the relationship between monetary policy and financial stability is now much more recognized. Accordingly, ensuring financial stability through the use of macroprudential measures has become one of the major tasks of central banks. Thus, central banks are now much more actively involved in ensuring financial stability in the post-crisis environment. There is also a more cautious policy stance with regards to capital flows. Latin American countries had already used related tools prior to the crisis but in the aftermath of the crisis countries such as Turkey and some Eastern European countries have also joined the group. Lastly, reserve requirements are now used much more frequently by many more countries.

3.4   ARE THE SHIFTS IN DEVELOPING COUNTRIES' CENTRAL BANKING ENOUGH?

It is now widely recognized that mainstream macroeconomic thinking underestimated the importance of some lessons learnt by previous generations. The 'great moderation' led to a misperception that financial markets are self-regulating, although history is actually full of financial crises.[39] In other words, mainstream thinking, by adopting a single minded approach focused on inflation, turned its back on historical experience of central banking in which financial stability was among the key goals (if not the chief goal), of central banking. At the same time it appeared to forget the lessons of the Great Depression and turned a blind eye to the Japanese deflation.[40]

We have seen that the recent practice of central banking in developing countries can be classified as a shift from the previous framework in some respects. The narrow view of central banking is being abandoned in both academia and policymaking. Now, central banks are expected to target multiple objectives through multiple instruments. In this vein, they are expected to take *ex ante* measures in order to dampen procyclicality of the financial system. However, there are still several important inconsistencies and gaps within new central banking theories and practices.

First, even the adoption of the existing framework is problematic for some policymakers. A recent questionnaire answered by central bankers and economists throughout the world reveals that there is wide confusion over the analysis of what has happened, why it happened and what should now be done (Carre et al., 2013). Central bankers recognize the weaknesses of the pre-crisis conception of monetary policy. Nevertheless they don't have a clear cut agenda about what to do.[41]

Second, although, as mentioned before, in the aftermath of the crisis, a very low inflation target is challenged due to zero-lower-bound considerations, debates over the proper rate of targeted inflation still focus on a very narrow range of inflation (between 2 and 4 percent) maintaining that low inflation is for the benefit of the society.[42] In this sense, all inflation targeting countries still define themselves as inflation targeters and declare that their main objective is to ensure price stability. However, the recent evidence appears to be at odds with their presumption. It is more likely that there is a nonlinear relationship between inflation and economic growth. For instance, Anwar and Islam (2011) suggest that there is a threshold level of inflation up to which inflation positively affects output growth. More importantly, in today's world, the hampering impact of inflation on growth, if there is any, remains subordinated by the huge uncertainties regarding the future path of the economy, which affects economic agents' spending decisions adversely. Inflation targeting does not have a proposal for this damaging problem, and maintaining a focus on inflation at the expense of ignorance of output concerns may even exacerbate the situation. Hence, it remains unclear that low inflation leads to improved growth performance. There are more serious problems in achieving robust economic growth, which should be handled with a broader vision as to monetary policy.

Third, in addition to the misspecification of low inflation as a key for robust economic growth, affecting it through conventional policy tools is also problematic. Although in practice many developing countries have to resort to the exchange rate as an anchor to curb inflation in the new framework, interest rate decisions are once again set mainly in line with the inflation target. However, the effectiveness of monetary policy in determining the level of output and inflation is subject to question, even in advanced countries.[43] What is more, setting policy interest rates is more ineffective in determining inflation due to the aforementioned different characteristics of the economies of developing countries. Hence, we can argue that, in the case of developing countries, the diagnosis was not true (low inflation is what is needed to achieve high and stable growth), nor were the policy tools that were chosen correct.

Fourth, the new post-crisis framework sticks to the ineffectiveness of monetary policy in longer horizons.[44] Theoretically, monetary policy is still assumed to have no impact on long run growth. Thus, the role attached to central banks is still related to short term concerns. Central banks should focus on what they can do, that is, price stability and output stabilization and should not attempt to target long term growth through conventional monetary policy.[45]

In line with this, the new framework does not assume growth related objectives for central banks. Besides the ineffectiveness of interest rate policy on growth, it also does not have room for other nonconventional policy tools. For instance, it lacks credit allocation and exchange rate policies through which investment can be directed into strategic sectors. In the new framework, employment concerns are absent and structural transformation of productive capabilities are out of the policy agenda. The stabilization role of the central bank now rules the day and there is no mention of the developmental roles that were once assumed by most central banks. However, as Epstein (2006) argues, a balance between these two historical objectives may be desirable in the sense that a developmental role can complement a stabilization role through redirecting investment from speculative areas (which proved very costly during and after the crisis) to productive areas.[46]

Fifth, the new framework has another major deficiency as far as developing countries are concerned. With the existence of massive financial flows, the effectiveness of monetary policy is likely to be reduced. Flexible exchange rates may not be panacea to that problem. External finance can substitute for domestic funding and the main macroeconomic variables such as credit growth and exchange rates are themselves affected by financial flows.[47] Hence, even in the presence of a flexible exchange rate regime, external developments are likely to shape domestic economic conditions, posing challenges for an independent monetary policy. In fact, as can be seen from Figure 3.3, the correlation of capital flows with credit growth, GDP growth and real effective exchange rate is strong in our sample of developing countries.[48]

Central bankers in developing countries have taken measures (described above) in order to dampen the effect of capital flows on domestic financial conditions. However, in their current form these measures are inadequate and a much more systematic management approach is needed.[49] In this respect, we can argue that in the absence of a new international financial architecture (that helps individual countries to coordinate their policies by taking into account the impact of their policy choices on their counterparts), the current framework remains unchanged in that it cannot insulate the developing world from the impact of external financial shocks.[50]

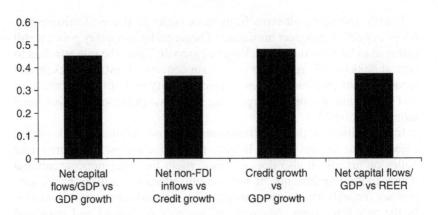

Source: IMF (International Financial Statistics), World Bank (World Development Indicators), BIS and authors' calculations.

Figure 3.3　Average of correlations between capital flows and macroeconomic indicators over countries (1990–2014)

This argument is particularly important in the current environment in which policy decisions of the central banks of advanced countries, particularly the Federal Reserve, can expose developing countries to potential dangers. In the aftermath of the crisis, the abundant liquidity made available to financial markets has stimulated, once again, the search for yield activity. Consequently, the developing countries' economies witnessed:

- large capital inflows with an accumulation of foreign exchange reserves
- high credit growth
- domestic currency appreciation
- worsening current accounts.

In this way, these years were very reminiscent of the boom phase of what is called a 'developing country Minskian cycle' by Frenkel and Rapetti (2009: 689).

Consistent with the new framework and having benefited from the available policy space for a more cautious stance with respect to capital flows, the developing world has tried to contain systemic risks associated with abundant liquidity. But the resilience of their economies is not tested yet. Macroprudential policies have provided a shield but the degree of their effectiveness remains contentious. What is more, in the case of an abrupt change in market sentiments triggering capital outflows, developing

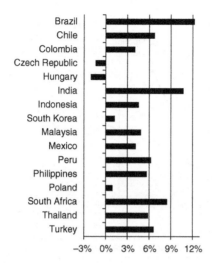

Source: IMF, International Financial Statistics.

Figure 3.4   Percentage changes in dollar exchange rate from March–May to June–August 2013

countries are likely to be affected heavily. A good indicator of that is the impact of the Federal Reserve's (Fed) policy decisions on economic conditions in developing countries. We know that tapering (the gradual reduction of asset purchases by the Fed) news has led to hikes in interest rates and significant depreciation of currencies in developing countries, as Figures 3.4 and 3.5 illustrate.[51]

In this regard, it is important to note that the Fed is trying to make this transition gradually; hence the impact is not abrupt. However, as the markets expect that higher global interest rates materialize in the near future, the magnitude of outflows is likely to increase. As a result, the main macroeconomic indicators in developing countries can deteriorate rapidly.

Along these lines, it is very interesting to observe the reactions of the financial markets to the Fed's statements by analyzing every sentence word by word. Even speculations about whether the Fed will remove the phrase 'considerable' from its statements, indicating that the target for the federal funds rate will be kept low for a considerable time, could result in excessive fluctuations in financial markets of developing countries for a few days. This reiterates the high level of exposure of developing countries to external developments.

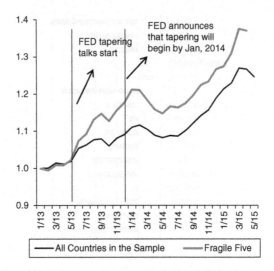

Notes: Following Aizenman et al. (2014) we set the dollar exchange rate of each country equal to 1 for January 2013. Then we took the average of the index across countries. The sample is the same with that of Figure 1. Fragile Five consists of Brazil, India, Indonesia, South Africa and Turkey.

Source: IMF, International Financial Statistics and authors' calculations.

Figure 3.5   *The change in dollar exchange rates of developing countries (average across countries)*

3.5   CONCLUDING REMARKS

The recent experiences of both advanced countries and developing countries during and after the global economic crisis have revealed the problems within the mainstream macroeconomic theory. In response to the crisis, the narrow view of central banking has been abandoned by both academia and policymakers. Financial stability concerns gained ground and usage of multiple instruments to target multiple objectives became much more acceptable. However, the resulting modified framework is far from a radical shift and the core of the previous consensus is preserved. The new framework sticks to the ineffectiveness of monetary policy in longer time horizons. Growth and employment concerns are absent; structural transformation of productive capabilities is out of the policy agenda; there is limited scope for restrictions to capital inflows. In the case of an abrupt change in market sentiments triggering capital outflows, developing countries are likely to face huge challenges. At that point the resilience of the modified approach to central banking will be tested especially in the developing world.

In general, the macroeconomic performance of developing countries in the near future depends on the exit strategies of advanced countries.[52] Changes in current central banking in developing countries would not make much difference in this process. Given the existing international architecture and central banking practices in developing countries, the three most likely scenarios for developing countries are as follows: The first possibility is that interest rates gradually increase as the Fed raises short term rates over 2015. Restoring high returns in advanced countries would mean that advanced countries reclaim their attractive roles. This development is likely to trigger reversals in capital flows to developing countries, further exacerbating the ongoing processes of depreciation, rises in interest rates and decreases in stock markets. As the magnitude of reversals increases, so does the likelihood of a full-fledged financial crisis in some countries.

In scenario two, the abandonment of an aggressively easy monetary policy proceeds very slowly and a reversal is always possible in case the recovery in real sectors remains subdued in advanced countries. In this case, capital inflows to developing countries are likely to continue, increasing asset prices, fueling credit growth and appreciating the currency, all of which may create financial fragilities. In this case, we assume that developing countries would continue to develop their macroprudential frameworks. Nevertheless, given that the effectiveness of macroprudential policies is open to question, the challenge will continue as developing countries endeavor to shield their economies from external developments. In this case, even if developing countries manage to avoid financial turmoil, their growth prospects will be bleak. The years following the crisis are illustrative in this sense. Most developing countries remained unsuccessful in restoring both their export and growth performances during 2011 to 2014, as Figures 3A.1 and 3A.2 demonstrate. In this vein, if the recovery of advanced countries remains subdued, the demand for developing countries' exports will be limited, posing challenges especially to export oriented economies.[53]

In scenario three, the prolonged expansionary monetary policy and ignorance of necessary regulatory steps in advanced countries creates considerable danger through ensuing high risk taking behavior, increases in leverage, and sharp rises in asset prices. This progress can result in many problems in advanced countries if it results in asset and credit bubbles formed in a similar way before the crisis. As a result, developing countries would be adversely affected by the volatility of financial flows related to developments in advanced countries. With its current version until now, modified monetary policy in advanced countries, seemingly, tries to

save the day. However, the current framework is still subject to considerable threat coming from the financial sector given its inability to turn the
tide. The resilience of developing countries in this respect after adopting a new monetary policy framework will be tested throughout the new
developments.

NOTES

1. Inflation targeting can be defined as a framework by which a central bank conducts
    its monetary policy through the announcement of quantitative point/range targets for
    inflation with the explicit declaration that it will pursue price stability as its primary
    goal.
2. This term refers to the assumption that price and output stability reduces the possibility
    of unstable asset prices, thereby ensuring financial stability.
3. In one of the pioneer studies, Bernanke and Gertler (2001) use a simulation method to
    show that there is no significant gain from responding to asset prices beyond the level
    required by the inflation targeting rule.
4. Within this framework, interest rate smoothing was accepted to be optimal in order to
    decrease uncertainty about monetary policy (Woodford, 2003).
5. These include Armenia (2006), Brazil (1999), Chile (1999), Colombia (1999), the
    Czech Republic (1997), Ghana (2002), Guatemala (2005), Hungary (2001), Indonesia
    (2005), Israel (1997), Mexico (2001), Peru (2002), the Philippines (2002), Poland (1998),
    Romania (2005), Serbia (2006), Slovakia (2005), South Africa (2000), Thailand (2000)
    and Turkey (2002).
6. See, among others, Mohanty and Klau (2001), and Benlialper and Cömert (2015).
7. For an analysis of transmission mechanisms in low income countries, see Mishra and
    Montiel (2012).
8. With regards to the asymmetric response to exchange rate movements, we should make
    a distinction between inflation targeting developing countries and other developing
    countries. Whereas an asymmetric stance appears to be the case for inflation targeting
    developing countries, some other developing countries adopted a competitive exchange
    rate policy. Among them are Argentina and some Asian countries, which intervened to
    absorb abundant liquidity in the foreign exchange market. See, for instance, Frenkel and
    Rapetti (2008), Akyüz (2010), Pontines and Siregar (2012) and Rajan (2011).
9. For such argument, see Benlialper and Cömert (2015), Barbosa-Filho (2006) and
    Galindo and Ros (2009).
10. In this article we focus mostly on this set of countries. In the selection process we
    tried to include the most important developing countries in terms of their share in
    the world economy. Hence, we listed developing countries according to their GDP
    and excluded oil dependent economies (such as Saudi Arabia and the United Arab
    Emirates) whose macroeconomic conditions depended heavily, and much more
    explicitly compared to our sample, upon external shocks. We also excluded countries
    that implemented more heterodox policies in the recent past (for example, China and
    Argentina) in order to focus on the shift from a mainstream design. These country
    cases are subject to other research and need to be carefully investigated for a hetero-
    dox policy agenda. The resulting sample leaves us with a relatively homogenous set of
    countries both in terms of the characteristics of their economies and their monetary
    policy stances.
11. However, at this juncture we must make a distinction between countries on the basis of
    export products. Countries producing minerals and related energy products benefited
    most as energy prices increased. Exporters of agricultural goods did not witness a

profound change in their terms of trade and exporters of manufactured goods even suffered from increasing commodity prices (Griffith-Jones and Ocampo, 2009).

12. In this respect, it is important to make some caveats about the differences in economic performance in different regions. For instance, whereas Asian developing countries were characterized by high saving rates and current account surpluses, the case is different for African countries and Eastern Europe. Countries in these regions generally suffered from high current account deficits and external debt, and fueled their growth through capital inflows, which rendered the financial systems of these countries fragile. On the other hand, countries can also be decomposed within the same region. This is the case for Middle Eastern countries where oil exporting countries' and others' economic characteristics are significantly different. Nevertheless, it remains clear that developing countries, overall, enjoyed low levels of inflation and high GDP growth.

13. As a case study, Benlialper and Cömert (2015) analyze the determinants of inflation in Turkey during the period under consideration. Since the exchange rate appears as one of the most important determinants of inflation in Turkey, it is apparent that Turkish monetary authorities benefited from appreciation of their currency to fight with inflation. Although other econometric researches are needed, it is very likely that a generalization can be applied to other developing countries, the economic structures of which have much in common with Turkey.

14. The reason we use real exchange rate data is that even depreciation in nominal exchange rates lower than the inflation level may decrease the inflation level. Real exchange rate appreciation, on the other hand, puts a downward pressure on inflation.

15. On the other hand, it is true that after 2009 developing countries resumed their growth and outreached the performance of advanced countries, reviving 'decoupling' arguments. This was mostly related to the fact that the impact of the recent crisis on the economies of developing countries did not last long and remained relatively small in magnitude compared to previous crises. Cömert and Çolak (2014) claim that this is due to the extraordinary nature of the recent crisis in that advanced countries did not fully fulfill their safe haven roles. In this sense, the resilience of the economies of developing countries is not tested yet. However, even with that in mind, one can observe that their performance has fallen behind that which was achieved before the crisis and now it is widely accepted that they cannot return to their pre-crisis performance in the near future due to unfavorable global conditions. We will discuss these issues in more detail in the fourth section.

16. Among others, see Blanchard et al. (2010), Mishkin (2013), Svensson (2009) and Hahm et al. (2011).

17. Costs other than loss in output are mentioned in Hahm et al. (2011). These include very slow growth (typical in the aftermath of financial crises), deterioration of government budget balance and erosion of the central bank's ability to manage the economy.

18. See Eichengreen et al. (2011), Blanchard et al. (2010) and Blinder (2010) for a role attached to central banks.

19. The interaction of interest rate policy and policy measures for financial stability is analyzed in detail in IMF (2012a) and IMF (2013b).

20. Here, we should note that, in contrast with the bulk of the literature, we are using the term 'monetary policy' in such a way that both 'interest rate policy' and some parts of 'macroprudential policy', parts that are implemented by central bank, are subsumed. The literature takes monetary policy synonymous with interest rate policy by virtue of the simple framework of the 'new consensus' in which the only policy tool of the central bank is short term policy rates. However, we believe that all policy tools of the central bank that effect monetary conditions should be regarded as part of the monetary policy toolkit.

21. IMF (2012a) makes the case for using interest rate policy for financial developments in certain conditions: 'in models where macroprudential policy is absent or time invariant, but in the presence of financial sector distortions, it is optimal for monetary policy to consider financial shocks. In such contexts, optimal monetary policy responds to the

growth in credit (in addition to the output gap and deviations of inflation from target). By extension, when macroprudential policy is imperfectly targeted, it can be desirable for monetary policy to respond to financial conditions' (IMF, 2012a: 5).

22. Those who are against the use of interest rate policy for financial concerns claim that policy interest rates are too blunt to deal with bubbles forming in specific sectors (Blanchard et al., 2010). A contractionary policy in response to developments in a specific sector would mean throwing out the baby with the bathwater. In this sense, more targeted policy tools emerge as the most suitable instruments. Controversy surrounds the effectiveness of interest rate policy in dealing with financial imbalances. After all, in order to dampen increases in asset prices, very sharp movements of interest rates are needed which may have many side effects. Furthermore, an active use of interest rates to correct financial imbalances may risk price stability given that one instrument is used for more than one policy objective and, thereby, erodes the credibility of an inflation targeting central bank. With respect to the bluntness of interest rate policy, Agenor and Da Silva (2013) suggest that the bluntness of interest rate policy may even be advantageous given that it is more difficult to circumvent increasing borrowing costs emanating from an increase in interest rates. On the other hand, the impact of macroprudential policy can more easily be circumvented through various mechanisms. Moreover, some authors claim that macroprudential policy is more subject to political pressure than interest rate policy due to the fact that it affects financial institutions more directly (Hahm et al., 2011; Agenor and Da Silva, 2013). Regarding the effectiveness of interest rate policy, some claim that even small changes in interest rates may affect leverage decisions of some segments of financial institutions and moderate asset price increases (Trichet, 2009).

23. We will analyze the relevance of the trilemma argument for developing countries in the next section. Central bank independence, on the other hand, remains to be the only intact principle of the new consensus in post-crisis central banking experience.

24. We should again distinguish Asian countries that still have current account surpluses and others. However, as Table 3.2 shows, the surpluses of Asian countries diminished in 2010 and 2011 as well.

25. See IMF (2012b) for instance.

26. Some authors interpret the new framework as enhanced and enriched versions of inflation targeting (Cespedes et al., 2012). However, especially in developing countries, we think that inflation targeting regimes lost their core (one target, one instrument, transparency, simplicity, and so on). Independent of what we call the new framework, it is evident that there is a substantial change in how central bankers approach monetary policy. In the case of Indonesia, for instance, Perry Warjiyo (the deputy governor of the Indonesian central bank) states that: 'a mix of monetary and macroprudential policy measures is required to deal with the multiple challenges of "the impossible trinity" and the preservation of monetary and financial system stability. Even though interest rate policy is still the primary instrument, monetary policy needs to work through all available transmission channels, including interest rates, exchange rates, money and credit, and expectations. These considerations form the basis for the monetary policy framework adopted in Indonesia since mid-2010. Starting from the inflation targeting framework, we have added macroprudential measures to manage capital flows and safeguard financial system stability. We call this an enhanced inflation targeting framework based on a monetary and macroprudential policy mix' (Warjiyo, 2013: 156).

27. Lim et al. (2011) and Moreno (2011) are examples of similar classifications. A detailed literature about macroprudential measures can be found in Galati and Moessner (2011). Here, in this part we will not try to explore how these measures work practically. Nor will we present arguments about how policy tools can be enhanced or be coordinated. For these issues, readers are referred to FSB, IMF and BIS (2011), IMF (2013b) and Galati and Moessner (2011).

28. Some statements from central bankers about this issue are as follows. 'Nevertheless, the sudden and prolonged surges in foreign exchange flows can threaten the conduct

of monetary policy. Moreover, if these capital flows are not managed appropriately, they can have negative implications, such as real exchange rate misalignments, credit and asset price booms, inflationary pressures, overheating, and financial imbalances that can culminate into a full-blown financial crisis' (Bangko Sentral NG Pilipinas, 2011: 17). 'The diagnosis was that domestic banks could take advantage of the ample liquidity in global markets to significantly increase their funding abroad, and then invest those resources in BRL-denominated domestic assets, including loans, thus capturing the interest rate differential. There were concerns that such behavior could leave banks overexposed to currency mismatch and overly dependent on foreign liquidity, and hence vulnerable in the event of a large shock to the exchange rate or a rapid reversal of inflows' (Da Silva and Harris, 2012: 30).

29. This part draws upon a wide range of resources including journal papers, presentations, speeches, working papers and annual reports, some of which were published by national central banks. For the interested reader, the list of some references used in this study is given in Table 3A.1 in the Appendix. The list contains sources for policies implemented in some individual countries.

30. At this juncture we should note that we consider CFM measures as part of the general macroprudential policy toolkit in contrast to the bulk of the literature (see, for instance, Lim et al., 2011). Following Epstein et al. (2003), we argue that it is really hard to separate CFM techniques and other prudential tools since they usually affect the same set of variables and hence are complementary in general.

31. In the words of the Governor of the central bank of the Philippines: 'the crisis has made it clear that the objectives of financial stability and monetary stability are intertwined ... complementary at times ... and yet, at times also, conflicting. The presence of financial stability enhances monetary stability and vice versa. But the tools to address financial stability could weaken monetary stability. Again, this effect could go the reverse direction as well' (Tetangco, 2012: 2). Similarly, the Polish central bank claims: 'Excessive and long-term reduction in interest rates amidst low inflation and simultaneous fast economic growth may lead to rapid asset price growth, thus increasing the risk of so-called speculative bubbles. Rapid asset price growth is accompanied by the likelihood of asset price deviation from the levels justified by fundamentals, which increases the risk of an abrupt and significant decline in asset prices in the future. This poses a threat to financial system stability, and consequently, in the longer term, to sustainable economic growth and price stability' (National Bank of Poland, 2011: 7).

32. According to the Malaysian central bank: 'It was recognised that leaving the Overnight Policy Rate (OPR) at a low level for a sustained period could give rise to financial imbalances and create distorted incentives for economic agents, leading to the mispricing of risks, financial disintermediation and excessive credit growth' (Bank Nagara Malaysia, 2011: 82).

33. CBRT succinctly explains its new framework as follows: 'in order to contain macrofinancial risks driven by global imbalances, the Central Bank enhanced the inflation targeting regime and designed a new monetary policy strategy. Accordingly, the Central Bank started to take macro-financial stability into account as much as economic conditions permit while preserving the primary objective of maintaining price stability. Within the framework of this new structure, the Central Bank designed a policy mix in which the interest rate corridor, which is formed between the overnight borrowing and lending rates, and required reserves are jointly employed besides the policy rate to ensure the diversity of instruments that is required by the monetary policy implemented to achieve multiple goals' (Central Bank of the Republic of Turkey, 2011: 2).

34. Monetary authorities in Turkey also tried to influence the composition of inflows by an active use of the corridor. In the expansion period, they widened the corridor in order to create short term interest rate uncertainty and thereby discourage short term capital flows. Interested readers can see Kara (2012) and Aysan et al. (2014) for a summary of the new policy framework developed by the Turkish central bank.

35. For more details about ROM, see Aysan et al. (2014), Değerli and Fendoğlu (2013) and Alper et al. (2013).
36. Different roles of reserve requirements as a policy tool and their impact are discussed in detail in Tovar et al. (2012), IMF (2012a), and Montoro and Moreno (2011).
37. Borio and Shim (2007) give a good account of the macroprudential policies that are implemented in both advanced countries and developing countries before the crisis.
38. We should note that most of the policy tools discussed above were used in a counter-cyclical manner. When capital inflows and concomitant credit growth were strong they were used to counteract these forces. However when risk sentiments of international markets increased and led to reversals in capital flows (especially in the second half of 2011 and in the first months of 2012) these tools were used in the opposite direction by easing credit conditions.
39. Stiglitz (2013: 2) brilliantly calls this: 'the ability of ideology to prevail over the lessons of history and theory'. On the other hand, Masaaki Shirakawa strikingly makes the case for a watchful eye on financial markets and makes a caveat for the dangers created by an excessive focus on inflation: 'In retrospect, however, when we look back at how bubbles were formed and then developed into financial crises, the most significant imbalance that destabilized the macroeconomy emerged on the financial front instead of the price front' (Shirakawa, 2013: 375–377).
40. The similarities between the crisis in Japan and the US are recognized by the former governor of the Bank of Japan, Masaaki Shirakawa. Interestingly he also mentions that he feels a sense of 'déjà vu' in this respect (Shirakawa, 2010).
41. For instance, the approach of Ben Bernanke indicates that there is a reluctance to admit that the main tenets of the mainstream approach to monetary policy are based on false presumptions. He argues that the recent crisis was a failure of management and design related issues rather than of theoretical foundations (Bernanke, 2010).
42. In this chapter we do not make an attempt to suggest an optimal monetary policy for the society as a whole. However, we believe that optimal monetary policy differs from one segment of the society to others. For discussion about the differential impacts of monetary policy on different layers of society, see Palley (2011).
43. Cömert (2013) presents empirical evidence suggesting a gradual decline in effectiveness of monetary policy in the US.
44. In this sense, the assumptions about the vertical Philips curve are left unchallenged. In this regard, Palley (2011) presents an alternative theory.
45. This principle is criticized by especially Post-Keynesian economists. For instance, Fontana and Palacio-Vera (2007) present some of the important rejections to the neutrality of monetary policy in the long-run. Taking into account the path dependency of the economy yields different results with those of New-Keynesian models. In the presence of path dependency, permanent changes in aggregate demand may have long-run implications for the level of unemployment and output indicating the 'long-run non-neutrality of monetary policy'.
46. It is obvious that central banks cannot easily implement developmental policies within the current domestic and global financial structure. However, we argue that current domestic and global financial structure should be questioned in order to increase effectiveness of central banking policies to tackle with both financial instability and address some developmental concerns. In this sense, of course, within the current structure, central banks cannot even effectively address inflation and financial stability concerns.
47. Rey (2013) goes further and makes the case for the presence of 'dilemma' rather than 'trilemma', meaning that in a world of free capital mobility independent monetary policy is not possible independent of the chosen exchange rate regime.
48. Here we should note that what we referred to as credit growth is only a proxy. The data for ratio of domestic credit to private sector over GDP is obtained from the World Bank and we calculated the percentage change in the nominal credit stock. Then, the resulting change in credit stock is adjusted for inflation since developing countries had high inflation levels during the 1990s. It is very likely that using credit growth data directly

instead of a proxy leads to higher correlations. For the exchange rate, we should note that there were many countries who fixed their exchange rates until the 2000s. Moreover, even after adopting inflation targeting, these countries made interventions to decrease the volatility of their exchange rate and also to fight with depreciation pressures. Hence, the impact of inflows on foreign exchange markets is also expected to be higher.

49. While international institutions such as the IMF tolerated capital controls in developing countries after the crisis, they have now returned to their neo-liberal agenda, which dictates financial deregulation. For an argument about this issue see Epstein (2013).

50. Borio (2011) points to the deficiencies of 'country-centric' approaches. He emphasizes that the safety of individual countries cannot be ensured by themselves. It can only be evaluated in a global context. Hence a more 'global-centric' approach is called for.

51. There is now an emerging literature on the impact of Fed tapering news on the economies of developing countries. A few examples are Aizenman et al. (2014), Mishra et al. (2014) and Eichengreen and Gupta (2014). All these papers analyze the impact of tapering announcements on some indicators in emerging markets such as stock markets, exchange rates, foreign reserves and government bond yields. Here, we only focus on the impact on exchange rates.

52. This part draws upon some arguments made in Cömert and Çolak (2014).

53. Eichengreen (2009) elaborates the case for mounting risks for export led growth in the new environment.

REFERENCES

Agenor, P-R. and L.A.P. Da Silva (2013), *Inflation Targeting and Financial Stability, A Perspective from the Developing World*, Inter-American Development Bank.

Aizenman, J. (2010), 'Macro prudential supervision in the open economy and the role of central banks in emerging markets', *Open Economies Review*, 21 (3), 465–482.

Aizenman, J. (2011), 'Trilemma and financial stability configurations in Asia', Asian Development Bank Institute, Working Paper Series no. 317.

Aizenman, J., M. Binici and M.M. Hutchison (2014), 'The transmission of Federal Reserve tapering news to emerging markets', NBER Working Papers, 19980.

Akçelik, Y., A.F. Aysan and A. Oduncu (2013), 'Central banking in making during the post-crisis world and the policy-mix of the central bank of the Republic of Turkey', *Journal of Central Banking Theory and Practice*, 1 (2), 5–18.

Akyüz, Y. (2010), 'The global economic crisis and Asian developing countries: impact, policy response and medium-term prospects', Third World Network Global Economy Series, no. 27.

Alper, K., H. Kara and M. Yörükoğlu (2013), 'Alternative tools to manage capital flow volatility', BIS Papers no. 73.

Anwar, S. and I. Islam (2011), 'Should developing countries target low, single digit inflation to promote growth and employment?', International Labor Office, Employment Sector, Employment Working Paper, no. 87.

Aysan, A.F., S. Fendoğlu and M. Kılınç (2014), 'Macroprudential policies as buffer against volatile cross-border capital flows', Central Bank of the Republic of Turkey, Working Paper, no. 14/04.

Bangko Sentral NG Pilipinas (2011), '2010 Annual Report', Volume 1, retrieved January 5, 2015 from www.bsp.gov.ph/downloads/publications/2010/annrep2010. pdf.

Bank Nagara Malaysia (2011), 'Annual Report, 2010', retrieved January 5, 2015 from www.bnm.gov.my/files/publication/ar/en/2010/ar2010_book.pdf.

Bank Nagara Malaysia (2012), 'Annual Report, 2011', retrieved January 5, 2015 from www.bnm.gov.my/files/publication/ar/en/2011/ar2011_book.pdf.

Barbosa-Filho, N. (2006), 'Inflation targeting in Brazil: is there an alternative?' *Political Economy Research Institute, Alternatives to Inflation Targeting*, no. 6. Retrieved January 5, 2015 from www.peri.umass.edu/fileadmin/pdf/inflation/barbosa_paper6.pdf.

Başçı, E. (2012), 'Monetary policy of central bank of the Republic of Turkey after global financial crisis', *Insight Turkey*, 14 (2), 23–36.

Benlialper, A. and H. Cömert (2015), 'Implicit asymmetric exchange rate peg under inflation targeting regimes: the case of Turkey', forthcoming in *Cambridge Journal of Economics*, doi: 10.1093/cje/bev073.

Bernanke, B.S. (2010), 'On the implications of the financial crisis for economics', Speech at the conference co-sponsored by the Center for Economic Policy Studies and the Bendheim Center for Finance, Princeton University, Princeton, New Jersey, September 24, 2010, retrieved February 13, 2015 from www.federalreserve.gov/newsevents/speech/bernanke20100924a.pdf.

Bernanke, B.S. and M. Gertler (2001), 'Should central banks respond to movements in asset prices?', *American Economic Review*, 91 (2), 253–257.

Blanchard, O., G. Dell'Ariccia and P. Mauro (2010), 'Rethinking macroeconomic policy', IMF Staff Position Notes, 2010/03.

Blinder, A.S. (2010), 'How central should the central bank be?', *Journal of Economic Literature*, 48 (1), 123–133.

Borio, C. (2011), 'Central banking post-crisis: what compass for uncharted waters?' Bank for International Settlements Working Papers, no. 353.

Borio, C.E.V. and I. Shim (2007), 'What can (macro)-prudential policy do to support monetary policy?', Bank for International Settlements Working Papers, no. 242.

Calafell, J.G. (2013), 'Challenges for macroprudential policy and the Mexican case', Fifth Summit Meeting of Central Banks on Inflation Targeting, Santiago de Chile, November 15–16, 2013.

Carre, E., J. Couppey-Soubeyran, D. Plihon and M. Pourroy (2013), 'Central banking after the crisis: brave new world or back to the future?', CES Working Papers, 2013.73.

Central Bank of the Republic of Turkey (2011), 'Monetary and exchange rate policy for 2012', retrieved January 5, 2015 from www.tcmb.gov.tr/wps/wcm/connect/d9476bf5-b8d2-4d5c-bc59-4d1af564c9bf/Mon_Exc_Pol_2012.pdf?MOD=AJPERES&CadvancedcountriesHEID=d9476bf5-b8d2-4d5c-bc59-4d1af564c9bf.

Cespedes, L.F., R. Chang and A. Velasco (2012), 'Is inflation targeting still on target? The recent experience of Latin America', NBER Working Paper 18570.

Chai-Anant, C. (2012), 'Incorporating macro-prudential instruments into monetary policy: Thailand's experience', Presentation in Monetary Policy Workshop on Strengthening Macroprudential Frameworks, Imperial Hotel, Tokyo, Japan, March 22, 2012.

Cömert, H. (2013), *Central Banks and Financial Markets: The Declining Power of US Monetary Policy*, Cheltenham, UK and Northampton, MA, USA: Edward Elgar Publishing.

Cömert, H. and S. Çolak (2014), 'Can financial stability be maintained in developing countries after the global crisis: the role of external financial shocks?', Economic Research Center, Working Papers, 14/11.

Da Silva, L.A.P. (2013), 'Riding the global financial cycle: Brazil's experience with capital flows and macro-prudential policies under unconventional monetary policy', retrieved January 5, 2015 from www.bcb.gov.br/pec/appron/apres/Apresentacao_Luiz_Pereira_II_IMF_Financial_Stability_and_Risk_Forum_14_03_2014.pdf.

Da Silva, L.A.P. and R.E. Harris (2012), 'Sailing through the global financial storm: Brazil's recent experience with monetary and macroprudential policies to lean against the financial cycle and deal with systemic risks', Banco Central Do Brasil, Working Paper Series no. 290.

Değerli, A. and S. Fendoğlu (2013), 'Reserve option mechanism as a stabilizing policy tool: evidence from exchange rate expectations', Central Bank of the Republic of Turkey, Working Paper, no. 13/28.

Eichengreen, B. (2009), 'Lessons of the crisis for emerging markets', Asian Development Bank Institute, Working Paper Series no. 179.

Eichengreen, B. and P. Gupta (2014), 'Tapering talk, the impact of expectations of reduced Federal Reserve security purchases on emerging markets', The World Bank Policy Research Working Paper Series 6754.

Eichengreen, B., M. El-Arian, A. Fraga, T. Ito, J. Pisani-Ferry, E. Prasad, R. Rajan, R. Ramos, K. Reinhart, H. Rey, D. Rodrik, K. Rogoff, H.S. Shin, A. Velasco, B.W. di Mauro and Y. Yu (2011), 'Rethinking Central Banking', Brookings Institution, Washington, DC.

Epstein, G. (2006), 'Central banks as agents of economic development', UNU-WIDER Research Paper no. 2006/54.

Epstein, G. (2013), 'Developmental central banking: winning the future by updating a page from the past', *Review of Keynesian Economics*, 1 (3), 273–287.

Epstein, G., I. Grabel and K.S. Jomo (2003), 'Capital management techniques in developing countries: an assessment of experiences from the 1990's and lessons for the future', Political Economy Research Institute Working Paper Series, no. 56.

Financial Stability Board, International Monetary Fund and Bank for International Settlements (2011), 'Macroprudential policy tools and frameworks, Update to G20 Finance Ministers and Central Bank Governors'.

Fontana, G. and A. Palacio-Vera (2007), 'Are long-run price stability and short-run output stability all that monetary policy can aim for?', *Metroeconomica*, 58 (2), 269–298.

Frenkel, R. and M. Rapetti (2008), 'Five years of competitive and stable real exchange rate in Argentina, 2002–2007', *International Review of Applied Economics*, 22 (2), 215–226.

Frenkel, R. and M. Rapetti (2009), 'A developing country view of the current global crisis: what should not be forgotten and what should be done', *Cambridge Journal of Economics*, 33, 685–702.

Galati, G. and R. Moessner (2011), 'Macroprudential policy – a literature review', Bank for International Settlements Working Papers, no. 337.

Galindo, M. and J. Ros (2009), 'Alternatives to inflation targeting in Mexico', *International Review of Applied Economics*, 22 (2), 201–214.

Griffith-Jones, S. and J.A. Ocampo (2009), 'The financial crisis and its impact on developing countries', United Nations Development Programme Working Paper, retrieved January 5, 2015 from www.undp.org/content/dam/aplaws/

publication/en/publications/poverty-reduction/economic_crisis/the-financial-crisis-and-its-impact-on-developing-countries/Griffith-Jones_Ocampo_UNDP_18_Feb_2009.pdf.

Hahm, J-H., F.S. Mishkin, H.S. Shin and K. Shin (2011), 'Macroprudential policies in open emerging economies', *Proceedings*, Federal Reserve Bank of San Francisco, November, 63–114.

Huh, I., J. An and D. Yang (2013), 'The effect of Korea's macro-prudential measures', *World Economy Update*, 3 (3).

International Monetary Fund (IMF) (2012a), 'The interaction of monetary and macroprudential policies', Background Paper, retrieved January 5, 2015 from www.imf.org/external/np/pp/eng/2013/012713.pdf.

International Monetary Fund (IMF) (2012b), 'The liberalization and management of capital flows: an institutional view', retrieved February 13, 2015 from www.imf.org/external/np/pp/eng/2012/111412.pdf.

International Monetary Fund (IMF) (2013a), 'Brazil: technical note on macroprudential policy framework', IMF Country Report, no. 13/148.

International Monetary Fund (IMF) (2013b), 'The interaction of monetary and macroprudential policies', retrieved February 13, 2015 from www.imf.org/external/np/pp/eng/2013/012913.pdf.

Kara, A.H. (2012), 'Küresel Kriz Sonrası Para Politikası' (Monetary Policy after Global Crisis, in Turkish), Central Bank of the Republic of Turkey, Working Paper, no. 12/17.

Kara, A.H. (2013), 'Capital flows, financial stability and monetary policy', Presentation in Anadolu International Conference in Economics, June 19, 2013, Eskişehir, Turkey.

Kenç, T. (2013), 'Financial stability and macroprudential policies', retrieved January 5, 2015 from www.tcmb.gov.tr/wps/wcm/connect/229e1b70-38a6-454e-86d5-66d3f17e74a6/Kenc_FinancialStability.pdf?MOD=AJPERES&Cadvanced countriesHEID=229e1b70-38a6-454e-86d5-66d3f17e74a6.

Kenç, T., M.I. Turhan and O. Yıldırım (2011), 'The experience with macroprudential policies of the central bank of the Republic of Turkey in response to the global financial crisis', The World Bank Policy Research Working Paper Series 5834.

Kim, J. (2014), 'Macroprudential policies in Korea: key measures and experiences', *Financial Stability Review*, 18, 121–130.

Lim, C., F. Columba, A. Costa, P. Kongsamut, A. Otani, M. Saiyid, T. Wezel and X. Wu (2011), 'Macroprudential policy: what instruments and how to use them?', International Monetary Fund Working Paper 11/238.

Marshall, E. (2012), 'Implementing macroprudential policies in Chile', Presentation in Macroprudential Policies to Achieve Financial Stability, Punta del Este, Uruguay, February 29–March 2, retrieved January 5, 2015 from www.imf.org/external/np/seminars/eng/2012/macro/pdf/marshall.pdf.

Mishkin, F.S. (2013), 'Central banking after the crisis', Central Bank of Chile Working Papers no. 714.

Mishra, P. and P. Montiel (2012), 'How effective is monetary transmission mechanism in low-income countries? A survey of the empirical evidence', International Monetary Fund Working Paper 12/143.

Mishra, P., K. Moriyama, P. N'Diaye and L. Nguyen (2014), 'Impact of Fed tapering announcements on emerging markets', International Monetary Fund Working Paper 14/109.

Mohanty, M.S. and M. Klau (2001), 'What determines inflation in emerging market economies?', Bank for International Settlements Papers, no. 8.

Montoro, C. and R. Moreno (2011), 'The use of reserve requirements as a policy instrument in Latin America', *BIS Quarterly Review*, March 2011, 53–65.

Moreno, R. (2011), 'Policymaking from a "macroprudential" perspective in emerging market economies', Bank for International Settlements, Working Paper no. 336.

National Bank of Poland (2011), 'Report on monetary policy implementation in 2010', retrieved January 5, 2015 from www.nbp.pl/en/publikacje/o_polityce_pienieznej/implementation2010.pdf.

Nijathaworn, B. (2010), 'Macroprudential policies and capital flows – managing under the new globalization', Conference on Macroprudential Policies, Shangai, October 18, 2010.

Palley, T.I. (2011), 'Monetary policy and central banking after the crisis: the implications of rethinking macroeconomic theory', Macroeconomic Policy Institute, Working Paper 8/2011.

Park, Y.C. (2011), 'The role of macroprudential policy for financial stability in East Asia's emerging economies', Asian Development Bank Institute, Working Paper Series no. 284.

Pontines, V. and R.Y. Siregar (2012), 'Exchange rate asymmetry and flexible exchange rates under inflation targeting regimes: evidence from four East and Southeast Asian countries', *Review of International Economics*, 20 (5), 893–908.

Rajan, R.S. (2011), 'Management of exchange rate regimes in emerging Asia', Asian Development Bank Institute Working Paper Series no. 322.

Rey, H. (2013), 'Dilemma not trilemma: the global cycle and monetary policy independence', Proceedings – Economic Policy Symposium – Jackson Hole, Federal Reserve Bank of Kansas City.

Se, O.H. (2013), 'Loan-to-value as macro-prudential policy tool: experiences and lessons of Asian emerging countries', Duisenberg School of Finance Policy Paper no. 33.

Shirakawa, M. (2010), 'Revisiting the philosophy behind central bank policy', Speech at the Economic Club of New York, April 22, 2010. Retrieved February 13, 2015 from www.boj.or.jp/en/announcements/press/koen_2010/data/ko1004e.pdf.

Shirakawa, M. (2013), 'Central banking: before, during and after the crisis', *International Journal of Central Banking*, 9 (1), 373–387.

Sinha, A. (2011), 'Macroprudential policies: Indian experience', speech at Eleventh Annual International Seminar on Policy Challenges for the Financial Sector, Washington, DC, June 1–3, 2011, retrieved January 5, 2015 from http://rbidocs.rbi.org.in/rdocs/Speeches/PDFs/DGSMP150611.pdf.

Stiglitz, J. (2013), 'A revolution in monetary policy, lessons in the wake of the global financial crisis', The 15th C.D. Deshmukh Memorial Lecture delivered at Taj Mahal Place, Mumbai, January 3, 2013.

Svensson, L.E.O. (2009), 'Flexible inflation targeting – lessons from the financial crisis', speech at the workshop 'Towards a new framework for monetary policy? Lessons from the crisis', Amsterdam, September 21, 2009.

Terrier, G., R. Valdes, C.E. Tovar, J. Chan-Lau, C. Fernandez-Valdovinos, M. Garcia-Escribano, C. Medeiros, M-K. Tang, M.V. Martin and C. Walker (2011), 'Policy instruments to lean against the wind in Latin America', International Monetary Fund Working Paper 11/159.

Tetangco, A.M. (2012), 'Contemporary challenges to monetary policy', speech at the BSP International Research Conference, Manila Peninsula Hotel, retrieved January 5, 2015 from www.bsp.gov.ph/events/2012/ccmp/downloads/2012_BSP-CCMP_Opening_Remarks_Tetangco.pdf.

Tovar, C.E., M. Garcia-Escribano and M.V. Martin (2012), 'Credit growth and the effectiveness of reserve requirements and other macroprudential instruments in Latin America', International Monetary Fund Working Paper 12/142.

Trichet, J-C. (2009), 'Credible alertness revisited', remarks at the Federal Reserve Bank of Kansas City symposium on Financial Stability and Macroeconomic Policy, Jackson Hole.

Warjiyo, P. (2013), 'Indonesia's monetary policy: coping with volatile commodity prices and capital inflows', BIS Papers chapters, in Bank for International Settlements (ed.), *Globalisation and inflation dynamics in Asia and the Pacific*, vol. 70, 149–159.

Woodford, M. (2002), 'Financial market efficiency and the effectiveness of monetary policy', *Economic Policy Review*, 8 (1).

Woodford, M. (2003), 'Optimal interest-rate smoothing', *The Review of Economic Studies*, 70 (4), 861–886.

Zhang, L. and E. Zoli (2014), 'Leaning against the wind: macroprudential policy in Asia', International Monetary Fund Working Paper 14/22.

APPENDIX

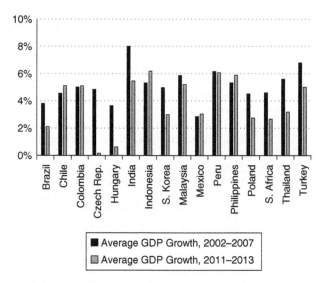

Source: World Bank (World Development Indicators).

Figure 3A.1   Change in average GDP growth of selected countries

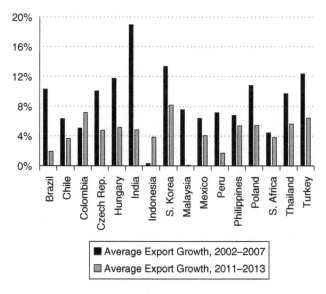

Source: IMF (World Economic Outlook).

Figure 3A.2   Change in average export growth of selected countries

Table 3A.1   Some studies presenting macroprudential policies implemented in some developing countries

Country/Regions	References
Brazil	Da Silva (2013); Da Silva and Harris (2012); IMF (2013a)
Chile	Marshall (2012)
India	Sinha (2011)
Indonesia	Warjiyo (2013)
Korea	Kim (2014); Huh et al. (2013)
Malaysia	Bank Nagara Malaysia (2011); Bank Nagara Malaysia (2012)
Mexico	Calafell (2013)
Thailand	Chai-Anant (2012); Nijathaworn (2010)
Turkey	Kara (2012); Kara (2013); Kenç (2013); Aysan et al. (2014); Kenç et al. (2011); Başçı (2012); Akçelik et al. (2013)
Latin America	Tovar et al. (2012); Terrier et al. (2011)
Asia	Zhang and Zoli (2014); Se (2013); Siregar (2011); Park (2011); Aizenman (2011)
Cross country studies	Moreno (2011); IMF (2012a); Aizenman (2010); Lim et al. (2011)

4. Monetary transmission in Africa: a review of official sources[1]

Rex A. McKenzie

4.1 INTRODUCTION

This chapter focuses on the efficacy of monetary policy in Africa. We ask two sets of related questions. First, how are increasing volumes of cross border flows, a rise in pan-African banking and an increased momentum towards regional integration (new emergent processes) changing financial arrangements in Africa? Second, what explains the historical weakness in the African monetary transmission mechanism (MTM) and what can be done about it? The MTM is the sequence through which the monetary policy decisions of the authorities express themselves on price and output levels. There is a fairly well developed body of literature on the MTM that comes from the professional economists of the World Bank, Bank for International Settlements (BIS) and the International Monetary Fund (IMF). It may be because the questions that concern us are technical in nature, or it may be neglect, but on the academic side, with regard to Africa, this type of literature is relatively underdeveloped. The aim of this chapter is to review these official sources. The exercise offers a theoretical (non VAR)[2] route to the answers to our questions for students, teachers, central bankers, policymakers and those in civil society that may need such answers. The review reveals a disjuncture in the literature; on the one hand, the official sources posit that the credibility of the monetary authorities is the key variable in promoting monetary policy objectives. Yet, in actuality, the literature assumes away the possibility of using monetary policy to promote credible and coherent policy because it is unable to conceive of a broader role for the monetary policy of the central banks.

Like almost everything else in this area written since 2008, there is an underlying preoccupation with risk and destabilization of the economy that is framed by the seismic events of the 2007/2008 Great Recession. Thus, the first object of our enquiry is monetary transmission in Africa during and after the recent crisis. The chapter is arranged as follows: reflecting the underlying motivation for the chapter, Section 4.2 explains how Africa was affected by the 2007/2008 crisis. Section 4.3 discusses regional integration and reviews the associated rise of pan-African banks. Section 4.4 describes two new features of the capital inflow picture. First, there are the deepening investment linkages with Brazil, China, India and, conspicuously, Malaysia, who have all become important sources of Foreign Direct Investment (FDI) for Africa and, second, a marked increase in interregional FDI. Section 4.5 discusses the interaction between monetary transmission and monetary policy. Section 4.6 concludes. In general, the new forms of banking, their associated capital flows and the tendency towards regional integration are processes that bring a degree of financial depth to monetary arrangements. However, the biggest challenge to effective monetary policy lies in the unknown size and scope of informal sector activities that mediate the policy. Where the sector is large, interest rates do not reflect liquidity and credit conditions, and the MTM is often weak and unresponsive. In these circumstances until African countries can rebase their economies and provide more jobs in the official sector, monetary policy remains a blunt instrument with a weak MTM.

4.2 THE GREAT RECESSION IN AFRICA

The crisis itself had a differential impact across the continent and many countries were spared the more damaging slowdown in economic activity that ensued in the North Atlantic countries simply because they were not well integrated into the world system and because financial arrangements were undeveloped. Thus, the transmission channels were muted. Where the crisis did hit, it did so with a vengeance. In the decade leading up to the Great Recession, Africa experienced accelerated economic growth averaging annual increases in real GDP of 6 per cent per annum. Growth stuttered immediately after the events of 2007/2008 and declined to 1.1 per cent in 2009 (Luvhengo, 2010). At the depth of the crisis the International Labour Organization (ILO, 2010) estimates showed that unemployment increased appreciably by between 1 and 4 million from 2008 to 2009. In addition, the ILO estimates showed unemployment and working poverty[3] increased up to 15 per cent in 2009 as a result of the crisis. All told, rates of poverty, working poverty and unemployment reverted to 2003 levels. Trade and current account balances deteriorated across the continent but particularly so in the oil exporting countries. Worsening current account balances were accompanied by rising fiscal deficits leading to twin deficits in several countries (Brixiova et al., 2011).

In the years leading up to the Lehman's bankruptcy in 2008, Africa had benefited from a prolonged energy and commodity boom driven by demand mostly emanating from India, Brazil and China.[4] In the aftermath of the collapse there was a contraction in demand; the prices of mineral ores, oil and other primary goods declined and the perennial concerns about Africa's poor growth and development performance reclaimed centre stage in any discussion of Africa's future prospects. In 2010 the International Monetary Fund's (IMF) Global Economic Outlook reported that Brazil would grow by 5.5 per cent, Russia by 4 per cent, India by 8.8 per cent and China by 10 per cent. The forecasts were accurate and this growth once again fuelled demand for commodities. In general, the fastest growing countries in 2008 declined the most in 2009 and the least growing countries in 2009 rebounded the most in 2010 (Brixiova et al., 2011). Thereafter, Africa and other commodity rich economies again derived the benefit of rising commodity prices. In 2011 commodity prices were expected to reach their pre-crisis era levels, but in both 2011 and 2012 GDP growth slowed in the BRIC countries; China's GDP declined to 9.3 per cent and 7.8 per cent, and India's to 6.6 per cent and 4.7 per cent (World Bank Data). But, with regard to Africa, the initial dire projections[5] were tempered as SSA's GDP rose to 4.7 per cent and the region attracted foreign direct investment worth a 'near record' US$43 billion (up 16 per cent in 2012) largely driven by coal, oil and gas discoveries in Angola, Mozambique and Tanzania (World Bank, 2014).

In 2014 the World Bank reported:

> weaker demand for metals and other key commodities, combined with increased supply, could lead to a sharper decline in prices. In particular, if Chinese demand, which accounts for about 45 per cent of total copper demand and a large share of global iron ore demand, remains weaker than in recent years and supply continues to grow robustly, copper and iron ore prices could decline more sharply, with significant negative consequences for the metal-producing countries. (World Bank, 2014: 15)

Also in 2014 economic growth in sub-Saharan Africa increased to 5.2 per cent, driven largely by increasing investment aimed at exploiting the region's natural resources and developing infrastructure (World Bank, 2014). According to the Bank's estimates, economic expansion in sub-Saharan Africa is projected at 5.4 per cent for 2015. By 2014 it was clear that the demand for commodities coming from the BRICs would not return to pre-crisis levels. China, Brazil and India still required raw materials and fossil energy for their own growth and development purposes, but growth in those countries slowed and the prices of the various raw materials have declined accordingly. In the first quarter of 2014 Chinese GDP grew at 7.4 per cent (the slowest rate of increase since the third quarter of

2012), thereby escalating concerns of China's ability to act as a sustained engine of growth for the rest of the world.[6]

With regard to the trajectory of trade in the aftermath of the global financial crisis, a Brixiova and Ndikumana (2013) comparison between the EAC, SACU and SADC regional groupings is instructive. In general, the EAC region's lack of integration into global financial markets protected it from the direct consequences of the crisis. The more indirect financial channels had a muted impact largely attributed to the fact that, in the EAC, the banks primarily fund their loans from deposits. According to the authors, the crisis was therefore transmitted primarily through trade (and in some cases also foreign investment, aid, remittances[7] and tourism receipts). In contrast, studies by Ncube et al. (2012a and 2012b), and Ncube and Ndou (2013), show that South Africa (and therefore all of SACU), which is closely integrated into the global financial system, was directly affected through both financial and trade channels. Interestingly, Brixiova and Ndikumana (2013: 5) also found that, 'the deeper intra-regional trade in the EAC region as well as the EAC region's trade links with the rest of Africa have increased the community's resilience to global output shocks'. The lesson appears to be that in order to withstand a global shock of the magnitude of the Great Recession countries need 'to diversify[8] their geographical composition of trade to include fast growing economies, both in Africa and other regions' (Brixiova and Ndikumana, 2013).

There were at least two other mitigating factors. First, 'food' accounted for most of the EAC's total exports and the financial crisis unfolded contemporaneously with a food crisis. The consequent rise in food prices made the EAC far less vulnerable to the global slump than it otherwise would have been. In the EAC region, a combination of countercyclical policies, public investment and the upward thrust of world food prices came together to cushion and mitigate the more deleterious effects of the crisis that had enveloped the rest of the world. This is in stark contrast to the crisis of 1991 in which the EAC nations grew at a slower pace than the world economy (Brixiova and Ndikumana, 2013). Second (and for Africa in general), because most of the private capital flows to Africa take the form of FDI, Africa's exposure to the global credit crunch was less severe (Brixiova et al., 2011). On balance, insofar as integration into the world system is concerned, SSA is the least integrated region and so SSA in particular was insulated from the full impact of the financial crisis. In general, FDI flows to Africa are in small, absolute amounts but in 2009 SSA was the recipient of more net FDI inflows than other countries and regions (Brixiova et al., 2011). With regard to official capital inflows aimed at mitigating the crisis, SSA has received smaller gross and net amounts (relative to GDP and in absolute terms) than other developing regions except Asia. Asia has been in the vanguard of the global recovery (Brixiova et al., 2011).

With respect to the balance of payments for EMEs and frontier market countries, the effects of the crisis were related to portfolio flows. South Africa's current account deficit is one of the highest in the world and it is funded by large portfolio inflows. South Africa was particularly hard hit by the retreat and volatility of these inflows and, in response, the South African banks cut their lending to branches in other countries (Brixiova et al., 2011). The impact on the banking system then reverberated throughout the rand area. The banking sector in South Africa was also affected by the sharp decline in equity prices during the crisis, which further negatively impacted private consumption via the wealth effect (Brixiova et al., 2011).

In Nigeria the banking system was also negatively affected by the crisis. The banks had expanded lending significantly in the pre-crisis period. The lending was primarily funded by foreign financing and it was this financing that dried up first. Nigeria's banks were also engaged in margin lending for equity investments. With the sharp decline in equity prices, banks' assets declined accordingly. In addition, some of the banks also had sizeable off balance sheet instruments that concealed nonperforming loans. Christensen (2011: 47) observes that this 'was a home-made problem accentuated by the global financial crisis'. Ultimately, in August 2009 the Central Bank of Nigeria was forced to intervene in five banks. The ensuing liquidity support totalled US$2.8 billion (2.5 per cent of nonoil GDP) (Christensen 2011: 47). Other countries in which declines in local equities affected the banking sector included Kenya and Uganda in East Africa.

In general, Africa did not experience currency mismatches on the balance sheets of the government, banks or the private sector. Consequently, currency valuation losses in the face of significant local currency depreciations were limited. Africa nevertheless suffered from the indirect effects of the crisis on the balance sheets of the banks. Thus, a fall in export demand and commodity prices induced a decline in the quality of bank loan portfolios. 'In addition, interest rate spreads increased and the availability of foreign credit declined. Equity markets declined across the board in line with equity markets globally. Likewise, African currencies depreciated in line with developments in other emerging regions' (Christensen 2011: 47).

The foregoing represents a brief recapitulation of the crisis in Africa. The period after the crisis (post-2008/2009) has been characterized by an increase in cross border flows, the spread of pan-African banking and an increase in issue of debt by the authorities. These developments pose challenges and yield opportunities at one and the same time. The challenges lie in their combined ability to transmit the negative effects of financial excess from country to country when coupled with the lax management and loose arrangements that characterized the run up to the crisis in the developed markets of the US and UK. The opportunities come from the much needed financial deepening and financial integration that can enhance growth and transform the continent. Two points remain to be made; first, the continent's financial integration into the world economy and its financial depth are markedly underdeveloped. While this lack of depth was important in shielding Africa from the full effects of the crisis, it constrains growth in GDP and makes for the general arrested development of the African continent.[9] Second, the banking systems in Africa are characterized by relatively large interest margins that reflect, among other things, an absence of competition, the lack of financial infrastructure and the riskiness of lending when combined with weak property rights (Christensen, 2014). From a monetary policy point of view, the authorities would like to use interest rates as they are used in other parts of the world, that is, to allocate savings and credit so that they could influence the value of key financial indicators such as the interbank interest rate (Christensen, 2014). Globally, integration with international markets would enforce a convergence of prices that is both desired and necessary if the continent is to move forward.

4.3   REGIONAL FINANCIAL INTEGRATION AND PAN-AFRICAN BANKS

The theoretical rationale for integration comes from Lewis (1950) in his *Industrialisation of the British West Indies*. The basic idea is that integration allows smaller economies to scale up and enjoy the benefits of economies of scale. Regional integration as an aspiration of African countries was given tremendous impetus by Kwame Nkrumah, George Padmore, Jomo Kenyatta and other pan-African leaders of the post-independence era who envisaged it as a step on the way to a United States of Africa with full economic and political union. The ratifying of the AU's Sirte Declaration of 1999[10] has given the process a more contemporary impetus.

Drawing on Lewis (1950), the EAC Treaty, signed in 2000, committed the five participating countries of Burundi, Kenya, Tanzania, Rwanda and Uganda to establishing a customs union (established in 2005), a common market (July 2010) and a monetary union (Christensen, 2014). Significant steps have been taken towards harmonizing the regulatory environment for financial banking and services. In addition, preparations have begun for a common payment and settlement system for the five member states, which would allow settlement in local currencies (IMF,

2011). There appears to be the necessary political will to see the process through to its conclusion and, by all indications, we are to see a fully integrated EAC region. On the way there are obvious difficulties to overcome. As Christensen (2014: 15) notes, the countries have different monetary and exchange policy frameworks. The countries involved are Kenya, Uganda, Tanzania, Rwanda and Burundi. Kenya and Uganda have the more sophisticated systems where the authorities utilize what the author calls a 'responsive set of policy rates'. In contradistinction, Burundi, Rwanda and Tanzania employ a monetary target framework. Among the banks only the Kenyan banks have so far established a regional presence (Christensen 2014: 15) and, perhaps most importantly, 'it appears that expansionary monetary policy works differently in the different countries; in Kenya and Uganda it lifts prices significantly but raises output in Uganda, Burundi, and Rwanda'.[11] Going forward, a functioning East African banking system will rely on an in depth understanding of these differences and their dynamic interaction with each other. In general we can say that, among the five countries, a banking system that supports growth and development will, first of all, require progress in ensuring property rights and, secondly, a working system for the resolution of contractual disputes (Christensen, 2014).

In general, Africa has a bank based system where banks dominate the financial system. In large part because of the imperialist history, banks from Britain, France and the other imperial countries have held the larger share of the banking business. This is now changing because of the entry of new pan-African banks. Pan-African banks are banks formed with African capital that have subsidiary banks in other African countries. In the West African Economic and Monetary Union (WAEMU) pan-African banks accounted for approximately one third of credit institutions operating in 2011 with nearly half of the total balance sheet. The major pan-African banking groups come from South Africa, Nigeria, Togo and Morocco.

The foreign activity of Nigerian banking groups is new. According to Alade (2014: 83), the Nigerian banks expanded after a consolidation phase in the banking industry that started in 2004 and resulted in a tenfold increase in the capital base. The greater proportion of the Nigerian banks' expansion came via an increase in branch networks in the domestic market and the opening of subsidiaries in other African countries.[12] The largest bank in Morocco is Attijariwafa Bank. After the global financial crisis enveloped the eurozone, Attijariwafa started opening subsidiaries in sub-Saharan francophone countries. What is altogether new about these banks is that they reach a part of the population that the longstanding traditional banks have ignored. Attijariwafa in Morocco, African Bank in

South Africa and the other pan-African banks generally lend to small and medium sized enterprises that have otherwise been ignored by the traditional banks.[13]

The expansion of pan-African banks is gaining momentum across Africa. These banks know the conditions very well and are (in theory) in a position to transfer know how to the other countries in which they operate. What is different about these banks is that they are self-funded; as such they provide a degree of insulation from credit and liquidity shocks that have affected other regions. Early studies cited in Christensen (2014) and initial indications suggest that, in countries where they account for a significant share of banking business, pan-African banks are:

1. Improving the market clearing effectiveness of the interbank and foreign exchange markets;
2. Creating competition in the bank sector;
3. Reaching the population in rural areas that previously had no access to banking services; and
4. Spreading technology and financial services to non-banked areas.

Risk diversification and greater profit opportunities for shareholders are the main benefits for the parent company, while recipient banking systems benefit through increased intermediation and improved efficiency (resulting from technological advancement), and reduced interest rates and efficiency improvements as a result of increased competition (see Alade, 2014: 83).

The growth of these banks with the accompanying financial deepening makes for an increased mobility of goods and capital. With respect to trade integration, this would mean a reduction in the costly delays at African ports of entry, which in general constitute 1 per cent of the selling price of the commodity (Ncube et al., 2014). We would also anticipate African intra continental trade, which now stands at 10 per cent of all trade with the rest of the world, to rise towards the 60 per cent average of other regions (Ncube et al., 2014). There would be some contribution to employment and some alleviation in food shortages. We are already seeing much of this in the EAC, perhaps most starkly where the benefits of professionals offering services in several countries (without needing work permits) are already manifest in a region that has historically been bereft of skills and management.

In this manner, the emergence of pan-African banking promises to transform financial arrangements, deepening and strengthening the hold of an indigenous banking system that appears to be far more inclusive than the traditional financial institutions.

4.4 SOUTH–SOUTH FDI

Private cross border flows are made up of foreign direct investment (FDI), portfolio investment and other investment. With regard to Africa, there are two new features of the capital inflow picture. First, there are the deepening investment linkages with Brazil, China, India and, conspicuously, Malaysia, who have all become important sources of FDI for Africa, and second, a marked increase in interregional FDI (World Bank, 2014).

China is the leading southern investor in Africa by a considerable margin. Chinese FDI to Africa increased from US$200 million in 2000 to US$2.5 billion in 2011 (Busse et al., 2014) with about 40 per cent of this total holdings invested in South Africa (Rangasamy and Mihaljek, 2011).[14]

Despite the rapid increase, actual volumes are fairly small, both in terms of African GDP and total FDI inflows in Africa. According to Busse et al. (2014), average Chinese FDI flows to Africa in 2000 and 2011 amounted to only 5 per cent of total FDI inflows to Africa. Nevertheless, according to the UNCTAD (UNCTAD WIR, 2013), China is the biggest and largest proponent of South to South investment in Africa.[15]

4.4.1 Foreign Direct Investment

FDI flows into sub-Saharan Africa have grown nearly six fold over the past decade. The flows increased from about US$6.3 billion in 2000 to US$35 billion in 2013. While this is still just 2.5 per cent of total global flows, 'it represents an unprecedented size of investment capital in most African countries' (UNCTAD, 2014).

Rangasamy and Mihaljek (2011) show interesting cross regional variations within Africa. Emerging markets showed a strong increase in FDI from 2002 to 2008. But from 2008 to 2010 the crisis led to the halving of FDI in these markets. In this period, by contrast, portfolio inflows exhibited strong growth in 2010, exceeding FDI by US$5 billion. Pre-crisis, the EMEs were the largest recipients of net portfolio flows, especially in 2006 to 2007. But their reversal in 2008 was deep and pronounced. In contrast, FDI inflows to the frontier markets and financially developing countries were essentially undisturbed by the crisis. The outflows from these countries were confined to portfolio and other investment categories. These were large and significant outflows. In the frontier market countries other investment inflows recovered in 2009 and 2010.

In 2013 FDI inflows to Africa rose by 4 per cent to US$57 billion, fuelled by international and regional consumer seeking flows, and infrastructure investments. Africa's middle class is said to have expanded by 30 per cent from 2007 to 2015, and now totals approximately 120 million people.[16] It is at this market that much of the FDI is now aimed. The extractive industries continue to be a destination for FDI, but consumer oriented markets are now starting to drive FDI increases (UNCTAD WIR, 2013). These markets include consumer products such as foods, information technology (IT), tourism, finance and retail, and similarly driven by the growing trade and consumer markets, infrastructure FDI showed strong increases in transport and in information and communication technology (ICT) (UNCTAD, 2014: 38). Between 2003 and 2012, 15 countries accounted for some 80 per cent of the total FDI inflow. The largest inflows go to sectors where the region has a comparative advantage (that is, agriculture and natural resources) or where returns are high[17] (that is, construction[18]). Nigeria, Mozambique and South Africa received the largest amounts of FDI. They were followed by Ghana, DRC, the Congo and Sudan (all above US$2 billion).

Intraregional investments are also increasing with South African, Kenyan and Nigerian corporations accounting for the lion's share. Most of the outflows were directed to other countries in the continent, paving the way for investment driven regional integration. With respect to intraregional FDI, the share of African countries in South Africa's FDI stock grew from 5 per cent in 2000 to 22 per cent in 2008. South Africa is not only a major recipient of FDI, but also a major source of FDI in Africa. According to UNCTAD (UNCTAD WIR, 2013), South Africa was the second most important investor in Africa (from developing countries) in 2012 after Malaysia. The rise in outward FDI flows from Africa in 2012 to US$14 billion was mainly due to large flows from South Africa directed at mining, the wholesale sector and health care products. South Africa holds the fifth largest stock of FDI in Africa, with the largest proportion in Mauritius, followed by Nigeria and its neighbours Mozambique and Zimbabwe. According to the IMF's CDIS, in 2012 it also had a sizeable stock of FDI in Ghana, DRC, Tanzania and Zambia.

According to UNCTAD (2010), 'there were a total of 2,250 South African projects in African countries in 2009, in areas such as infrastructure, telecommunications, energy and mining'. In 2013, South African outward FDI almost doubled to US$5.6 billion, driven by investments in telecommunications, mining and retail investors[19] (UNCTAD, 2014). The other main investors were Angola and Nigeria, with flows mostly directed to neighbouring countries. Unlike foreign investment, where the extractive industries are the main focus of attention, intra African projects are concentrated in manufacturing and services: '97 per cent of intra-African investments target non-primary sectors compared with 76 per cent of investments from the rest of the world, with a particularly high difference in the share that targets the manufacturing sector'[20] (UNCTAD, 2014).

The other main targets for intraregional FDI flows are finance (especially banking) and business services.

With respect to greenfield investments, there are three key aspects: first, it is the service sector that is driving investment; second, roughly 40 per cent of all greenfield investments by number of new projects are concentrated in finance and business services, low technology consumer products and wood furniture; third and last, recently announced greenfield projects show rising inflows in the textile industry and high interest by international investors in motor vehicle industries (UNCTAD, 2014). Between 2009 and 2013, the share of cross border greenfield projects, which is the major investment type in Africa, originating from other African countries has increased to 18 per cent from about 10 per cent in the period 2003 to 2008. All major investors, namely South Africa (7 per cent), Kenya (3 per cent) and Nigeria (2 per cent), more than doubled their shares. The gross value of cross border intra African acquisitions grew from less than 3 per cent of total investments in 2003 to 2008 to more than 9 per cent by 2013 (UNCTAD, 2014).

In general, intraregional FDI appears to be an increasingly important mechanism through which Africa can reduce its dependence and satisfy its increasing demand out of its own resources. Furthermore, 'intra-African investment helps African firms enhance their competitiveness by increasing their scale, developing their production know-how and providing access to better and cheaper inputs'[21] (UNCTAD, 2014, 43).

4.4.2 Net Portfolio Flows

The data show that, for Africa's EMEs net portfolio, capital inflows were increasing before the crisis. Among the EMEs, South Africa has been the preeminent recipient of net portfolio inflows. Rangasamy and Mihaljek (2011), estimate that some US$30 billion in portfolio capital flowed out of Africa when the crisis struck in 2008. After small net outflows in 2009, 'portfolio capital flows recovered strongly with some US$25 billion returning to the continent' in 2010 (Rangasamy and Mihaljek, 2011).

In addition to South Africa, which received net portfolio inflows of US$4.6 billion per year on average, Nigeria was the other big recipient of net portfolio inflows between 2000 and 2009 (US$0.7 billion per year). Since 2009, other countries, including Ghana, Kenya, Tanzania, Uganda and Zambia, have started to attract increasing amounts of portfolio inflows.[22]

4.4.3 Other Investment Flows

Other investment is mostly made up of cross border bank lending to African countries and deposits placed by African countries in foreign banks. Between 2001 and 2005, these were negative but stable. In 2006 the outflows jumped to almost US$75 billion due to large placements of deposits by some oil exporting countries (in particular Nigeria) in overseas banks. Since 2008 the pattern of these flows has reversed. As the crisis began and foreign investors withdrew from Africa and other emerging markets, many African countries withdrew their deposits from overseas banks to compensate for the loss of liquidity in local markets. This resulted in net inflows of other investment of about US$10 billion per year.

Claims of BIS reporting banks (which consist mainly of cross border loans to African countries), with regards to all sectors in Africa, doubled between 2001 and 2010, with total amounts outstanding of close to US$160 billion in the third quarter of 2010 further increasing to US$195 billion by the fourth quarter of 2014 (BIS, 2014). One stark difference between Africa and other developing regions of the world is that the continent on average holds more deposits in BIS reporting banks than it does loans received from them. According to Rangasamy and Mihaljek (2011: 7), the 'imbalance reflects the underdevelopment of Africa's financial systems in general and its banking systems in particular'. It suggests that a large share of the revenue from exports is not intermediated by local banks. About 60 per cent of these funds are recycled back to the continent in the form of cross border loans by recipient banks (Rangasamy and Mihaljek, 2011).

Cross border capital flows in Africa increasingly reflect three key factors; first, the *Africa Rising* narrative. This is very much a twenty-first century development; according to this official story, sound macroeconomic policies (aimed primarily at restraining inflation) and the good governance practices that the various governments had all instituted in the previous decade have combined to give Africa a far more robust institutional fabric that can now support profit making. In short, by dint of these changes Africa is decidedly more market friendly and ripe for investment. Thus, there is a greater optimism among foreign investors about private sector activity and the economic potential of Africa. Second, financial flows now reflect the shift in emphasis from North–South to South–South relations, in particular the growing role of the major BRICs such as Brazil, China, India and South Africa.[23] Third, because of the proliferation of pan-African banking groups and the WAEMU and EAC regional trade initiatives, there has been increasing integration of financial markets in Africa.

4.5 MONETARY TRANSMISSION AND MONETARY POLICY

The literature identifies four main pillars for responsive and effective monetary policy:

1. Secondary markets that are deep enough to promote the sale and resale of financial paper that strengthen the central bank's ability to manage the interbank interest rate and the money stock (Mishra et al., 2010).
2. A degree of competition in the banking sector such that changes in policy rates induce changes in market rates (Christensen, 2014; Kuttner and Mosser, 2002; Davoodi et al., 2013).
3. A long term bond market that ultimately helps to establish a market based term structure of interest rates that retires the inverted yield curve that so often characterizes the more undeveloped financial arrangements (Christensen, 2014).
4. Regional and international financial integration so that arbitrage between domestic and foreign financial assets can bring about price convergence (Christensen, 2014).

These would be the pillars upon which a credible central bank's communication with the general public on the conditions, expectations surrounding inflation, employment and output would form the basis of a functioning market. The big question that remains to be answered is how far have the emergent post-crisis trends, described in the previous sections, gone in establishing the four preconditions for effective and responsive monetary policy? In particular, we want to know more about the MTM and its effectiveness in transmitting monetary policy.

There are six channels through which policy can influence the real economy. Answers to our questions therefore come from six different directions. Each channel affects one or more macroeconomic variables, ultimately impacting through aggregate demand and/or supply on inflation and output. At the very outset it is to be noted that the heterogeneity reported by the various authors poses significant challenges for officials. For example, if monetary policy increases interest rates say in Kenya, and the same policy leads to an increase in the monetary base in Uganda, then the first question to arise is: what exactly do we mean when we describe monetary policy as expansionary or contractionary?

If Africa is to manage its growth process in a way that avoids the excess and the boom and bust of the last global crisis, the authorities must establish these framework conditions and must then manage the constituent parts of the monetary transition mechanism. The literature differentiates between six main channels for the transmission of monetary policy:

1. The interest rate channel
2. The money channel
3. The exchange rate channel
4. The credit channel
5. The asset price channel
6. The expectations channel.

The money channel is the oldest and perhaps the most well-known of the channels that make up the MTM. Changes in reserve money that are transmitted to broad money through the money multiplier aggregate demand are assumed to move in tandem with money balances that finance transactions with consequent effects on nominal and real GDP as well as the price level. In economies with a high share of currency in circulation, reserve money will weaken the central banks' ability to influence the cost conditions in the economy. As a result, regulating a small part of reserve money, namely bank reserves, will not be as effective. Alternately, bank excess reserves are high as they are in many African countries as the central bank's ability to regulate the market for bank reserves is again weakened. In such cases the central banks' actions in no way constrain bank lending; instead, banks simply draw on these balances when they need to make loans[24] (Kuttner and Mosser, 2002).

With respect to the interest rate channel, we have already stated that African authorities would like to use this option in order to manage monetary conditions in the economy. Theoretically, increases in nominal interest rates mean that the real rate of interest also increases. Together they make for an increase in the cost of capital, which in turn leads to a deferral of consumption and/or a decrease in investment spending. This is how the mechanism is supposed to work, but Bernanke and Gertler (1995) found that, in the case of the US, the reaction to policy initiated changes in interest rates of a much larger magnitude than the interest elasticities for consumption and investment (Kuttner and Mosser, 2002). Insofar as cross border banking increases competition in domestic banking, it contributes to a reduction of interest rate margins and, in that the pan-African banks participate in open market operations, they contribute to an amplification of the interest rate channel (Alade, 2014; Christensen, 2014). This would apply to Uganda and Nigeria. It remains to be seen if the theoretical basis for the interest rate channel lies entirely in the Keynesian IS-LM construct.

We know from other experiences that, in open economies with flexible exchange rates, the exchange rate channel is a powerful transmission mechanism for monetary policy (Alade, 2014). This is certainly the case in South Africa, Ghana, Mauritius and Morocco (Christensen, 2014). In these countries a monetary contraction would have the effect of raising interest rates, thus causing the local currency to appreciate in value. Alternately, monetary expansion would reduce the real interest rate and lead to a depreciation of the currency. The theoretical basis for the operation of this channel within the MTM lies in uncovered interest parity (UIP). Essentially, UIP posits that any expected future changes in the nominal exchange rates are the result of the differentials between the domestic and foreign interest rate. Theoretically, UIP means that the monetary policy authorities can influence the exchange rate and thereby the relative prices of goods both domestic and foreign (Davoodi et al., 2013). Where pan-African banks are actively participating in the local foreign exchange market they have the effect of changing monetary conditions and consequently the exchange rate. This is the case in Nigeria where these banks are active in the foreign exchange auction. Christensen (2014) reports that in Malawi these banks withdraw or inject (depending on the conditions) foreign currency that in part comes from the parent. Further, because a sizeable proportion of foreign currency deposits and lending is undertaken by the pan-African banks there is scope for currency substitution. So, here again the capacity to influence monetary policy is augmented by the workings of a more responsive exchange rate channel. On the other hand, the capacity to transmit macroeconomic shocks from region to region is a by-product of this closer integration.

The literature on the subject distinguishes between two types of credit channel: the bank lending channel and the balance sheet channel. As far as the bank lending channel is concerned, a monetary contraction decreases bank reserves and bank deposits as well as degrading the quality of bank loans that are available. The balance sheet channel works in such a manner as to influence net worth both of businesses and households. Here monetary contractions would lower the net worth of firms by reducing both cash flows and the value of collateral. As a consequence, lending, investment and output would all be reduced (Bernanke and Gertler, 1995; Davoodi et al., 2013).

To the extent that pan-African banks are able to bring about improvements in the local payments system and modernize the infrastructure, it will be possible for them to increase the intermediation ratio, that is, the ratio between lending and deposits. Alade (2014) reports that in the WAEMU pan-African banks have increased competition in the credit market and, according to Christensen (2014: 19), they have also stimulated the interbank market and helped strengthen the transmission mechanism of monetary policy. Further, pan-African banks are also more willing to serve non-prime borrowers than the major international banks and thereby have made a contribution to the strong growth in intermediation that has occurred in Uganda. In this case the credit channel of the monetary policy transmission mechanism is made more responsive to monetary policy initiatives (Christensen, 2014: 19).

The asset price channel played a very important role in the lead up to the subprime crisis. The rise in the value of the Dow Jones had the effect of increasing financial wealth and thereby the financial resources of households. This increase contributed to an expansion of output that aimed to satisfy the increase in consumption demand. The house price appreciation that accompanied the lead up to the crisis also worked in a similar manner.

Thus asset price increases/decreases contribute to wealth effects that in turn influence the MTM.[25] The asset price channel has become more important among some of the frontier market economies (with relatively developed financial markets). Several bond issues have had the effect of deepening the local markets and the COMESA-EAC-SADC Free Trade Area initiative between the Common Market for East and Southern Africa (COMESA), the East African Community (EAC) and the Southern African Development Community (SADC) aimed at creating one single solitary exchange for the region with a common regulatory and accounting framework for 26 countries would have the effect of strengthening the workings of monetary policy in the region.

4.6   CONCLUSION

This chapter has sought to report on the aftermath of the Great Recession of 2008 in Africa and to examine the workings of monetary transmission in Africa. Specifically, we examined three post-crisis developments: (a) an increased momentum towards regional integration, (b) the rise of pan-African banking, and (c) an increase in cross border flows, and enquired as to their effects on the MTM in Africa. The effects of the crisis were unevenly spread and differed from region to region. The EAC by virtue of its lack of integration into global financial markets was insulated and protected from the more damaging consequences of the crisis. Here the effects of the crisis were largely transmitted through trade. In the SACU region, which is more integrated into the global financial system, both the financial and trade channels were important transmission mechanisms. In general, we found that in order to withstand a global shock of the magnitude of the Great Recession countries needed to diversify their trading partners so as to include fast growing economies both in Africa and other regions.

There are three main findings with regard to the operation of the MTM in Africa. The official literature is clear and unequivocal. Pan-African banking and the regionalization thrust of the authorities are both important tendencies in establishing the four pillars for effective monetary and responsive policy. It follows that the MTM is playing an increasing part in the transmission of monetary policy to the real economy. In terms of bolstering the MTM, there is uniform agreement across the BIS literature (Jeanneau, 2014; Christensen, 2014; Alade, 2014; all in BIS Papers #76, 2014) that monetary arrangements in Africa would benefit from a freer flow of information and greater cross border collaboration including contingency plans. This would require improvements in both the regulatory and supervisory arrangements.

Second, the huge size of deposits maintained by Africa's BIS reporting banks suggest relatively low levels of intermediation and competition. Thus the benefits that would accrue as a result of increased cross border flows are withdrawn from the local economy and stored up in BIS banks. Deposits of this size can limit the effectiveness of monetary policy and weaken the responsiveness of the MTM.

Third and last, BIS surveys of central banks suggest that the expectations channel is important in the operation of the MTM. In South Africa it is already regarded as one of the important transmission mechanisms. In Kenya the expectations channel is also becoming more and more important. The same applies to Mauritius. Unfortunately, research output on the expectations channel in Africa is relatively undeveloped and, until researchers catch up with events, this important expectations feature of the MTM remains unexamined. The need for research work in this area is reinforced by the example of Nigeria.

Nigeria carried out a rebasing of its GDP[26] in 2014 and, as a consequence, the economy expanded by 87 per cent making it Africa's largest economy by GDP (ahead of South Africa by quite some margin).

Rebasing deepens our knowledge of the Nigerian economy by taking into account new economic activity in telecommunications, construction, financial services and other new sectors. If repeated throughout Africa,[27] the more robust GDP data and information point to a significant problem with the official literature on the MTM in Africa. A large part of the increase in GDP is explained by the fact that the rebased GDP now includes activities in the informal sector. Without a grasp of the size and scope of this sector, interest rates cannot reflect the liquidity conditions. The informal economy requires its own currency in circulation and gives birth to its own expectations channel that can diminish the relevance of the MTM and the effectiveness of monetary policy.

In general, the big problem with almost all of the official literature is that it assumes that the success of monetary policy lies solely in its ability to restrain inflation. But if the monetary authorities in Africa are to be credible, as the literature insists, monetary policy must also be used to support employ-ment generating objectives. What the rebasing profoundly demonstrates is an urgent need for the central banks to do more than target inflation; they must target jobs as well. The MTM (despite the new emergent processes analyzed in earlier sections) remains weak in proportion to the size of the informal sector. If the size and scope of the informal sector is a function of the lack of jobs in the official sector, as many studies suggest, it follows that the monetary authorities can only enhance the credibility of monetary policy by addressing employment as well as inflation. The official literature is deep and technically insightful as far as it goes. Its weakness lies in its inability to conceive of a broader role for the monetary policy of the central banks.

NOTES

1. I am indebted to my colleagues in the Political Economy Research Group at Kingston University where an earlier version of this chapter was presented and to Paul Auerbach and Gary Dymski who read and commented on earlier drafts. Notwithstanding their interventions any remaining errors and mistakes are entirely my own.
2. Vector Autoregessive Models used by econometricians to measure linear dependency in time series analysis.
3. The working poor are those living on less than US$1.25 a day or less.
4. Weisbrod and Whalley (2011), use growth accounting methods to show how Chinese FDI contributed to an additional one half of a percentage point or above to GDP growth in the 2005 to 2008 pre-crisis period.
5. See the IMF Survey Magazine, 3 February 2009, for a good example of the dire type of forecasts and projections that typify the period.
6. The data here is taken from a report in the *Financial Times*, 16 April 2014.
7. It's worth noting that The World Bank estimates that sub-Saharan Africa received remittances in the amount of US$32 billion in 2013, up 3.5 per cent in 2012 and equal to roughly 2 per cent of the region's GDP.
8. In Kenya, Uganda and Tanzania, the top three products account for less than 40 per cent of total exports, well below levels in the SACU (Brixiova and Ndikumana, 2013). According to the authors, the EAC's deeper intra-regional trade and its fewer trade ties with advanced economies strengthened its capacity to reduce export volatil-ity and mitigate global output shocks. Further, unlike the case of the SACU where the small countries export mostly to South Africa, the EAC's regional trade is better diver-sified among various members and other countries in the region (Sudan, Democratic Republic of Congo). This underscores the importance of export diversification and trading with fast growing economies.
9. Growth is important because, as Benjamin Friedman (2006) says, 'economic growth more often than not fosters greater opportunity, tolerance of diversity, social mobil-ity, commitment to fairness, and dedication to democracy'. It follows that the absence of growth is always accompanied by xenophobia, intolerance and a negative attitude towards the poor.
10. Three financial institutions were established to facilitate inter-African trade. These were: the African Investment Bank (AIB), the African Monetary Fund (AMF) and the African Central Bank (ACB). It was agreed that it would be necessary to establish a single common currency in Africa in order to speed economic integration. The planning

for the African Monetary Fund and for the African Central Bank was supposed to be a phased process alongside the process of the full unification of Africa, leading towards the Union Government of Africa.

11. See World Bank (2011) in Christensen (2014).
12. United Bank for Africa (UBA) and Access Bank combined are operating in more than 20 countries on the continent (Alade, 2014: 83).
13. In Attijariwafa's case, it also finances large infrastructure projects.
14. In addition, Chinese private investors have also increased their presence in many African countries (Gu, 2009).
15. According to Busse et al. Chinese investment is a particularly important source of capital for certain African countries. Chinese FDI accounted for 52 per cent of FDI inflows in Zimbabwe, 26 per cent in Mauritius and 13 per cent in both South Africa and Zambia.
16. According to a World Bank/UNIDO survey of 713 potential investing firms from Brazil, India, South Africa and South Korea, new market access is the most important motivation of Southern outward FDI (nearly 70 per cent), followed by lower production costs (20 per cent) and acquisition of natural resources and inputs (5 per cent) (UNCTAD, 2014).
17. Angola recorded the highest rates of return on FDI in 2011 with 87 per cent, followed by Nigeria (36 per cent) and Zambia (13 per cent) (World Bank, 2014).
18. 'In residential construction and in hotels and restaurants services, TNCs from South Africa, Kenya and Egypt were the leading investors in Africa by number of cross-border acquisitions deals. The high shares of intra-African investment targeting the manufacturing sector accord with evidence from trade statistics showing that the industry products that are most traded intraregionally are manufactured goods – especially those entailing low and medium levels of processing' (UNCTAD WIR, 2013: 40).
19. These include Bidvest, Anglo Gold Ashanti, MTN, Shoprite, Pick n' Pay, Aspen Pharmacare and Naspers.
20. Intra-African investments in the manufacturing sector concentrate in agri-processing, building materials, electric and electronic equipment, and textiles, while in the services sector African TNCs have been attracted to telecommunications and retail industries, especially in rapidly growing economies like those in Nigeria, Ghana, Uganda and Zambia.
21. All quarters of the literature welcome these emerging trends, but Bond (2014) finds that South Africa for one is motivated by sub-imperialist aspirations.
22. But several countries, in particular Egypt, experienced net outflows of portfolio capital during 2000 to 2009.
23. Forty of the top 50 companies that operate on a pan-African scale are South African in origin.
24. A high currency ratio might be due to (1) a lack of trust in the banks, (2) the inability of the banking sector to offer a return above that of cash and (3) the desire to hold cash may be tied to an intention to engage in illicit underground economy activities where cash is king.
25. For more on wealth effects, see Case et al., 2001.
26. Nigeria had not changed the base year for calculating the value of its GDP since 1990.
27. By the new rebased GDP, Nigeria's 2013 GDP stood at US$520 billion dollars – 25th largest in the world. Kenya and Ghana also rebased and experienced increases in GDP as a result.

BIBLIOGRAPHY

Alade, Sarah O. (2014), 'Cross-border expansion of Nigerian banks: has it improved the continent's regulatory and supervisory frameworks?' in M.S. Mohanty (ed.),

'The role of central banks in macroeconomic and financial stability', BIS Papers No. 76, Monetary and Economic Department, February.

Bernanke, Ben and Mark Gertler (1995), 'Inside the black box: the credit channel of monetary policy transmission', *Journal of Economic Issues*, 9 (4), 27–48.

BIS (2014), BIS reporting banks: Summary of international positions.

Blas, J. (2013), African countries race to issue bonds, 15 December 2013, FT.com, retrieved on 2 March 2016 from http://on.ft.com/PcC8ri.

Bond, Patrick, 2014, 'Which way forward for the BRICS in Africa, a year after the Durban summit?', Pambazuka News, Issue 673, retrieved on 2 March 2016 from http://bit.ly/1kL8JDs.

Brixiova, Zuzana and Léonce Ndikumana (2013), 'The global financial crisis and Africa: the effects and policy responses', in J. Epstein and M. Wolfson (eds), *Handbook of the Political Economy of Financial Crises*, Chapter 36. Oxford: Oxford University Press.

Brixiova, Zuzana, Léonce Ndikumana and Kaouther Abderrahim (2011), 'Supporting Africa's post-crisis growth: the role of macroeconomic policies', William Davidson Institute, Working Paper Number 1008, January.

Busse, Matthias, Ceren Erdogan and Henning Mühlen (2014), 'China's impact on Africa, the role of trade and FDI', SSRN Working Paper, 2014, retrieved on 2 March 2016 from http://ssrn.com/abstract=2426106.

Case, Karl E., Robert J. Shiller and John M. Quigley (2001), 'Comparing wealth effects: the stock market versus the housing market', NBER Working Paper No. 8606, November 2001.

Christensen, Benedicte Vibe (2011), 'Have monetary transmission mechanisms in Africa changed?', in Dubravko Mihaljek (ed.), 'Central banking in Africa: prospects in a changing world Monetary and Economic Department', BIS Papers No. 56, September.

Christensen, Benedicte Vibe (2014), 'Financial integration in Africa: implications for monetary policy and financial stability', in M.S. Mohanty (ed.), 'The role of central banks in macroeconomic and financial stability', BIS Papers No. 76, Monetary and Economic Department, February.

Collier, Paul (2013), 'Speech by Paul Collier', in M.S. Mohanty (ed.), 'The role of central banks in macroeconomic and financial stability', BIS Papers No. 76, Monetary and Economic Department, February.

Davoodi, Hamid R., Shiv Dixit and Gabor Pinter (2013), 'Monetary transmission mechanism in the East African community: an empirical investigation', International Monetary Fund, WP/13/39.

Economist, The (2011), April 20.

Financial Times (various issues).

Friedman, Benjamin (2006), The Moral Consequences of Economic Growth, New York: First Vintage Books.

Gu, J. (2009), 'China's private enterprises in Africa and the implications for African development', European Journal of Development Research, 21 (4).

Habiyarenye, A. and L. Soute (2010), The Global Financial Crisis and Africa's Immiserising Wealth, Research Brief, Number 1, United Nations University, Tokyo.

International Labour Office (ILO), January 2010, Global Employment Trends. Geneva, Switzerland, retrieved on 17 March 2016 from www.ilo.org/wcmsp5/groups/public/---ed_emp/---emp_elm/---trends/documents/publication/wcms_120471.pdf.

IMF Survey Online (2009), IMF to Assist Africa Hit Hard by Global Downturn, IMF Survey Magazine: Countries & Regions, retrieved on 2 March 2016 from http://bit.ly/1eyeNad.

IMF (2011), Regional economic outlook, sub-Saharan Africa, April.

IMF (2014), World Economic Outlook, 2014.

Jeanneau, Serge (2014), 'Financial stability objectives and arrangements – what's new?', BIS Papers No. 76.

Kuttner, K.N. and Mosser, P.C. (2002), 'The monetary transmission mechanism: some answers and further questions', Federal Reserve Bank of New York Economic Policy Review, 8 (1), 15–26.

Lewis, W. Arthur (1950), *Industrialisation of the British West Indies*, Barbados: Barbados Government Print Office.

Kuttner, Kenneth N. and Patricia C. Mosser (2002), 'The monetary transmission mechanism: some answers and further questions', FRBNY Economic Policy Review, May.

Luvhengo, Victor (2010), 'Unlocking Africa's abundant mineral resources', The Thinker, volume 21, www.thethinker.co.za.

Mishra, Prachi, Peter J. Montiel and Antonio Spilimbergo (2010), 'Monetary transmission in low income countries', IMF Working Paper WP/10/223, Washington DC.

Mohanty, M.S. (ed.) (2014), 'The role of central banks in macroeconomic and financial stability', BIS Papers No. 76, Monetary and Economic Department, February.

Ncube, Mthuli and Eliphas Ndou (2011), 'Working Paper 133 – Monetary policy transmission, house prices and consumer spending in South Africa: an SVAR approach', Working Paper Series 317, African Development Bank.

Ncube, Mthuli and Eliphas Ndou (2013), 'Monetary policy and exchange rate shocks on South African trade balance', African Development Bank, Working Paper No. 169, February.

Ncube, M., E. Ndou and N. Gumata (2012a), 'How are the US financial shocks transmitted into South Africa? Structural VAR Evidence', African Development Bank Working Paper No. 157.

Ncube, M., E. Ndou and N. Gumata (2012b). 'The impact of euro area monetary and bond yield shocks on the South African economy: structural vector auto-regression model evidence', African Development Bank Working Paper No. 161.

Ncube, M., Zuzana Brixiova and Qingwei Meng (2014), 'Can intra-regional trade act as a global shock absorber in Africa?', African Development Bank Group, Working Paper No. 198, February.

Quartey, Kwei (2012), Africa: Why Africa Is Turning to China, originally published in Foreign Policy in Focus, retrieved on 7 January 2013 from http://allafrica.com/stories/201301071472.html.

Rangasamy, Logan and Dubravko Mihaljek (2011), 'Capital flows, commodity price movements and foreign exchange intervention', in Dubravko Mihaljek (ed.), 'Central banking in Africa: prospects in a changing world Monetary and Economic Department', BIS Papers No. 56, September.

Sulaiman, Tosin (2014), 'African countries' debt undermines growth boom', Business Day, 20 March 2014, retrieved on 2 March 2016 from http://bit.ly/1ejvP0Q.

UNCTAD (2010), Cited in BIS Papers No. 56, 'Capital flows, commodity price movements and foreign exchange intervention', by Logan Rangasamy and Dubravko Mihaljek, retrieved on 17 March 2016 from http://www.bis.org/publ/bppdf/bispap56f.pdf.

UNCTAD WIR (World Investment Report) (2013), Global Value Chains: Investment and Trade for Development, New York and Geneva: United Nations.

UNCTAD (2014), 'World Investment Report 2014 – Investing in the SDGs: An Action Plan', UNCTAD/WIR/2014.

Vajs, Stephen (2014), 'Government debt issuance: issues for central banks', in M.S. Mohanty (ed.), 'The role of central banks in macroeconomic and financial stability', BIS Papers No. 76, Monetary and Economic Department, February.

Weisbrod, Aaron and John Whalley (2011), 'The contribution of Chinese FDI to Africa's pre crisis growth surge', National Bureau of Economic Research, Working Paper 17544, October 2011, Cambridge, MA.

World Bank (2013), 'An analysis of issues shaping Africa's economic future', Africa's Pulse, volume 8, October 2013, Washington, DC.

World Bank (2014), 'Foreign direct investment flows into sub-Saharan Africa', Science, Technology, and Skills for Africa's Development, March.

World Bank (2015), 'World Development Indicators', retrieved on 2 March 2016 from http://bit.ly/1pcMTL2.

World Bank (2015), 'Chapter 2 – Sub-Saharan Africa', *Global Economic Prospects*, January 2015, retrieved on 2 March 2016 from www.worldbank.org/content/dam/Worldbank/GEP/GEP2015a/pdfs/GEP2015a_chapter2_regionaloutlook_SSA.pdf.

PART II

Country cases

5. Commodities economy in times of crisis: Bolivia after the global financial meltdown

Orlando Justo and Juan E. Santarcángelo

5.1 INTRODUCTION

During the last two decades of the twentieth century the economic reality of many Latin American nations changed after a disappointing period of neo-liberal policies that aggravated their macroeconomic performance and stability. The twenty-first century has witnessed increasing criticism and concerns about the effectiveness of these policies, as well as a rise in leftist governments in the Latin American region. As one of these Latin American countries, Bolivia has implemented a set of policies aimed to change the country's institutional and economic arrangement during the administration of Evo Morales of the Movimiento al Socialismo (MAS), and has embraced, alongside Venezuela and Ecuador, a development strategy that is usually referred as '21st century socialism'.[1]

This strategy has focused on balancing the interests of this diverse country's ethnicities and reorganizing institutions that have historically marginalized the indigenous sector. The government has shifted from past neo-liberal policies to giving the state a more relevant role in the economy, nationalized the hydrocarbons sector, increased transfer payments to help a vast segment of the population living in poverty and passed a new constitution.

In 2008 the international financial system was heavily tested by a major financial crisis that originated in the United States. Millions of American borrowers failed to pay back the mortgage loans that had been easily acquired in the previous years during the so called 'real estate bubble'. The banking system was shaken and liquidity issues forced federal regulators in the US to rescue several financial institutions trying to provide stability to the financial system and the American economy. In a globalized economy it was just a matter of hours before this financial disruption expanded worldwide.

This global financial crisis caught Bolivia in the middle of its reform process, and its economy was heavily exposed to the imbalances of the financial system, but the country has managed to overcome this situation with relative success. The main objective of this chapter is to explore the factors that made it possible for the Bolivian government to pass through this critical situation. The study argues that, rather than a sound and specific economic plan, Bolivia has enjoyed a period of high commodity prices, which has allowed the Morales administration to obtain huge revenues from the state controlled natural resources, and implement large government spending on social programs to alleviate the negative consequences of the crisis. In other words, while many developed countries have been suffering the consequences of the shocks in global financial markets and have faced serious liquidity problems, Bolivia has enjoyed a period of large inflows of cash from the high price of its export commodities. This has served to lessen the negative effects of the crisis, but also to hide some of the structural problems of the Bolivian economy, which have not yet been resolved.

The first part of the chapter goes through the economic reforms implemented under the Morales administration. The second section explores how Bolivia has experienced this crisis, and the final part summarizes the main findings and possible future implications for the Bolivian economy.

5.2   EVO MORALES AND MOVIMIENTO AL SOCIALISMO: A 'NEW BOLIVIA'

Historically, Bolivia has been the poorest country in Latin America. In 2003 the total population living in poverty was 67.3 percent, this situation being extremely critical within the rural sector, where almost 80 percent of the population lived under this condition. The fragility of the democratic institutions has historically been a major issue in Bolivia. Throughout the twentieth century the country had more than 50 heads of state, including presidents, military juntas and government juntas, with no clear commitment regarding the destiny of the nation. Victor Paz Estenssoro was elected president in 1985 when the country had experienced seven months of economic turmoil, with a hyperinflation of over 4,000 percent. Paz Estenssoro, following the advice of Harvard based economist Jeffrey Sachs and Gonzalo Sánchez de Lozada, implemented a neo-liberal program aimed at reshaping the economic structure of the country, giving markets primacy over all other social mechanisms. These policies, which were known as the *New Economic Policy* (Nueva Política Económica), represent a shift from the path followed by Bolivia since the beginning of the

1950s, one which was deepened during the 1990s by the administrations of Jaime Paz Zamora, Gonzalo Sánchez de Lozada and Hugo Bánzer. Among the most relevant reforms were the deregulation of markets, the privatization of state-owned enterprises, the decline in the power of labor unions, and the reduction in the size, public spending and participation of the state in economic activities (Morales, 1992).

Fifteen years of neo-liberal policies reshaped the Bolivian economy, and the traditionally marginalized indigenous sector emerged as an active left political force. They confronted the World Bank fiercely over the Cochabamba water privatization in a dispute called *Guerra del Agua*. The struggle reached its peak with the removal of Presidents Gonzalo Sánchez de Lozada in October 2003 and Carlos Mesa Gisbert in June 2005 (Webber, 2011b). Subsequently, Evo Morales of the Movimiento al Socialismo was elected president of Bolivia on December 18, 2005 with a historic 54 percent of the popular vote (Webber, 2011a: 1). Morales became the first indigenous president in the republic's history, which represented not only the end of dominance by a minority white elite, but also prompted the participation of Bolivia's majority indigenous population in government (Kohl, 2010: 107).

Twenty-first century socialism pursues an alternative path to Soviet style socialism and the neo-liberal model. It aims to build on their mistakes, not by rejecting the market, but rather by opposing the control of foreign interests – mainly through multinational enterprises in the domestic economy. This project aims for a more active role of the state in the economy by the state controlling the nation's main natural resources, and for an effective redistribution of income. These imply a transformation of the institutional arrangement that allows correction of economic and social imbalances, while using the allocation benefits that innovation and entrepreneurship provide in a market economy (see Kennemore and Weeks, 2011; and Petras and Veltmeyer, 2009). In other words, it tries to build in the 'best of both worlds'.

The steps taken by the Morales administration since taking over the Bolivian government were strongly oriented in that direction. In May 2006 they nationalized the hydrocarbons sector and renegotiated the terms of the agreements they had with companies managing the oil and gas industries. As a result of this, the state obtained a 51 percent share of Yacimientos Petrolíferos Fiscales Bolivianos (YPFB, Bolivian Treasury Petroleum Fields), and ruled that the former owners would receive only 18 percent of total revenues, while the remaining 82 percent would be treasured by the state. The Morales government has taken over all telecommunications and electrical companies, even from national cooperatives, proposed the elimination of private pension plans, recreated a state airline company, nationalized two Swiss smelters and systematically pushed for state control over mineral resources from iron ore to lithium (Klein, 2011: 288). As a result, the state is becoming the dominant player in the national economy and has nationalized a total of 12 major foreign companies.

Also, in 2007 they created the Banco de Desarrollo Productivo (Productive Development Bank) and funded it actively through public investment. Likewise, in January 2009 they approved a new constitution that made explicit the commitment of government institutions to the country's sovereignty, and the equal rights of the diverse communities and ethnicities of the nation. Moreover, the Morales administration has begun several programs targeted at the poorest Bolivians, which include payments to low income families to increase school enrollment, an expansion of public pensions to relieve extreme poverty among the elderly, and payments for uninsured mothers to expand prenatal and postnatal care and to reduce infant and child mortality (Weisbrot et al., 2009b: 3). All these programs had an impressive impact on the living conditions of the poorest Bolivians, significantly improving their economic and social condition (the percentage of people living under the poverty line was almost 60 percent at the beginning of the Morales administration and in 2012 it was reduced to 38 percent).

At the same time and following the path of most Latin American countries, the Bolivian government distanced itself from the US and strengthened ties with allies in Latin America – such as Venezuela, Ecuador, Brazil and Argentina – as well as Asia. For instance, in 2007 Bolivia, with the neighbor countries listed above along with Paraguay, created the Bank of the South to reduce financial dependence on the international financial institutions by financing infrastructure and long run productive investment projects. The Morales administration has also worked closely with the Venezuelan government in the Bolivarian Alternative of the Americas (ALBA) to develop the oil and mining sectors, and it has increased its business relations with Iran and the Russian state gas company Gazprom (Kennemore and Weeks, 2011).

The Morales government also made major advances in providing access to land for the poorer groups in Bolivian society. The new administration gave a major boost to the 2002 land reform act, and from 2006 through mid 2009 had distributed some 31 million hectares to 154,000 peasants and farmers (some five times the amount distributed during the pre-2006 period), with a higher ratio now going to indigenous peoples than before (Klein, 2011: 290).

Despite significant transformations in the living conditions of many Bolivians (especially the poorest) and an impressive performance in economic growth terms, the academic literature is in the middle of an avid debate between what we can call detractors and supporters of the Morales regime. Regarding the former group, Morales' economic reforms have been questioned for not being as socialist oriented as his rhetoric implies, even from heterodox scholars. For instance, Petras (2013) claims that these reforms are orthodox economic policies typically found in the economic packages of the Washington based international financial institutions. He argues that Morales' administration has kept social spending and public investments at the same level as previous neo-liberal oriented regimes, and has managed to influence labor union leaders to negotiate salary agreements that do not provide real benefits to workers, especially in the rural sector, where a large segment of the population barely survive or live below the poverty line (Petras, 2013: 1). Kennemore and Weeks (2011) also claim that Morales' economic reforms, instead of being a radical change toward a socialist project, aim to take advantage of the surplus generated by the capitalist sector, using these funds to finance government spending with more pragmatism than ideological conviction. The authors also question the depth and long term viability of the social reforms implemented in favor of the traditionally marginalized Bolivian communities based mainly on large social spending. Haarstard and Andersson (2009) claim that through its nationalization programs the Bolivian government has secured joint ventures and profit sharing agreements with foreign companies, while maintaining favorable relations with the International Monetary Fund. On the other hand, Leiva (2008) challenges the ability of the Bolivian government to control the funds generated by the profit sharing schemes established with foreign companies in the oil and gas sector, as well as the scope of the nationalization process since foreign companies can still exploit the national resources under the name of the state owned Yacimientos Petrolíferos Fiscales Bolivianos (YPFB).

On the other hand, scholars who support (at least in some degree) the current transformations and economic measures taken by the Morales administration can be grouped into three main branches. The first one supports the idea that Morales' policies do not necessarily lead toward socialism but are firmly against neo-liberalism. A good example of this can be found in Klein (2011: 291), who argues that the 2009 change in the constitution was clearly a step toward a 'social constitution' as earlier defined by the Bolivian Constitution of 1938. The right to private property (individual and communal) was limited by its necessity to fulfill a social function and could not prejudice the collective interests of society (Article 56). Also, the constitution gave priority to national over foreign capital and stated that all foreign investments were to be completely subject to Bolivian law without exception (Article 320). The rights to strike and collectively bargain were also guaranteed.

The second group of supporters of the current regime, such as Weisbrot et al. (2009b: 30), recognizes the economic and social accomplishments of Morales' administration, while other authors such as Kaup (2010) go even further by criticizing the ability of the policies to significantly alter Bolivia's socioeconomic trajectory in order to develop a new developmentalist path (Kaup, 2010: 123).

Finally, the remaining authors of this group praise the significant impact that Morales' administration has had for the mestizo and indigenous populations, and praise many of the social programs for their favor of the poorest population and their impact on poverty. Siotos (2009) goes even further by affirming that the rise of Evo Morales' MAS party to power reflects a new neostructuralist model of development, governance and political economics (Siotos, 2009: 51).

5.3   BOLIVIA AND THE GLOBAL FINANCIAL CRISIS

The negative effects of the international recession caused by the so called 'subprime crisis' hit Bolivia like it did most countries worldwide. By the time this crisis exploded the Bolivian economy was being affected by other factors, such as declining export prices, falling remittances, the US revocation of trading preferential agreements, and lower foreign investments. The result of these negative shocks was reflected in a sharp decline in GDP growth during 2008, as shown in Figure 5.1.

The situation was aggravated during the 2008 to 2009 period, given the enormous dependence of the nation's economy on foreign trade. Exports carry a weight of over 40 percent of the Bolivian GDP and imports around 35 percent (World Bank, 2015). This is reflected in a severe fall in Bolivian exports growth of over 10 percent, as depicted in Figure 5.2.

In addition, Bolivia has an economic structure typical of a periphery economy, being a producer and exporter of primary products, as depicted in Figure 5.3, which makes it quite vulnerable to changes in global markets and to the volatility of commodity prices.

Along with the trade channels, financial mechanisms also contributed to worsening the Bolivian economic position by 2008. The current account, although having remained in surplus even after the peak of the crisis, has experienced a declining trend since 2008, as shown in Figure 5.4.

As mentioned above, family remittances were affected during the peak of the global crisis, heightening the economic downturn. Following the explosion of the 'subprime bubble' Bolivia experienced two consecutive years of declining inflows from personal remittances during 2009 ($1,057.39 MM)

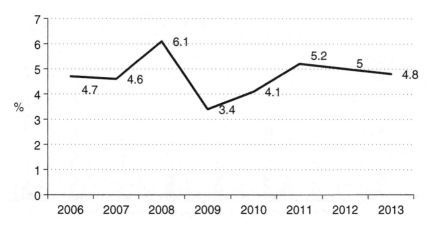

Source: Banco Central de Bolivia.

Figure 5.1 Real GDP growth

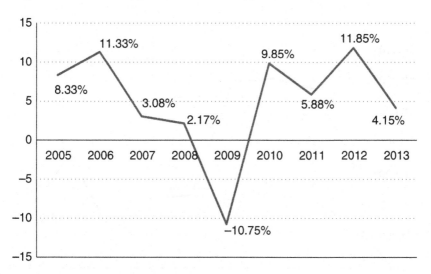

Source: World Bank Development Indicators, World Bank.

Figure 5.2 Annual exports growth (%)

and 2010 ($960.21 MM) in current US dollars. When observing remittances as a percentage of GDP, they went down from 6.81 in 2008 to 6.10 and 4.89 in the following two years (World Bank, 2015).

On the other hand, financial flows show an irregular behavior since the

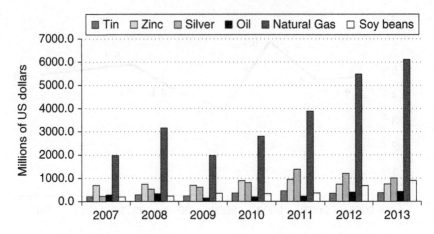

Source: Banco Central de Bolivia.

Figure 5.3   Main export items

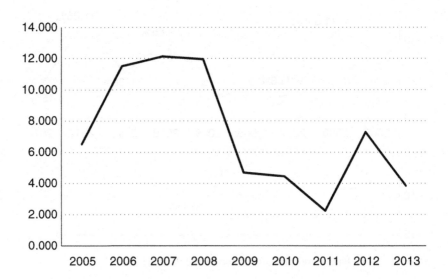

Source: World Bank Development Indicators, World Bank.

Figure 5.4   Current account (% of GDP)

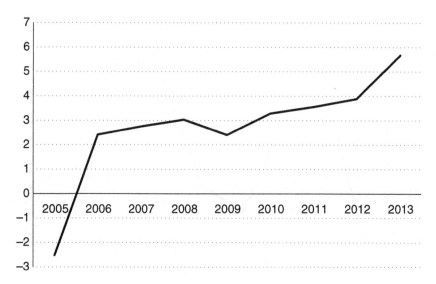

Source: International Financial Statistics, IMF.

Figure 5.5   Net direct investment (% of GDP)

collapse of the financial system. By observing these variables individually, we can notice that, although net direct investment was not severely
affected, it showed a slight decline during the peak of the crisis and a quick
and relatively steady recovery after 2009 (see Figure 5.5).

By contrast, portfolio investments and net other flows show an unstable trend. We can observe in Figure 5.6 that portfolio investments experienced a sharp decline from 2006, bouncing back in 2008 with an even
steeper growth from 2009, but entering again into a downturn in 2011.
Similarly, net other flows depict ups and downs going from an aggressive recovery since 2006 to a slight decline by 2008, which was reversed
a year later and, like portfolio investments, had a huge drop from 2011
(see Figure 5.7).

In spite of the unsteady behavior of these two variables and the declining tendency of the current account surplus, which enables a temporary
deficit in total net financial flows, they do not seem to have played a
prominent role in aggravating the economic position of Bolivia in the
aftermath of the crisis. As we can observe in Figure 5.8, the country's net
financial flows are positive from 2008, with just a slight drop by 2009,
which didn't last long. This shows that the Bolivian economy did not face
a severe financial shock in this period and FDI contributed positively to
this fast recovery.

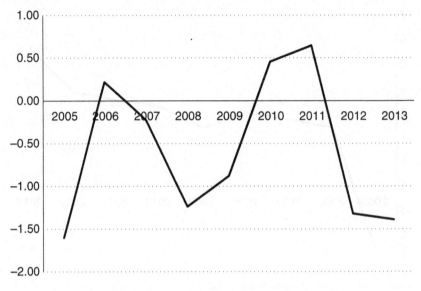

Source: International Financial Statistics, IMF.

Figure 5.6   Portfolio investment (% of GDP)

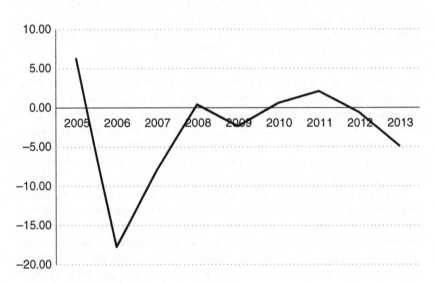

Source: International Financial Statistics, IMF.

Figure 5.7   Net other flows (% of GDP)

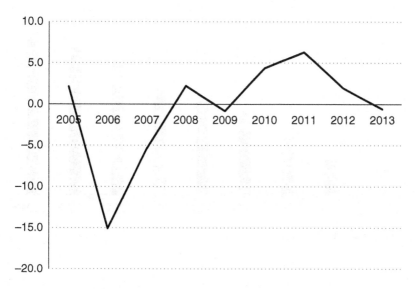

Source: International Financial Statistics, IMF.

Figure 5.8   Total net financial flows to Bolivia (% of GDP)

The 2008 to 2009 economic downturn in Bolivia appears, over time, to be a circumstantial incident rather than a long term recessionary gap, given the ability of the Bolivian economy to recover from these negative shocks by 2010. Unemployment, one of the most sensitive macroeconomic variables during recessions, rose during 2008 from 7.5 percent to 7.9 percent, but has maintained a declining trend since 2009 and by 2013 it was at 7.4 percent (Banco Central de Bolivia, 2014). Notice that when the crisis erupted this increase was of less than 1 percent, and just five years later, it was below the pre-crisis level. As of today, the rate of unemployment in Bolivia is one of the lowest in the Latin American region (ECLAC, n.d.). However, the lack of significant investment, especially in labor-intensive manufactures, has led to Bolivia having one of the largest informal labor markets in the Americas. It is estimated that 80 percent of the labor force today is employed in low production and low wage jobs in the informal sector or in subsistence agriculture (Klein, 2011: 289).

While most nations have been struggling to have their economies recovered from the subprime crisis and financial shocks have been rampant worldwide, Bolivia has enjoyed an inflow of funds that have provided stability to their financial system. The aftermath of the crisis, as well as the income derived from the nationalization of foreign firms, has left Bolivia

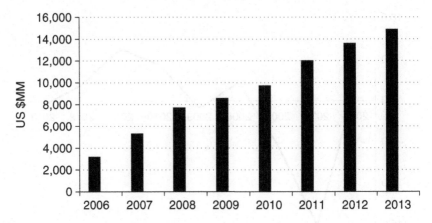

Source: Banco Central de Bolivia.

Figure 5.9   International reserves

with a solid international reserves position, as shown in Figure 5.9. At the same time, Bolivia did not experience severe declines in net financial flows (Figure 5.8), which liberated the local currency (Bolivian boliviano) from heavy external pressure. The currency depreciated mildly after 2008, but this was a trend that started before the crisis erupted, depreciating from 2007 to 2008 at a higher rate than during the post-2008 years (see Figure 5.10).

In spite of its structural economic challenges, in practice Bolivia has overcome this crisis with fewer difficulties than some of its industrialized

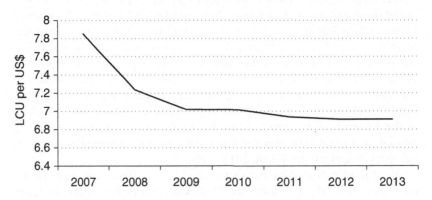

Source: World Bank Development Indicators, World Bank.

Figure 5.10   Exchange rate (period average)

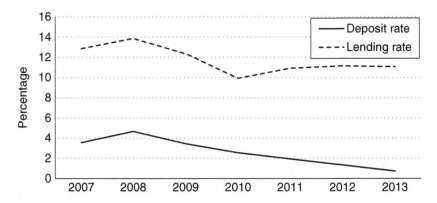

Source: World Bank Development Indicators, World Bank.

Figure 5.11   Interest rate

counterparts such as the United States and the European Union. This poses two immediate questions: how can this be explained, and does the Morales administration's twenty-first century socialism hold the key to overcoming the global financial crisis?

When the 2008 financial crisis expanded globally, it generated a sense of panic in the international financial system, which prompted firms, governments and private individuals to make adjustments and take preventive measures worldwide. The Bolivian government was not an exception, and as the effects of the crisis reached the domestic borders, the Morales administration implemented macroeconomic corrections.

In terms of monetary policy, the interest rates were reduced from 2008 to 2010 to stimulate domestic borrowing (see Figure 5.11), while the domestic credit provided by the financial sector increased during the same period, as shown in Figure 5.12. The Bolivian boliviano was allowed to depreciate, remaining quite stable relative to the US dollar from 2010, stimulating exports based on boliviano terms (Figure 5.10).

These macroeconomic mechanisms contributed toward alleviating the initial economic deceleration created by the crisis, but Bolivia also benefitted directly in the aftermath of the global recession from a sharp increase in the prices of its energy and mineral exports. The bonanza from the commodities sector that most of Latin America has enjoyed in the last decade has favored Bolivia as well. In spite of these prices suffering a negative shock during 2008, international markets recovered quickly, as we can observe in Figures 5.13 and 5.14. Thus, while the Bolivian government was immersed in trying to cope with the negative effects of the crisis, a sudden

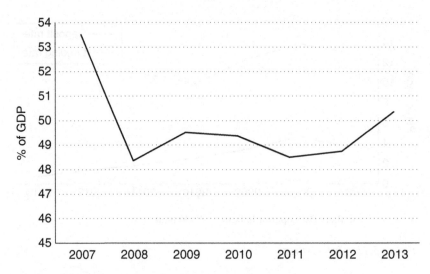

Source: World Bank Development Indicators, World Bank.

Figure 5.12   Domestic credit provided by financial sector

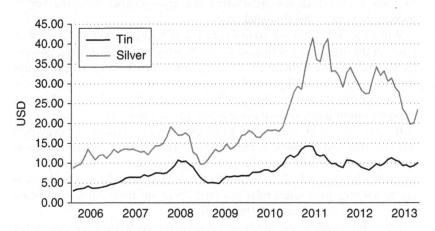

Source: Banco Central de Bolivia.

Figure 5.13   Price of export minerals: 2006–13 (monthly)

change in international market prices brought out a new, preferential scenario for the country. The exposure of the primary sector to the volatility of commodity prices, with the drop in commodity prices historically having a negative impact on Latin American economies, affected these

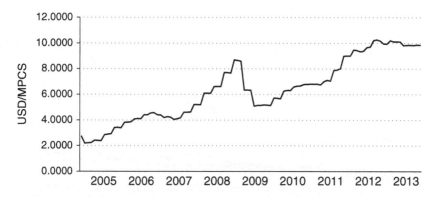

Source: Banco Central de Bolivia.

Figure 5.14 *Average export price of natural gas to Brazil: 2005–13 (monthly)*

peripheral economies with more prosperity this time – at least in the short term.

Bolivia's large number of commodity exports has provided the country with unusually large rents. Since a substantial part of this revenue (around 65 percent) is generated by the nationalized hydrocarbons sector, the Morales administration has received heavy cash inflows, which they have used to carry out an aggressive expansionary fiscal policy.

The Bolivian government also used fiscal policy mechanisms to alleviate the impact of the global recession in the country during 2009. The economic slowdown contracted slightly government spending this year, but the Morales administration gave priority to public-funded programs. These included public investment in economic activities and infrastructure, as well as an increase in transfer payments through the implementation of social programs in health care and education: *Bono Juancito Pinto* provides 200 bolivianos per year for enrolled students until 6th grade to stimulate education; *Renta Dignidad* is aimed at reducing extreme poverty in the elderly (those over 60 years), giving 1,800 bolivianos to those who collect Social Security and 2,400 bolivianos to those who do not receive retirement benefits; *Bono Juana Azurduy* grants 50 bolivianos to new mothers for four medical visits before birth, 120 bolivianos after childbirth and 125 bolivianos for each medical visit until the child turns two years old. This large fiscal spending was crucial for the country to overcome the trough of the downturn more effectively than most of its neighbors (Weisbrot et al., 2009a). As public income improved, the government took more ambitious steps, and government spending increased

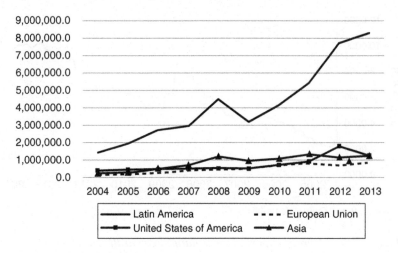

Source: Banco Central de Bolivia.

Figure 5.15   Exports to main trading regions ('000s US$)

abruptly from 2010, remaining quite high and stable (Banco Central
de Bolivia, 2014).

Another factor that helped Bolivia to ease the negative effects of the
crisis was a diversification of the destination of its exports. Increasing sales
to Latin America and Asia lessened Bolivia's dependence on the United
States during the subprime crisis. For instance, while Bolivian exports to
Latin America and Asia accounted for 63.4 percent and 4 percent of the
total exports in 2003, by 2013 these regions absorbed 68.1 percent and
9.9 percent respectively. During the same period, the relative weight of
exports to the United States decreased from 14.1 percent to 10.2 percent
(Banco Central de Bolivia, 2014).

Figure 5.15 illustrates this trend, showing the total value of Bolivian
exports by main regional partners. The increasing importance of
Latin American markets for Bolivian products is notorious, particularly
since the Morales administration's embracing of the twenty-first century
socialism project in 2006 alongside some of its neighbor countries. For
instance, exports to Brazil increased around 2.5 times from 2006 to 2013,
going from $1,591,923.5 to $4,042,444.3. Exports to Argentina went up
5.4 times, from $390,993.0 to $2,451,976.7, and exports to Ecuador grew
around 22.4 times in the same period, from $10,832.2 to $139,088.0 (Banco
Central de Bolivia, 2014).

Bolivia's foreign trade has also been redirected more aggressively
toward nontraditional trade partners such as China and Russia. Exports

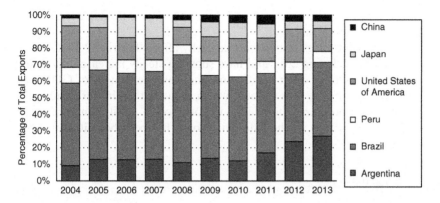

Source: Banco Central de Bolivia.

Figure 5.16   Bolivian main export partners

to Russia in 2006 were merely $2,909.4 but in 2012 they had already quadrupled, accounting for $13,073.0. China has now emerged in Latin America as a large importer of primary goods, and Bolivia has benefited from accessing this market, exporting goods for a value of $35,501.0 to China in 2006, and increasing this amount by almost nine times in 2013 when its exports to China accounted for $314,635.1 (Banco Central de Bolivia, 2014).

During the peak of the subprime crisis in 2008 to 2009, Bolivia managed to reduce its export dependence from the quite vulnerable American market and, as depicted in Figure 5.16, the relative weight of the United States as a total of Bolivian exports decreased during those two years, while neighbor countries and allies became escape valves for Bolivian exporters.

Financial channels have also contributed to Bolivia's economic recovery from the global meltdown. We mentioned above that at the peak of the crisis these mechanisms also contributed to the deceleration of the economy, but this situation was reversed relatively quickly. Foreign Direct Investment (FDI) inflows have increased steadily since 2009, as depicted in Figure 5.5. These investments have been absorbed mainly by the hydrocarbons and mineral sectors and, paradoxically, in spite of the alleged fear generated by the nationalization process on foreign investors, the data shows that since Evo Morales and the MAS won the presidency the country has managed to reverse a negative tendency in FDI inflows. The renegotiated agreements with the companies managing the oil and gas companies, and the freedom to negotiate agreements on behalf of YPFB, could have contributed to lessening these concerns. Likewise, the closer relations with Latin American and Asian allies gave Bolivia access to an alternative pool of investors.

Family remittances, which were critically affected during 2008 to 2010, bounced back during 2011 and have shown a steady increase in absolute dollar terms. On the other hand, remittances as a percentage of GDP have decreased during the same period, which suggests that, in this period of a commodities bonanza, the relative importance of family remittances on GDP has decreased, as the national account has been benefited by other inflows.

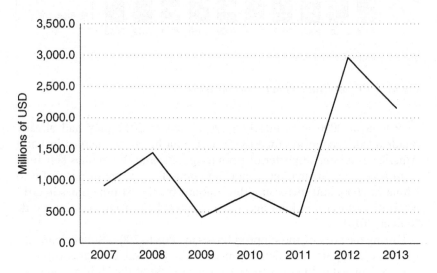

Source: Banco Central de Bolivia.

Figure 5.17   Trade balance

5.4   CONCLUSION

In summary, Bolivia has managed to survive the international financial crisis by relying on large cash inflows from commodity exports, heavy social spending as part of an expansionary fiscal policy, increased FDI inflows, and diversification of the export markets. However, Bolivia's production shows an economy that continues to provide primary products to global markets, which has been its historical position in the international division of labor. This is a pattern that in the past generated severe economic distortions under numerous conservative and military governments, and it has not, as yet, changed under Morales and the MAS project.

The Bolivian government is resting heavily on the wealth fueled by the high prices of commodity exports rather than on implementing a well structured economic development plan. This bonanza is mainly dependent on market conditions and is happily accepted by Bolivian policymakers as it hides the circumstantial nature of this short term prosperity. This situation leaves the country heavily exposed to the volatility of commodity prices and, if they fall, the actual shortcomings of the Bolivian economy will surface. Thus, the attractive source of cash from the exports of minerals and energy resources would be wiped out, which could drag the economy into economic difficulty. This situation poses many questions and potential threats. For instance, even though commodity prices still remain beneficial for Bolivia, Figures 5.13 and 5.14 show that prices of silver and tin have decreased lately, and the price of natural gas has experienced a reduction in its growing trend and remained flat. This situation is hurting the trade balance of the country, which shows a decline in trade surplus, as depicted in Figure 5.17.

The current economic status quo perpetuates the Bolivian economy's dependency on natural resources and primary goods, and this extractive strategy undermines the trustworthiness of an environmentally friendly policy aimed at counterbalancing the actively criticized damage associated with globalization models.

Despite the transformations achieved, there is much more to be done, especially to reduce extreme poverty and informal labor. The main economic challenge is still to figure out how to transform the country from its longstanding extractive economy to a more value added economy. It is time to start developing a sustainable long term development plan.

NOTE

1. The term '21st century socialism' is attributed to Heinz Dieterich, a German sociologist and former advisor of the late Venezuelan president Hugo Chávez.

REFERENCES

Banco Central de Bolivia (2014), *Estadísticas*, retrieved on March 3, 2016 from www.bcb.gob.bo/?q=estadisticas.
ECLAC (n.d.), CEPALSTAT. Databases and Statistical Publications – Economic Commission of Latin America and the Caribbean, retrieved on March 16,

2016 from http://interwp.cepal.org/cepalstat/Perfil_Nacional_Economico.html?
pais=BOL&idioma=english.

Haarstard, H. and V. Andersson (2009), 'Backlash reconsidered: neoliberalism
and popular mobilization in Bolivia', *Latin American Politics and Society*, 51
(4), 1–28.

International Monetary Fund (n.d.), *Balance of Payments Statistics*, retrieved from
www.imf.org.

Kaup, B. (2010), 'A neoliberal nationalization? The constraints on natural-gas-led
development in Bolivia', *Latin American Perspectives*, 37 (3), 123–138.

Kennemore, A. and G. Weeks (2011), 'Twenty-first century socialism? The elusive
search for a post-neoliberal development model in Bolivia and Ecuador', *Bulletin
of Latin American Research*, retrieved on March 3, 2016 from https://clas-pages.
uncc.edu/gregory-weeks/files/2012/04/Kennemore-and-Weeks2.pdf.

Klein, Herbert (2011), *A Concise History of Bolivia*, Cambridge: Cambridge
University Press.

Kohl, B. (2010), 'Bolivia under Morales: a work in progress', *Latin American
Perspectives*, 37 (3), 107–122.

Leiva, Fernando I. (2008), *Latin American Neostructuralism: The Contradictions of
Post-Neoliberal Development*, Minneapolis, MN: University of Minnesota Press.

Morales, J. (1992), 'Cambios y consejos neoliberals en Bolivia', *Nueva Sociedad*,
121 (September–October), 134–143.

Petras, J. (2013), 'The most radical conservative regime: Bolivia under Evo
Morales', *Global Research*, retrieved on March 3, 2016 from www.globalresearch.
ca/the-most-radical-conservative-regime-bolivia-under-evo-morales/5363248.

Petras, James and Henry Veltmeyer (2009), *What's Left in Latin America? Regime
Change in New Times*, Burlington, VT: Ashgate Publishing.

Siotos, M. (2009), 'Social movements and development in Bolivia', *Hydra Inter-
disciplinary Journal of Social Sciences*, 1 (1), 51–60.

Webber, Jeffery R. (2011a), *From Rebellion to Reform in Bolivia: Class Struggle,
Indigenous Liberation and the Politics of Evo Morales*, Chicago, IL: Haymarket
Books.

Webber, J. (2011b), 'Red October: left-indigenous struggles in modern Bolivia',
Historical Materialism Book Series, 29, Boston, MA: Brill.

Weisbrot, M., R. Ray and J. Johnston (2009a), 'Bolivia: the economy during the
Morales administration', CEPR, retrieved on March 3, 2016 from www.cepr.net/
documents/publications/bolivia-2009-12.pdf.

Weisbrot, M., R. Ray, J. Johnston, J.A. Cordero and J.A. Montecino (2009b),
'IMF-supported macroeconomic policies and the world recession: a look at
forty-one borrowing countries.' CEPR, retrieved on March 3, 2016 from www.
cepr.net/documents/publications/imf-2009-10.pdf.

World Bank (2015), *World Development Indicators*, retrieved on March 3, 2016
from http://data.worldbank.org/data-catalog/world-development-indicators.

6. The Brazilian economy after the 2008 global financial crisis: the end of the macroeconomic tripod's golden age[1]

Marcos Reis, Andre de Melo Modenesi and Rui Lyrio Modenesi

6.1 INTRODUCTION

In 1994, Brazil implemented an economic program called the Real Plan in order to rein very high levels of inflation. As in the case of many other anti-inflationary programs in developing countries at that time, the program was based on an exchange rate anchor. After the abandonment of the exchange rate anchor, in 1999, Brazil adopted a new economic policy based on what has become known as the macroeconomic tripod. The tripod consisted of inflation targeting (IT, hereafter), a floating exchange rate and primary budget surplus targeting. It prioritized the fight against inflation by essentially resorting to a single tool: the basic interest rate (known as the Selic rate). Indeed, during the tripod's golden age, inflation control was the primary objective. Thus, monetary policy was dominant over fiscal and exchange rate policy, which played secondary roles.

After the subprime crisis in 2008, Brazil's economic policy began changing. This was toward the end of President Luis Ignacio 'Lula' da Silva's second term (2007 to 2010). The shift was strengthened under President Dilma Rousseff (2011 to 2014).

A considerable number of changes were implemented to add new elements to the existing economic policy framework. Eventually, the policy framework became more flexible through the extension of its instruments, especially the incorporation of countercyclical measures and the adoption of economic and social goals other than controlling inflation. For this reason, what was originally an almost exclusively anti-inflationary policy evolved into a more flexible economic policy endowed with a wide set of instruments and aiming at other economic and social goals in addition to inflation control.

This chapter focuses primarily on the post-2008 developments and the economic policy framework's evolution since the 2011 euro crisis. The main findings of this chapter are as follows.[2] First, considering the main contagion channels, the Brazilian economy was affected by both (the subprime and euro) crises mainly through the credit, financial, trade and exchange rate channels in a sudden and intense but transient way. Second, fiscal policy began to be used as countercyclical compensation for the impacts of the crises on economic activity and employment. Third, financial stability became an explicit concern of the government, while the Brazilian Central Bank (BCB) provided liquidity to the banking system and the state owned banks avoided a credit crunch in the aftermath of the 2008 crisis. Fourth, the government continued its demand-led policy that increased the minimum wage. The legal minimum wage doubled in real terms from 2008 to 2014, a historical record, with positive effects on income distribution and aggregate demand. Fifth, foreign exchange rate policy, combined with capital controls, helped to avoid persistent appreciation of the Brazilian real that could have followed a massive inflow of short term speculative capital. Finally, inflation control became more flexible; the interest rate was lowered significantly and fiscal and other non-monetary tools aimed at price stabilization were adopted. In general, what we have seen during this period is an easing of the tripod's dictates.

This chapter is structured as follows. After this introduction, Section 6.2 offers an overview of the Brazilian economic policy prior to the onset of the subprime crisis. Section 6.3 explains how the transmission channels operated during the crisis and how the country was affected by both the subprime and eurozone crises. In Section 6.4, the economic policy responses to the crises are described in detail, focusing on the fiscal, monetary, exchange rate and capital control policies. Section 6.5 provides a short discussion regarding Brazil's new resilience to crisis. Finally, Section 6.6 offers concluding remarks.

6.2 MACROECONOMIC DEVELOPMENTS IN THE BRAZILIAN ECONOMY PRIOR TO THE SUBPRIME CRISIS

Before analyzing the effects of the 2008 subprime crisis, we present a brief overview of recent Brazilian economic policy and its macroeconomic results. The starting point is the implementation of the Real Plan of 1994. The results of the Real Plan are summarized, after which the implementation of the macroeconomic tripod, whose 'golden age' spanned from 1999 to 2008, is discussed.

6.2.1 Historical Background: From the Real Plan to the Macroeconomic Tripod – 1995 to 1998

After a period of rapid economic growth between 1945 and 1979, the Brazilian economy (and nearly all the other Latin American economies) stagnated during the 1980s and the beginning of the 1990s.[3] Real GDP per capita growth was near zero during this period and inflation was extremely high (reaching 2.477 percent in 1993, according to the Brazilian Central Bank). Despite several attempts to reduce its chronically high inflation, Brazil's growth continued at a slow pace and inflation persisted after the 1980s.

In this context, the theory of inertial inflation gained strength in the national debate.[4] In fact, the inertial component predominated in determining inflation dynamics, and price stability required the deindexation of the economy as a consequence. With the improvement of international liquidity conditions in the beginning of the 1990s and as a result of the foreign debt renegotiation through the Brady Plan the government was able to implement the Real Plan in mid-1994. The Real Plan was a price stabilization strategy based on the adoption of a new monetary standard and the implementation of an exchange rate anchor (Modenesi, 2005, Chapter 5).

The plan was highly successful in controlling inflation, as measured by the Consumer Price Index or CPI (in Portuguese, Índice de Preços ao Consumidor Amplo – IPCA).[5] The CPI fell sharply after the launch of the Real Plan, reaching levels that had not been observed for decades in the Brazilian economy. The plan was adopted in three stages: (1) short term fiscal adjustment due to a reverse Tanzi effect – a negative relationship between the (real) fiscal deficit and the CPI (Bacha, 1994); (2) monetary reform with the introduction of a new currency, the Brazilian real; and (3) the adoption of a pegged exchange rate system operating as a nominal anchor for inflation.

Monetary policy was conducted with the goal of managing the volume of international reserves. The high financing needs of the balance of payments (between 1995 and 1998 the accumulated current account deficit was $110 billion) coupled with the fragility of the newly found price stability were frequently cited as major reasons for the excessive monetary rigidity. Brazil has had one of the highest interest rates in the world in the same period, reaching a peak of 22 percent in March 1995. Moreover, the loose fiscal policy of President Cardoso's first term (1995 to 1998) and the generation of primary deficits have also been cited as causes of the rigidity in monetary policy. Accordingly, the real basic interest rate (Selic rate) approached 30 percent annually in 1998. From 1995 to 1998, the real Selic rate average surpassed 22 percent annually.

The Real Plan was successful in putting an end to historically chronically high inflation. It is notable that inflation was brought under control and never returned to the levels observed in previous years although it has remained relatively high by international standards.

However, the achievement of price stability came at a high cost insofar as it resulted in anemic economic performance and a drastic increase in the public debt. GDP grew at an average rate of approximately 3 percent, and the public net debt/GDP ratio increased by 40 percent between 1994 and 1999. The stabilization strategy generated other undesirable outcomes, such as an intensification of short term GDP fluctuations (or a pattern of stop and go), a sharp deterioration in the balance of payments (the current account deficit reached 4.3 percent of GDP in 1998), the adoption of an excessively tight monetary policy (or the maintenance of the Selic rate at high levels), an increase in unemployment which reached more than 9 percent in 1998 (according to the BCB statistics) and fiscal imbalance.

6.2.2   The Macroeconomic Tripod's Golden Age: 1999 to 2008

In 1998 to 1999, the Brazilian economy suffered a speculative attack that resulted in the abandonment of the pegged exchange rate system. Accordingly, a new economic policy framework grounded in the macroeconomic tripod was adopted, which consisted of: (1) an inflation targeting regime, (2) a floating exchange rate that was coupled with high capital mobility, and (3) primary budget surplus targeting.[6]

Monetary policy assumed primacy. The economic policy targeted price stability, which became the sole object of monetary policy (by means of a single instrument, the Selic rate). By contrast, fiscal policy was assigned a supporting role that was limited to not creating inflationary pressures. The macroeconomic tripod was asymmetric; inflation targeting influenced and restricted both the fiscal and the exchange rate policies.

The high interest rates attracted foreign investment in pursuit of arbitrage gains and contributed to an overvaluation of the Brazilian real. In turn, the overvaluation facilitated inflation control. The exchange rate became a key monetary policy transmission channel (Arestis et al., 2011; Modenesi and Araújo, 2013).

Roughly speaking, fiscal targets were achieved by cutting government expenditures, particularly investments. If any conflicts arose between inflation control and other macroeconomic goals, they were resolved in pursuit of price stability. Despite the fears of many, the exchange rate (BR$/US$) overshooting (following the abandonment of the pegged exchange rate system, the Brazilian real faced a huge devaluation) did not result in the return of high inflation, and price stability was eventually preserved.

With the consolidation of price stability, the Selic rate was expected to be reduced significantly. Indeed, after abandoning the pegged exchange rate, improvements in external accounts and the adoption of a tight fiscal policy (with a primary surplus of approximately 3.5 percent of GDP) were expected to decrease the Selic rate. However, these measures were not sufficient to cause a substantial decline in the Selic rate.

In 1999 to 2008, the average real Selic rate was higher than 10 percent per year, reaching 16 percent in 1999. The real Selic rate fell in a non-negligible manner, particularly after 2000. However, it remains high. For instance, from 1995 to 2008, the basic interest rate in Brazil remained always above the Latin America's average. Although the country was subject to a very high interest rate, inflation remained at relatively high levels. Between 1995 and 2008, inflation remained below 5 percent annually on only three occasions (in 1998, 2006 and 2007), resulting in an annual average rate of 8 percent for that period.

It is important to note that, according to the IMF, a strong reduction in inflation rates occurred in most Latin American countries between 1980 and 2008. In 1980, inflation was generally higher than 10 percent in Latin America. By 2000, inflation retreated to rates below 10 percent annually. For approximately half of Latin America inflation had retreated to less than 5 percent annually over the same period.

In short, since the Real Plan, monetary policy in Brazil has been marked by an excess of rigidity, which persisted even after the consolidation of price stability and the implementation of inflation targeting. In this sense, Brazilian monetary policy remains an anomaly when compared with its counterparts in the international arena.[7]

The tripod years were characterized by low growth, chronically high interest rates, high inflation (relative to other developing countries) and an overvalued currency. After 2003, GDP growth started to pick up, but was halted by the 2008 crisis, with the country suffering a recession in 2009 and an impressive recovery in the following year (Figure 6.1). With the cumulative effects of the 2008 and 2011 crises, the rate of growth became sluggish, but economic depression was prevented by the countercyclical measures addressing the impacts of the crises.

The formal labor market has improved in the last decade. Even during the economic slowdown after 2010 unemployment continued to decline. From 2003 to 2013, unemployment dropped from 12.9 percent to 4.3 percent. It is noteworthy that even after the economic crises experienced in the period, unemployment kept going down, revealing a resilience in the labor market despite the comparatively poor performance of GDP.

Unlike many countries that have experienced an increase in economic

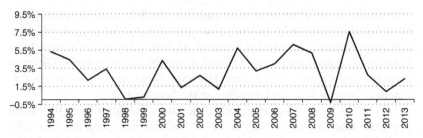

Source: Ministry of Finance of Brazil.

Figure 6.1   Real GDP growth (%) (1994–2013)

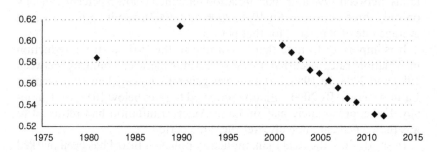

Source: Ministry of Finance of Brazil.

Figure 6.2   Gini index (1981–2012)

inequality in the last decade, Brazil has been reducing economic inequality. Figure 6.2 shows improvements in the Gini index from 1990 levels. We can divide this figure into two stages: (1) the first phase, characterized by controlled inflation since 1994. In this period the poor were adversely affected because they did not have access to sophisticated financial products with which to protect themselves from inflation, (2) a second phase, characterized by a much faster reduction of the index from the beginning of the Labor Party government of Luis Ignacio 'Lula' da Silva in 2003. The policies in this period were pro-poor and included policies such as a minimum wage increase, reduced unemployment, and income transfers through social programs (like the Bolsa Familia).[8]

Our review of the period shows that by 2008 Brazil's macroeconomic management had achieved the following: 1) low unemployment and lower income inequality, which contributed to growth supported by domestic demand; and 2) controlled inflation (despite the high cost of doing so).

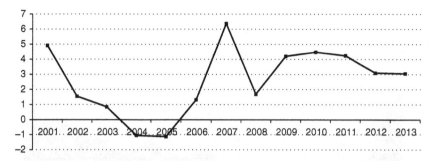

Source: International Financial Statistics, IMF.

Figure 6.3   Net financial flows (% of GDP)

6.3   THE IMPACT OF SUBPRIME AND EURO CRISES IN BRAZIL

To analyze the impacts of both global crises on the macroeconomic performance of the Brazilian economy, we focus on three transmission channels: financial, credit and trade channels. At the beginning of the subprime crisis, the Brazilian economy suffered capital flight through foreign loans and portfolio investments. In fact, there was an abrupt and enormous reversal in capital flows to Brazil; the outflow amounted to US$22 billion in the last quarter of 2008 alone.

The Net Financial Flows (NFF) before and after the beginning of the subprime crisis give a good insight/picture of what occurred. The NFF shows net acquisition and disposal of financial assets and liabilities. It measures how net lending to or borrowing from nonresidents is financed. A negative sign indicates an increase in Brazil residents' claims on nonresidents. Figure 6.3 shows the Net Financial Account of Brazil in the 2001–13 period. The impact of the crisis is clear. In 2007, the NFF experiences its peak in the sample, reaching 6.4 percent of GDP. The impact in 2008 is very strong, lowering the indicator from the previous peak to 1.7 percent. The recovery, however, was quick. During 2009–11 the economy experienced a positive inflow above 4 percent of GDP. In the following years, there is a slight decline but it remains positive and above 3 percent until 2013.

Turning now to the composition of financial flows to the Brazilian economy during this period, Figure 6.4 shows the trajectory of the three components of the net flows: portfolio equity, foreign direct investment (FDI) and other flows. Portfolio equity includes net inflows from equity

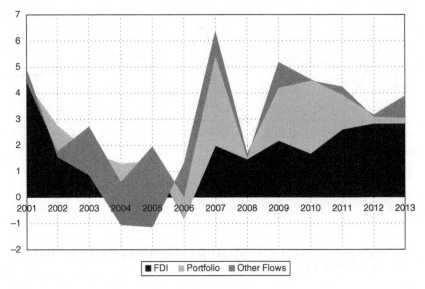

Source: International financial statistics, IMF.

Figure 6.4 Composition of financial flows to Brazilian economy (% GDP)

securities other than those recorded as direct investment.[9] FDI represents the net inflows of investment to acquire a lasting management interest (10 percent or more of voting stock) in an enterprise operating in an economy other than that of the investor and the remaining are included as 'other flows'.

Portfolio equity inflows suffered a sudden halt in 2008. They subsequently demonstrated an impressive recovery in 2009 and 2010. However, after 2011 their share had been heading downward. Thus, in 2012 and 2013 portfolio equity represented only a very small share of the total financial flows. On the other hand, FDI keeps its upward trajectory after 2007 and despite slight declines in 2008 and 2010 keeps consistently increasing its participation in the total flows. Lastly, 'other flows' also became negative after 2008, presenting a negative result (around 0.8 percent) in every year, except 2011 when a modest 0.3 percent positive result was observed.

Summing up, as a result of the contraction of the international market in the immediate aftermath of the 2008 subprime crisis, there was a sudden halt in capital flows to Brazil. The share of FDI in total flows increased considerably after 2009 and reached almost 3 percent of GDP in 2012 to 2013. Generally, financial flows recovered very quickly after 2009.

One should note the share of FDI (to total capital flows) has drastically increased, making for an improvement in the quality of financial flows to Brazil.

The deterioration of the financial markets in developed countries resulted in a sudden end to the inflow of external credit. The willingness to lend decreased so severely that even firms with strong balance sheets struggled to obtain foreign credit. Consequently, some of the most important domestic agents, including banks and firms that were main Brazilian export firms, had their liquidity tightened (De Paula et al., 2015).

As a result of the scenario described above, the domestic market for credit was inevitably turned into a link in the chain of transmission of the 2008 crisis. The recovery of the Brazilian economy from the financial impact of the subprime crisis is a notable achievement when compared with the performance of other affected economies. In fact, the negative effects of the crisis via the financial channels began to be reversed in a relatively short period of time in Brazil.

A good indicator of this rapid recovery was the annual growth rate of total domestic credit, which plunged from a peak of 34.5 percent in September 2008 to 15 percent in November 2009 and then began a sustained recovery in the middle of 2010 (BCB data). External lines of credit were also reestablished progressively in a relatively short period of time, which was mostly explained by the aggressive intervention of the BCB that began immediately after the subprime crisis. Between October 2008 and January 2009, the BCB acted as the lender of last resort and used both conventional and unconventional tools to enhance liquidity, enabling it to avoid a credit crunch with the decisive help of the public banks (see details in subsection 6.4.2).

With regard to trade it is to be noted that Brazilian exports are highly concentrated in commodities (nearly half of Brazilian exports in 2012 were commodities), which suggests that the economy is highly vulnerable to changes in commodity prices. This is an important threat to the Brazilian economy due to the high volatility of commodity prices.

In analyzing the impact of the crisis through the trade channel, we examine two indicators: total exports and the price of exports. Figure 6.5 shows the total exports on a monthly basis (with seasonally adjusted data) and the growth rate of exports for the 2008 to 2013 period. The 2008 crisis had a significant impact, decreasing exports from US$18.7 billion in July 2008 to US$10 billion in May 2009. However, in 2010 the exports started to increase and, at the beginning of 2011, the amount was already greater than in the previous peak (July 2008). Exports were dramatically affected by the subprime crisis, but the recovery was fast: exports reached a peak of more than US$24 billion (mid-2011). Following the euro crisis exports

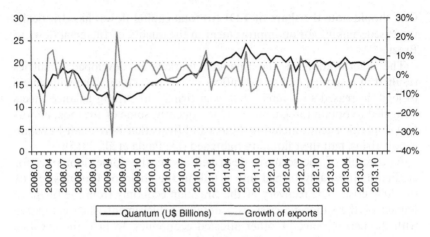

Source: Authors' elaboration with data from World Bank.

Figure 6.5   *Exports (seasonally adjusted, US billion) and exports growth rate (%)*

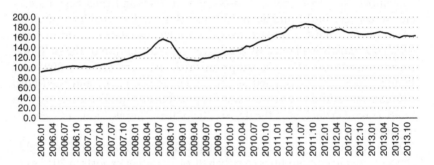

Source: World Development Indicators, World Bank.

Figure 6.6   *Export price index (2006=100) (2006–13)*

fell again, reaching a low of US$18.03 billion in mid-2012. After that, it remained relatively stable fluctuating around US$20 billion, and the exports growth rate fluctuated around zero.

The impressive recovery following the subprime crisis occurred due to a fast increase in the price of exports. The data from Figure 6.6 suggest that the variation in the export value is mostly explained by the variation in prices. The trajectory of the export price index is very similar to the result of the total exports. There is a peak in mid-2008 and at the beginning of the recovery at the end of 2009. By the end of 2010, export prices

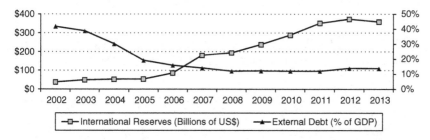

Source: Central Bank of Brazil.

Figure 6.7   External vulnerability indicators (2002–13)

surpassed the previous peak. Following the euro crisis, they have shown a slight downward tendency.

During 2002–13, the current account balance was positive during the period 2003–7. Although, even in its peak, in 2004, remained below a 2 percent surplus result. After 2007, it deteriorated sharply, maintaining its downward tendency and reaching its lowest result in the last year of the sample, 2013, when a negative 3.62 percent was observed.

A key change during the period is that Brazil has progressively accumulated foreign reserves. Between 2005 and 2013, regardless of both the subprime and the euro crises, the accumulation continued unabated. Figure 6.7 shows that the indicators for external vulnerability, represented by net external debt and international reserves, are currently low, particularly compared with former periods in which the country faced an external crisis.

The channel that most immediately reflected the impact of both crises in Brazil is the exchange rate (see Figure 6.14). There are three discernible periods: (1) the 57 percent sharp devaluation in the aftermath of the subprime crisis, from September to December 2008; (2) the recovery in the Brazilian real against the USD from January 2009 until July 2011, when the exchange rate decreased from 2.46 to 1.53 (an appreciation in domestic currency); and (3) a constant devaluation from August 2011 until the end of 2013.

Generally speaking, the transmission of the euro crisis via the credit and exchange markets can be said to have been sudden and intense but transient, mainly because the Brazilian economy became more resilient to crisis. It is notable that all of these developments are due in large part to the important economic policy changes initiated soon after the subprime crisis that were subsequently deepened, particularly after the euro crisis.

As a result, the overall impact of the subprime and euro crises on the macroeconomic performance of the Brazilian economy was relatively

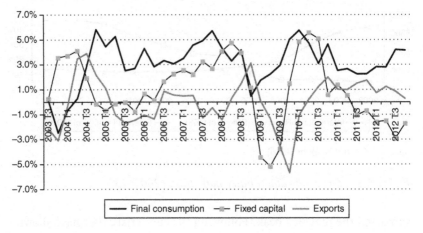

Source: IBGE.

Figure 6.8   Contribution to GDP growth (%) (2003–12)

limited. In fact, inflation did not spin out of control and the economy did not plunge into recession. Thus, Brazil's economy did not suffer the expected results of such crises as in the 1980s and 1990s.

According to De Paula et al. (2015), the GDP growth rate trajectory after the crisis can be divided into two periods: (1) in 2010, a fast recovery from the small recession experienced in 2009 with a significant increase in exports and final consumption; and (2) sluggish but positive growth characterized by strong final consumption in the years since 2010. Fixed capital and exports in particular exhibited downward trajectories (Figure 6.8).

Employment performance has been impressive and should be emphasized. An unlikely historically low unemployment rate was achieved in 2013. The flexibilization of the tripod, the active role played by the state in addressing the impact of the crises, anticyclical measures and payroll exemptions benefiting 45 economic sectors have all contributed to robust employment performance.[10] The labor market performance is the most positive macroeconomic achievement of the Brazilian economy over the last decade.

The public sector also demonstrated satisfactory performance; the primary surplus was maintained above 2 percent during 2008 to 2013, and net government debt has consistently decreased since 2006, reaching a low of 35 percent in 2012 (a detailed analysis follows in subsection 6.4.2).

In summary, the relevant transmission channels of the subprime crisis to Brazil's economy were the exchange rate, credit channels and exports, although the last one was negatively affected but presented a fast recovery.

The impact, although sudden and dramatic, was transient because the domestic economy had become more resilient to crisis as a result of important economic policy measures. There was no significant recession and no long employment plunge; inflation did not spin out of control and public accounts did not deteriorate significantly. In brief, Brazil did not experience these last two crises in the same way as it had the ones in the 1980s and 1990s.

There is no doubt that the global factors also played a very important role. The quick recovery of commodity prices, for instance, was led mainly by the aggressive countercyclical policy measures that China applied in 2009–10 which impacted the demand (and future demand) for natural resources. In addition, the massive global liquidity generated by the Quantitative Easing (QE) policies in advanced economies such as the USA, UK, eurozone and Japan created a huge capital availability on a global scale and the flowing of capital for emerging economies, such as Brazil, helped the countries to not face a hard Balance of Payment Constraint. Hence, both domestic and external factors helped the Brazilian economy to present good economic indicators from 2009 to 2013.

6.4 BRAZILIAN RESPONSE TO THE SUBPRIME AND EURO CRISES: MORE FLEXIBILITY IN IMPLEMENTATION OF MACROECONOMIC TRIPOD

The tripod was rigidly maintained in Lula's first term (2003 to 2006), and inflation and budget targets were pursued rigorously. In the absence of capital controls, the exchange rate served as the main anchor for inflation. By the end of the second Lula administration (2007 to 2010), a parsimonious flexibilization began with the reintroduction of countercyclical fiscal policy and some capital control measures. We will present the responses in two groups: (1) fiscal response, and (2) monetary, exchange rate and capital control measures.

6.4.1 Fiscal Response

After adopting the macroeconomic tripod in 1999, fiscal policy in Brazil was based on accruing a high primary surplus as a method to put public debt on a long term sustainable trajectory. Due to the size of the debt, and particularly the interest paid on the debt, there was no nominal surplus target.

With a better fiscal situation resulting from increased revenues due to the economic growth of previous years (2004 to 2007), the scope for countercyclical measures increased significantly, and the Ministry of Finance (MF) began to play a more important role in the inflation control strategy (for more details, see subsection 6.4.2). The largest activist fiscal policy was put in place in 2009 and has remained in place even after the acute phase of the crisis was over.

According to Barbosa (2010), the delay in monetary policy to stimulate economic growth immediately after the 2008 crash had to be compensated by fiscal policy. To mitigate the impact of the crisis, the government launched a stimulus package amounting to US$20.4 billion, which was equivalent to 1.2 percent of Brazil's GDP in 2009. This package aimed to boost aggregate demand and mitigate the negative impact of the crisis on the labor market and economic activity through three major channels: additional government spending, tax cuts and subsidies (Cunha et al., 2011), as detailed below.

Additional government spending
The increase in public spending covered four governmental initiatives: (1) an expansion of the Plano de Aceleração do Crescimento, that is, the Growth Acceleration Program (PAC); (2) the initiation of a program of government incentives and subsidies for housing construction, called Minha Casa, Minha Vida (that is, My Home, My Life), which was targeted at low and middle income households; (3) budget transfers to municipalities; and (4) an extension of unemployment insurance benefits.

Tax cuts
In December 2008, the government cut the Tax on Industrialized Products (IPI) for automobiles, motorcycles and trucks.[11] In 2009, the same rationale was extended to household appliances (so called white goods, for example, refrigerators, stoves and washing machines had their IPI cut by 10 percent on average), capital goods and inputs to civil construction. Tax cuts were also implemented for certain food items. As indicated by Barbosa (2010), the cost of all such temporary initiatives was below 0.5 percent of the 2009 GDP.

Subsidies
Lastly, the subsidies encompassed two elements. First, the government capitalized the Brazilian Development Bank (Banco Nacional de Desenvolvimento Economico, BNDES) with $40 billion to ensure resources for private and public investments. The policy of injection into the BNDES was maintained in 2010 with a further injection of $80 billion. In subsequent years, these injections continued in decreasing amounts.

Table 6.1   Fiscal responses to the crisis

Name of the program	Description
Plano de Aceleração do Crescimento (PAC)	The PAC was originally launched in 2007 and consisted of a set of economic policies and investment projects designed to accelerate economic growth in Brazil. When the crisis began, the government raised the original budget. In the end, the program had a budget of $200 billion for the 2007–10 quadrennium. In 2011, Roussef's government launched the so called PAC2, which had a budget of $600 billion to be spent during her four-year mandate.
Minha Casa, Minha Vida	The first stage of the program aimed to build 1 million new homes in 2009–10 for low- and middle-income families, with a maximum income equivalent to ten times the minimum wage. The initial budget was $6 billion for the first two years. The program was continued in Roussef's administration, and its budget was increased. At the end of 2013, the total amount spent in the program since its inception was approximately $130 billion.
Transfers to municipalities	Extraordinary budgetary transfers to local governments in 2009, which were equivalent to US$1.1 billion.
Extension of unemployment insurance	Extended the duration of unemployment insurance benefits by two months for workers whose sectors of the economy were more affected by the recession.

Source: Authors' elaboration based on official sources.

The subsidy is the difference between the interest rate that the National Treasury uses and the rate of the loans granted by the BNDES. Cunha et al. (2011) observed that these extra resources from the MF allowed the BNDES to increase its credit by 85 percent in 2009. The second element consisted of subsidies aimed at aiding the agricultural sector by reducing the cost of loans.

Even after the most critical periods of the international crises had passed, the government launched other countercyclical fiscal policies in 2013 to reactivate economic growth. The two biggest measures were: (1) payroll tax exemptions, which covered 45 sectors and had an estimated

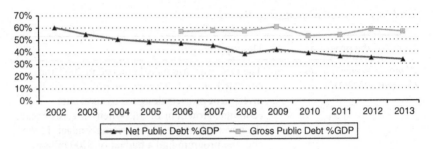

Source: Ministry of Finance of Brazil.

Figure 6.9   Gross and net government debt (% GDP) (2002–13)

$25 billion exemption for the first four years, and (2) a review of energy contracts, with an average reduction of 16.2 percent in the price of electricity for residential customers and 28 percent for the industrial sector.

What was the impact of these measures on government debt and the primary surplus? Figure 6.9 shows the trajectory of the liquid and gross government debt between 2002 and 2013. Gross government debt has remained nearly constant. Net government debt is exhibiting a clear downward trend. The difference between its maximum in 2002 (60.4 percent) and minimum in 2013 (33.62 percent) is significant. It is notable that, even after the crisis, this indicator continues on a downward trend, despite one year of growth in 2009.

There are two primary reasons for different trends of gross and net debt in Brazil: (1) subsidized loans to the BNDES and state enterprises, and (2) the issuance of bonds to acquire reserves and regulate the economy's liquidity. These operations expanded the gross debt but not the net debt.[12] The latter remained stable because the government was also increasing its assets with shares of the BNDES and companies alongside the accumulation of foreign reserves (Gentil and Araujo, 2012).

The net debt of the public sector has shown a constant declining trajectory. However, the economic literature frequently advises caution in examining the rate of net debt fluctuation due to two problems. The first problem is the possibility of not being fully paid on its assets. For instance, if the government holds a foreign sovereign debt and the issuing country default on its bonds. The second problem is the difference in the rate of remuneration on assets and liabilities. The interest rate paid on Brazil's debt is higher than the interest rate received on some of its assets as, for instance, the US Treasuries. This also happens domestically: the Brazilian Treasury transfers (lending or capitalization) to the BNDES are made with an interest rate mismatch because the bank lends at a rate lower than the

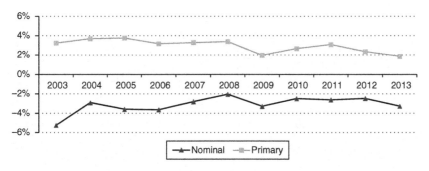

Source: Ministry of Finance of Brazil.

Figure 6.10   *Public sector primary and nominal balance (%) (2003–13)*

rate the Treasury pays to finance itself, resulting in a subsidy in BNDES transactions.

As explained above, the fiscal result is one of the targets of the macro-economic tripod. The government must pledge a primary surplus target and pursue it from the beginning of the year. Given the difficulty of pre-dicting the evolution of the economy in a given year, when the end of the year approaches and projections are not being fulfilled, the government resorts to accounting tricks to be able to deliver the results it promised. The government acted in this manner in 2011 and 2012, thereby opening itself up to various critics. The best solution would have been the use of a primary surplus target and commitment to the stability of public finances in the long term, a decision that would have allowed the government to pursue a countercyclical policy and establish a well-defined strategy of fiscal responsibility (De Paula et al., 2015).

Figure 6.10 shows that the primary surplus decreased slightly after the crisis but has remained positive and above 2 percent. Also, the nominal result remained between −3.28 percent and −2.47 percent, almost the same range that showed in the period before the subprime crisis, 2004–8. Hence, even with the decrease in the primary surplus, the nominal deficit did not increase. This result is explained by two primary causes: (1) the decrease in the basic interest rate (Selic), and (2) the positive effect of the countercycli-cal fiscal expenditure on the economy and consequently on tax revenue.

6.4.2   Monetary, Exchange Rate and Capital Control Policies

Immediately after the crisis, the Brazilian Central Bank and the Ministry of Finance were pulling in opposite directions. The BCB made the inflation

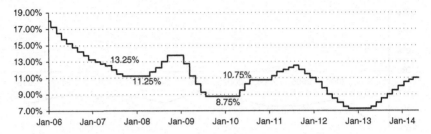

Source: Central Bank of Brazil.

Figure 6.11   Brazilian basic interest rate (%) (2006–14)

targeting regime even more rigid and there was tension and dysfunction among the central bodies responsible for economic policy. The end result was fiscal expansion with monetary tightening. While the MF was stimulating the economy, the BCB was raising interest rates. Figure 6.11 shows that even after the beginning of the subprime crisis the BCB raised the Selic (until the end of 2009) to avoid possible inflationary problems due to the devaluation of the Brazilian real in the aftermath of the crisis.

In 2011, however, the BCB began to act in a less conservative manner. The BCB anticipated and rightly utilized a window of opportunity to impose a less gradual reduction of the Selic rate. Thus, in the first years of Rousseff's government, the BCB distanced itself, albeit in a limited manner, from the overly conservative standard that had previously characterized the institution (Modenesi et al., 2013). A notorious example of this conservatism took place in late 2008. Despite the worsening of the subprime crisis (in late 2008) and in the face of clear signs of economic slowdown, the BCB maintained a tight monetary policy. In addition to favoring a more dramatic decrease in economic activity, a good opportunity to reduce the Selic rate was missed.

This new attitude was demonstrated at the Monetary Policy Committee meeting in August 2011 when, in a rather unexpected move that generated heavy losses for most financial market professionals, the committee decided to cut the interest rate. In this manner, the BCB directly bucked the consensus of the market (anticipating the expected value of the interest rate that was implied in the three months ahead SWAP-DI futures contracts). This decision was based on a more benign inflation outlook that was characterized by: (1) the threat of an intensification of the European crisis and the consequent maintenance of international interest rates at historically low levels, (2) a cooling of domestic economic activity, and (3) inflation rapprochement to the center of the inflation target.

Thereafter, the MF acted jointly with the BCB by raising the primary surplus target. Dissatisfaction with the reduced interest rate added to the dissatisfaction with the use of credit and macroprudential control measures, resulting in an angry reaction among market participants. As the euro crisis deepened, the government continued easing economic policy, providing continuity to the process of lowering the Selic rate, which reached a record low of 7.25 percent in October 2012.

To continue lowering the Selic rate, it was necessary to remove the Selic's virtual floor. This virtual floor had been established by the remuneration rule for the savings account, which was Brazil's most popular financial investment and annually yielded a fixed remuneration of 6.17 percent plus a variable rate (in Portuguese, taxa referencial de juros, or TR).[13] In practical terms, if the basic Selic rate fell below 8.5 percent per year, the yield of the savings accounts would be higher than the remuneration of the public bonds and, consequently, the National Treasury would find it difficult to sell Treasury Bills. Therefore, a new rule was adopted that fixed the remuneration of the savings accounts at 70 percent of the Selic rate (plus the TR) when the Selic fell below 8.5 percent per year. Although this change was technical, it was not politically trivial; on the contrary, without this adjustment the government's entire economic policy could have been jeopardized. It eliminated the historical floor and enabled the BCB to continue to lower the Selic rate.[14]

As noted by De Paula et al. (2015), the BCB was engaged in significant liquidity enhancing measures for the banking system between October 2008 and January 2009, including: (1) additional insurance deposits for small and medium sized banks, (2) a reduction in reserve requirements that resulted in an expansion of liquidity in money markets of approximately 3.3 percent of the GDP (Barbosa, 2010),[15] and (3) the creation of incentives for larger financial institutions to purchase the loan portfolios of small and medium sized banks.

The BCB was successful in acting as the lender of last resort using both conventional and unconventional tools.[16] However, even with aggressive intervention, which served to prevent a credit crunch, there was still a sharp contraction in private sector lending. The total domestic credit growth rate reached a peak of 34.5 percent annually in September 2008 and fell sharply during the next 14 months, reaching a low of 14.9 percent annually in November 2009. Figure 6.12 serves to illustrate the importance of state owned banks in ameliorating the private sector credit crunch. The contraction of private sector credit was countered by credit expansion by the state owned banks.

In December 2010, the BCB made two policy changes aimed at cooling aggregate demand and inflationary pressures that were again building

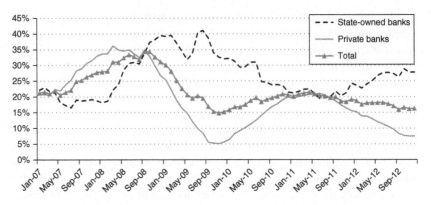

Source: Central Bank of Brazil.

Figure 6.12 Total credit growth rate (%) by bank ownership (12 months)

up. First, it introduced liquidity measures aimed at making lending more expensive. Specifically, the BCB sought to increase bank reserve requirements. Second, macroprudential measures aimed at restricting credit growth were introduced.

The first sought to raise the reserve requirements.[17] When analyzing the BCB's monetary and exchange rate response to the crisis, it is imperative to first note that decreasing the interest rate was the most remarkable event. Notably, from the end of 2012, it was important to advance a strategy of price stabilization, which required a change both in the diagnosis of and the strategy to combat inflation.

The BCB began to recognize that cyclical demand pressures are only one of the components of inflation and that it was not the BCB's exclusive responsibility to decrease inflation. The BCB admitted the relevance of structural inflationary pressures resulting from the supply side that had to be addressed by non-monetary instruments managed by the MF. In this manner, some of the measures discussed in the previous section regarding fiscal policy were also undertaken to help the BCB control inflation.

The direct attack on cost push inflationary pressures was an unprecedented innovation in contemporary Brazilian history, particularly after the Real Plan. The most striking effort was the revision of tariffs in the electricity sector,[18] which was explicitly announced as a measure to combat inflation. Other tax cuts operated in the same manner, particularly with respect to reducing employers' contributions to the payroll to decrease the cost of labor.

The deindexation of financial assets, an anachronistic residue of the time of high inflation, was another important step taken by the MF. The share of public debt indexed to the Selic rate was significantly reduced (to less than 30 percent).[19] Concomitantly, the average maturity of public debt increased.

In short, there has been a major change in the treatment of inflation. Despite the various alarms, the commitment to price stability was not relaxed but strengthened. First, since the BCB was better prepared to achieve the inflation target due to the availability of a wider set of instruments, it did not have to rely solely on the Selic rate. Second, the MF acted in coordination with the BCB to maintain stability. The recognition that inflation in Brazil is not correlated only with the level of economic activity (or demand) is a breakthrough. The fight against the structural pressures of cost and the deindexing of financial assets (to Selic rate) facilitates the work of the BCB.

Capital control policy

First of all, it is important to note that some authors argue that the effectiveness of capital controls is a matter that is subject to ideological bias (see Modenesi and Modenesi, 2008).[20] For the Brazilian recent case, Chamon and Garcia (2013) argue that the use of capital controls was not effective in halting the appreciation of the real against the US dollar after the 2008 crisis and that the determining factor in reversing the process of currency appreciation was the cut in interest rates. However, even if one accepts the argument that capital controls were not important in mitigating the effects of exchange rate overvaluation, it must be recognized that other goals were achieved. Taxing short term flows indicated to the market that the government would intervene with respect to the exchange rate when necessary. Consequently there was less volatility in the exchange market.

A tax on financial operations (in Portuguese, Imposto sobre Operações Financeiras, or IOF) was the primary tool used to curb the immediate post-crisis appreciation of the real. The 6 percent tax on foreign capital inflow in the fixed income market (bonds), derivatives and funds, and on foreign exchange transactions is notable. At total, 22 different capital control measures were adopted in Brazil during 2009–13, with 13 tightening policies and eight loosening policies measures. After March 15, 2012, only loosen policies (7 in total) were adopted. For a complete description of the policies adopted, see Chamon and Garcia (2013).

The use of capital controls aimed to reduce the volatility and the overvaluation of the exchange rate. A massive inflow of foreign currency results in an appreciation in the real exchange rate. Thus, in general, the measures adopted aimed to discourage the inflow of short term capital, thereby reducing the volatility of capital flows and exchange rate fluctuations. Exchange rate fluctuations were mediated by capital inflow controls that helped avoid more severe overvaluation of the Brazilian real. The

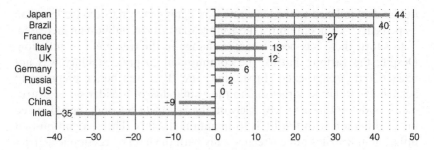

Source: Authors' elaboration based on data from World Economics.

Figure 6.13   Percentage of currency over/under valuation for March 2013

government's objective was to avoid the economy becoming more vulnerable and dependent on the international liquidity cycle.

The currency during the last decade was very volatile and most of the time overvalued. For instance, according to data from the BIS, the coefficient of variation of the real exchange rate in Brazil for the period 2004–11 was 17 percent, while the average of Latin America was 6 percent. Regarding its competitiveness, Figure 6.13 compares ten countries' currencies in March 2013 and shows that the Brazilian real was overvalued by approximately 40 percent when compared to the American dollar, trailing only the Japanese yen. Other developing countries, such as China and India, had undervalued currencies, making them more competitive. Brazil's interest rate differential in relation to the rest of the world makes the country a prime destination for speculative capital influxes that are seeking short term gains in carry trades.

As Sales and Barroso (2012: 18) note, 'The environment of high liquidity in the global markets may justify emerging markets' use of unconventional policy tools. Macroprudential measures, including capital controls, foreign exchange interventions and accumulation of international reserves, have higher payoffs in this environment.' This seems to be very much the case in Brazil.

6.5   THE CURRENT SITUATION: IS THE BRAZILIAN ECONOMY NOW MORE RESILIENT AGAINST CRISIS?

From a historical perspective, the Brazilian economy was deeply affected during various international crises over the last few decades, namely the Mexico crisis (1994 to 1995), the Asian financial crisis (1997), the Russian financial crisis (1998) and the Argentine economic crisis (2001 to 2002). However, the economy showed good resilience during the recent crisis. Despite growth slowing after 2011, the subprime and euro crises did not affect the country as deeply as former crises.

In the last decade, Brazil was considered one of the most important emerging market countries and was included in the so called BRICS (Brazil, Russia, India, China and South Africa). Currently, Brazil also belongs to a less desirable group called the Fragile Five (Turkey, Brazil, India, Indonesia and South Africa). According to some international analysis, these countries are considered particularly vulnerable to an exodus of foreign capital as the prospect of higher interest rates diverts funds back to the US in search of higher returns. This is an example of how emerging markets are very volatile and, especially, how the perceptions about them can change very fast under the eyes of the financial market. This oscillation poses a threat for the long term development strategies since it makes it more difficult for the countries to make medium and long term plans due to their dependency on external factors and (financial) markets humors.

For instance, many emerging markets suffered the effects of the Federal Reserve's tapering in the beginning of 2014,[21] including Argentina, Turkey, South Africa and Russia.[22] As a prime candidate for contagion, Brazil has been steadily increasing interest rates to combat inflation and a weakening real. This change in the external scenario posed a big challenge for the Brazilian economy since the economic policies implemented to curb the crisis were made in a favorable (after mid-2009 at least) external scenario. A change in this positive scenario can force the government to again change its economic policy and a failure to do so can result in an economic crisis in the future.

Since mid-2011, the real has nominally depreciated 46 percent against the US dollar (Figure 6.14). In 2013 alone, the loss in value of the national currency was 12 percent. Despite the appreciation of the dollar, the current account deficit in Brazil increased from 2.1 percent of GDP in 2011 to 3.7 percent in the 12 month period ending in October 2013. The real depreciates and the external deficit increases (IBRE, 2014).

The current account deficit has increased in quarters. In the third quarter of 2013, the deficit grew to 3.6 percent of GDP, the biggest increase since the first quarter of 2002. In 2006, there was a surplus of $13 billion in Brazil's foreign accounts. This surplus gradually eroded to a deficit of $54 billion in 2012, and $81 billion in 2013. By 2012, the entry of foreign direct investment (FDI) surpassed the deficit. In 2013, however, there was only $64 billion in FDI, a reduction of $17 billion. The increase in the current account deficit in 2013 was primarily caused by the deterioration of the trade balance. There is an indication that the Balance of Payment

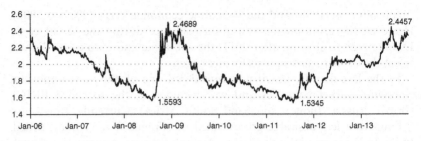

Source: Central Bank of Brazil.

Figure 6.14   Exchange rate BRL/USD (December 2006 to December 2013)

constraint to growth can impact the Brazilian economy. Developing countries running large deficit current accounts become too vulnerable to the 'humor' of international financial markets and this is a point that should be considered by the government.

Another point of fragility is the export composition. Commodities represented nearly half of Brazil's total goods exports in 2012, making the external position highly vulnerable to large swings in commodity prices.

The main difference between the recent two crises and previous ones is the amount of international reserves held by the authorities. Brazil has more foreign exchange reserves than required for external financing. Whereas Turkey's foreign reserves would last five months, Argentina's four months and South Korea's eight months, in Brazil there was a stock of reserves covering eighteen months of external financing. In this sense, a currency crisis in the short term is unlikely but the foreign reserves should not be viewed as a 'panacea' since a deep change in the international market can trigger a massive capital inflow. In this case, the reserves can be used to diminish the volatility but are unlikely to be able to stop the trend.

This huge increase in foreign assets decreased the net external debt (Figure 6.15). After the end of 2006, Brazil became a creditor in foreign currency, reversing a longstanding reputation as a significant international debtor.

This combination of lower net external debt and larger international reserves represents a significant improvement in the Brazilian external situation. Unfortunately, this development is not an indication that the country will escape external crises unscathed. Developing countries are particularly prone to external imbalances. Then, although this achievement should be celebrated, it comes at a cost and imbalance in the external sector and changes in international liquidity conditions still pose a threat to the Brazilian economy.

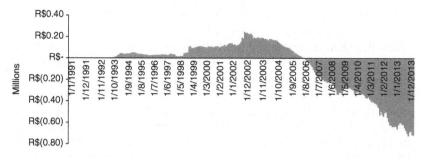

Source: Central Bank of Brazil.

Figure 6.15 Brazil's net external debt (1991–2013)

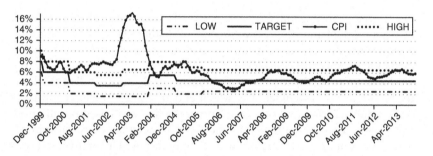

Source: Central Bank of Brazil.

Figure 6.16 Target bands and actual inflation (%) (December 1999 to December 2013)

Inflation is being held within the target, albeit consistently in the upper segment of its target range (see Figure 6.16). Going forward a continued depreciation of the real would assume a greater importance if the Fed's tapering in the US leads to an overshooting for the Brazilian real and a rapid rise in inflation. This was the situation in 2002 when the high exchange rate pass-through made Brazil a prime candidate for contagion.

Even though the economic performance in the aftermath of the crisis was not superb, with regard to its peers, Brazil performed relatively well, remaining slightly above the Latin American average. According to data from the World Bank, amongst the largest Latin American economies, Mexico and Venezuela were the worst GDP per capita performers during the 2008 to 2013 period (respectively, 0.6 percent and 0.4 percent average growth per year). Brazil's growth rate averaged 2.2 percent and remained above the region's average, 1.7 percent.

The Brazilian economy appears to be more resistant to external turbulence when compared to its performance during previous international crises, although it should also be borne in mind that international crises still pose a serious threat to Brazil. Unfortunately, Brazil may still face difficulties in the short and medium term, in particular, a slowdown in the Chinese economy (directly impacting on commodity prices and trade) and the possible increase in interest rates in developed markets might present difficult challenges for the Brazilian economy in the short term.

6.6　CONCLUSION

Due to the subprime and euro crises, Brazil's economic policy framework began a gradual and progressive process of change. This process was analyzed in this chapter, and the background of its recent historical paradigmatic phases was also considered.

The first phase, from 1999 to September 2008, can be called the macroeconomic tripod's golden age, which ended with the Lehman Brothers bankruptcy. During this period, economic policy was based on inflation, fiscal (primary surplus) targeting and flexible exchange rates. In terms of macroeconomics, performance was disappointing. Unemployment was chronically high and the period was marked by relatively high inflation despite a high basic interest rate and low GDP growth.

The period from September 2008 to the end of 2010 was the next phase. It was a period of struggle between two leading institutions; the MF and BCB had conflicting reactions to the subprime crisis. Immediately after the crisis, the MF adopted expansionary measures (indeed fiscal policy began to be used as countercyclical compensation for the impact of the crises on economic activity), whereas the BCB engaged in monetary policy tightening. However, eventually they began to act in tune, and the flexibilization of the tripod was initiated.

The third period spans from 2010 to the present. The tripod easing process was intensified. The MF played a more active role in inflation control by using non-monetary measures. Additionally, capital controls were tightened, taxes were cut (energy and food) and public commercial banks reduced their spreads, thereby increasing the supply of credit and financing.

From an analytical perspective, the process of economic policy relaxation was implemented in two complementary lines. First, economic policy was progressively better supported to achieve inflation control. Inflation control, which had been performed almost exclusively using the interest rate, was approached with a new set of tools, mainly unconventional (non-monetary) tools such as macroprudential measures and tax exemptions (for energy and food). A process of diversifying the instruments used to fight inflation was one of the main features of the period.

Complementarily, another relevant change was the relaxation of the monetary policy itself. Interest rates were kept at significantly lower levels, and this helped to support aggregate demand. This clearly was not price stabilization at any cost. As with the diversification of economic policy targets, fiscal policy was utilized to sustain demand by offering incentives for investment and stimulating consumption.

Change was also implemented at the operational level, with the MF playing a more active and collaborative role with the BCB to combat inflation. Joint measures to contain ethanol and electric energy prices were noteworthy in this regard. The MF also intervened more actively to curb the appreciation of the Brazilian real by introducing capital (inflows) controls. The BCB, in turn, adopted non-monetary (macroprudential) measures that were complementary to the interest rate movements to control credit. These measures were an attempt to diversify the MF instruments and create distance from the rigidity inherent in the exclusive use of the interest rate as prescribed by the orthodox macroeconomic tripod.

Regarding macroeconomic performance, inflation did not spin out of control and the economy is not in recession, which would ordinarily be expected after such crises. Brazil's economy performed relatively well compared with other economies. In this sense, one may affirm that the economic policy has been relatively successful until 2013. Even though the growth rates are not high, a low unemployment rate was achieved at the end of 2013. This result should be considered the most positive macroeconomic achievement of the Brazilian economy in the aftermath of the crises.[23]

Finally, it can be said that the Brazilian economy presents a more diversified set of instruments and stronger fundamentals to deal with future economic crisis than in the previous decades. However, the country is still quite dependent on the global scenario and some factors such as a decline in commodity prices and higher interest rates in developed countries can represent a threat to the country's economic performance especially in a period when the (partial) changing in the macroeconomic regime is still ongoing.

NOTES

1. We are grateful to the anonymous reviewers for their comments, helpful suggestions and for the research support of Lucas Bressan de Andrade and Matheus Vianna. The usual caveats apply.

2. The impact and responses to the crises given by the Brazilian economy were previously analyzed in other works. Among them, Barbosa (2010) highlighted the importance of three factors: (1) a comfortable level of international reserves to prevent contagion, (2) a social protection mechanism to help countercyclical policies, and (3) a 'heavy' prudential regulation, not only to prevent the crisis but also to fight its effects. De Paula et al. (2015) argued that the reaction in 2009 to 2010 was favored by a commodities boom and a low level of household indebtedness, conditions that were not present in 2011 to 2012.

3. The average real GDP per capita annual growth rate from 1945 to 1980 was 4.12 percent. In the 1980s and 1990s, it was 0.62 percent and 1.37percent respectively.

4. See, for instance, Lopes (1984) and Arida and Resende (1984).

5. The IPCA (Amplified Consumer Price Index) is measured monthly by the IBGE (Brazilian Institute of Geography and Statistics). The IPCA is considered the official inflation index of the country.

6. From a theoretical standpoint, the macroeconomic tripod is consistent with the *New Consensus on Macroeconomics*. Its theoretical core is given by the confluence of monetarism, new classical and real business cycle theory. The natural rate of unemployment (and the consequent acceptance of the neutrality of money in the long run, that is, monetary policy does not affect real variables, such as GDP and employment, sustainably) and the rational expectations hypothesis are among the two most relevant assumptions shared by this large group of economists (Blinder, 1981; 1997; Taylor, 1993; 2000; Allsopp and Vines, 2000; Romer, 2000). Accordingly, the tripod is a policy regime that radically opposes Keynes' theory, which is based on the principle of effective demand and the denial of the neutrality of money. For a critical view, see Arestis and Sawyer (2005), Lavoie (2004) and Setterfield (2004; 2005).

7. Modenesi and Modenesi (2012) list five themes that explain the 'problem of interest rates in Brazil', reduced efficacy of the monetary policy, pro-conservative convention in the monetary policy, multiple interest rate equilibria, fiscalism and jurisdictional uncertainty.

8. Despite its improvement in recent years, the Gini index in Brazil remains one of the highest in the world. The following data from the World Bank presents the Gini index in 2011 in several developing countries, including Brazil: Brazil (0.531), Nigeria (0.488), Mexico (0.470) and Argentina (0.445). Thus, there remains considerable room for improvement with respect to Brazil's income distribution. The country remains far from the OECD average (0.320) and compares poorly to other developing countries, as seen above.

9. Portfolio equity includes shares, stocks, depository receipts and direct purchases of shares in local stock markets by foreign investors.

10. One should note that the decrease of the labor force has also played a relevant role in reducing the unemployment rate.

11. The reduction of the rate of the IPI was 100 percent on cars with a maximum 1,000 cm^3 engine capacity (from 7 percent to zero) and 50 percent on cars between 1,000 cm^3 and 2,000 cm^3 engine capacity (13 percent to 6.5 percent for gasoline cars and 11 percent to 5.5 percent for cars on ethanol/flex fuel). Similar reduction rates also applied to trucks and similar (light commercial) vehicles (IPEA/DIMAC, 2009).

12. Portfolio equity includes shares, stocks, depository receipts and direct purchases of shares in local stock markets by foreign investors.

13. The gross debt of General Government 'covers the total responsibility for debts of federal, state and local (including direct and indirect administration) with the private sector, the financial public sector, the Central Bank and the rest of the world. In the other hand, the Net Public Debt is the consolidated net debt of the nonfinancial public sector and BCB with the financial system (public and private), nonfinancial private sector and rest of the world' (BCB, 2015).

14. It should be noted that the new rule provides for the unwanted indexing of savings income to the basic interest rate against the imperious detachment of the financial assets of the basic interest rate.

15. Reserve requirements, which are historically high in Brazil, were reduced from 53.0 percent to 47.0 percent for sight deposits (October 2008) and from 19.0 percent to 17.5 percent for time deposits (September 2009).
16. After the subprime crisis, many central banks (led by the Federal Reserve Bank) have engaged in so called unconventional monetary policy.
17. The second goal would be moderation of household indebtedness.
18. It should be noted that the attempt to reduce electricity tariffs has proven to be unsustainable. In 2015, electricity tariffs will be increased by approximately 40 percent on average.
19. The LFT (in Portuguese, *Letras Financeiras do Tesouro*) is a Federal government bond indexed to the Selic rate.
20. Capital controls had been misinterpreted as a practice of left wing governments: a former President of the BCB once declared that he had been 'an opponent of heterodoxy for more than 40 years and I am thereby perfectly justified in calling for an IOF for capital inflows . . . without being accused of leaping onto the bandwagon of the stupid leftist point of view that says that controlling capital flows leads to a more efficient monetary policy' (Pastore, *apud* Modenesi and Modenesi, 2008: 565). In their view, 'the defense of capital controls, as pioneered by Keynes and developed by Tobin, Davidson . . . Stiglitz, and Rodrik, is not the fruit of an ideological conviction' (Modenesi and Modenesi, 2008: 565).
21. This reference is to the reduction of the Federal Reserve's quantitative easing or bond buying program. This move is expected to diminish international market liquidity, thus affecting the emerging markets.
22. In January, the Argentine peso fell 23 percent, the most dramatic peso depreciation since the country's 2002 financial crisis. The Turkish lira fell 6 percent in January; at its low point, the lira was down 9 cent from January 1. The South African rand fell 7.5 percent in January, its weakest level since 2008. Additionally, the Russian ruble fell 7 percent in January, a five year low.
23. According to Modenesi et al. (2015), for most orthodox economists the macroeconomic tripod was discharged, or at least disfigured, and for some replaced by a Keynesian policy. Accordingly, Keynesians judged the latter proposition senseless, arguing that the prevailing economic policy does not fulfill the requirements of a Keynesian policy. In fact, from a Keynesian viewpoint, the Brazilian economic policy enclosed a serious contradiction: '[o]n the one hand, macroeconomic policy is still based on monetary regime dominance . . . and on the other hand, countercyclical economic policies have been managed' (Cunha et al., 2014: 537). Besides that, there is a lot of criticism, especially regarding Roussef's administration (De Paula et al., 2015). On the other hand, for a large group of heterodox economists (Post Keynesians, Sraffians, Marxists, and so on) tripod's flexibilization represents (broadly speaking) an improvement. This chapter does not address this academic debate.

REFERENCES

Allsopp, C. and D. Vines (2000), 'The assessment: macroeconomic policy', *Oxford Economic Review*, 16 (4), 1–32.

Arestis, P. and M. Sawyer (2005), 'New consensus monetary policy: an appraisal', in P. Arestis, M. Baddeley and J. McCombie (eds), *The New Monetary Policy: Implications and Relevance*, Cheltenham, UK and Northampton, MA, USA: Edward Elgar Publishing, 7–22.

Arestis, P., Fernando Ferrari Filho and Luiz F. de Paula (2011), 'Inflation targeting in Brazil', *International Review of Applied Economics*, 25 (2), 127–148.

Arida, P. and Andre L. Resende (1984), 'Inertial inflation and monetary reform in

Brazil', Paper prepared for the Conference Inflation and Indexation, Institute of International Economics, Washington, DC, December.

Bacha, E. (1994), 'O fisco e a inflação: uma interpretação do caso brasileiro', *Revista de Economia Política*, 14 (1), 5–17.

Barbosa, N. (2010), 'Latin America: counter-cyclical policy in Brazil: 2008–09', *Journal of Globalization and Development*, 1 (1), 1–12.

Blinder, A.S. (1981), 'Monetarism is obsolete', *Challenge*, September–October, 35–43.

Blinder, A.S. (1997), 'A core of macroeconomic beliefs', *Challenge*, July–August, 36–44.

Brazilian Central Bank (BCB) (2015), 'Fiscal Data'. Frequently asked question series. Retrieved on September 8, 2015 from www4.bcb.gov.br/pec/gci/ingl/focus/FAQ%204-Fiscal%20Data.pdf.

Chamon, M. and Marcio Garcia (2013), 'Capital controls in Brazil: effective?', Discussion Paper 606, Rio de Janeiro: Department of Economics, Pontifícia Universidade Católica do Rio de Janeiro.

Cunha, A.D., M. Prates and F. Ferrari Filho (2011), 'Brazil responses to the international financial crisis: a successful example of Keynesian policies?', *Journal Panoeconomicus*, 58 (5), 693–714.

De Paula, L.F., A.M. Modenesi and M.C. Pires (2015), 'The tale of the contagion of two crises and policy responses in Brazil: a case of (Keynesian) policy coordination?', *Journal of Post Keynesian Economics*, 37 (3), 408–435.

Gentil, D.L. and V.L. Araujo (2012), 'Public debt and foreign liabilities: where is the threat?', Discussion Paper 1, Brasília: Instituto de Pesquisa Econômica (IPEA).

International Monetary Fund (IMF) (2012), 'Coping with high debt and sluggish growth', *World Economic Outlook*, October, Washington, DC: IMF.

Instituto Brasileiro de Economia (IBRE) (2014), 'Uma história de dois câmbios: preços relativos não se moveram ainda' (Carta do IBRE), *Conjuntura Econômica*, 68 (1).

Instituto de Pesquisa Econômica Aplicada /Diretoria de Estudos Macroeconômicos (IPEA/DIMAC) (2009), *Impactos da redução do imposto sobre produtos industrializados (IPI) de automóveis*, Nota Técnica IPEA, August, Brasilia: IPEA.

Lavoie, M. (2004), 'The new consensus on monetary policy seen from a post Keynesian perspective', in M. Lavoie and M. Seccareccia (eds), *Central Banking in the Modern World: Alternative Perspectives*, Cheltenham, UK and Northampton, MA, USA: Edward Elgar Publishing, Chapter 1.

Lopes, F. (1984), *O choque heterodoxo: combate à inflação e reforma monetária*. Rio de Janeiro: Campus, 1986.

Modenesi, A.M. (2005), *Monetary Regimes: Theory and Experience of the Real*, Barueri: Manole.

Modenesi, A.M. and E. Araújo (2013), 'Price stability under inflation targeting in Brazil: empirical analysis of the monetary policy transmission mechanism based on a VAR model, 2000–2008', *Investigación Económica*, January–March, 283, 99–133.

Modenesi, A.M. and R.L. Modenesi (2008), 'Capital controls and financial liberalization: removing the ideological bias', *Journal of Post Keynesian Economics*, 30 (4), 561–582.

Modenesi, A.M. and R.L. Modenesi (2012), 'Quinze anos de rigidez monetária no Brasil', *Revista de Economia Política*, 32 (3), 389–411.

Modenesi, A.M., N.M. Martins and Rui L. Modenesi (2013), 'A modified Taylor Rule for the Brazilian economy: convention and conservatism in 11 years of inflation targeting (2000–2010)', *Journal of Post Keynesian Economics*, 35 (3), 463–482.

Modenesi, R.L., A.M. Modenesi and P. Fontine (2015), 'Restructuring the economic policy framework in Brazil: genuine or gattopardo change?', *Revue de la régulation*, 17 (Spring), 1–33.

Romer, D. (2000), 'Keynesian macroeconomics without the LM curve', *Journal of Economic Perspective*, 14 (2), 149–169.

Sales, A.S. and J.B. Barroso (2012), 'Coping with a complex global environment: a Brazilian perspective on emerging market issues', Working Papers Series, 292, Brasília: Brazilian Central Bank.

Setterfield, M. (2004), 'Central banking, stability and macroeconomic outcomes: a comparison of new consensus and Post Keynesian monetary macroeconomics', in M. Lavoie and M. Seccareccia (eds), *Central Banking in the Modern World: Alternative Perspectives*, Cheltenham, UK and Northampton, MA, USA: Edward Elgar Publishing, Chapter 2.

Setterfield, M. (2005), 'Central bank behaviour and the stability of macroeconomic equilibrium: a critical examination of the "New Consensus"', in Phillip Arestis, Michelle Baddeley and John S.L. McCombie (eds), *The New Monetary Policy*, Cheltenham, UK and Northampton, MA, USA: Edward Elgar Publishing, Chapter 3.

Taylor, J.B. (1993), 'Discretion versus policy rules in practice', Carnegie-Rochester Conference Series on Public Policy, 39, 195–214.

Taylor, J.B. (2000), 'Teaching modern macroeconomics at principles levels', *American Economic Review*, 90 (2), 90–94.

7. The global financial crisis: impact and response from Malaysia[1]

Shankaran Nambiar

7.1 INTRODUCTION

The Malaysian economy has been hit by crises, but the financial crisis of 2008 was quite unlike some of the crises experienced in the past. The 2008 crisis presented an extraordinary challenge, because the trigger came from external sources, and demands a serious reconsideration of Malaysia's growth strategy. The 1997 crisis, for instance, required temporary measures, such as instituting capital controls, and more fundamental measures, such as the restructuring of the banking and financial system. The 2008 crisis would require new ways of thinking about how Malaysia could reposition itself since the crisis questions the very assumptions on which the country's growth strategy is based.

This crisis led to a decline in consumer demand from the United States (US), the European Union (EU) and Japan. It led to a softening of export led growth in Malaysia. Malaysia cannot rely entirely on domestic demand to drive the growth of its economy. This means that a rebalancing of growth is called for and, along with it, a reexamination of national strategies that emphasize domestic consumption and investment. This does not imply that exports and export related activities should be dismissed. Some of the crucial questions that demand attention relate to how domestic investment and consumption can be boosted.

This chapter attempts to argue that the effects of the global financial crisis were transmitted to Malaysia mainly through the trade and financial channels (James et al., 2008). It begins by providing a brief background to the 2008 crisis. It then discusses the impact of the crisis on trade in Malaysia. The third section analyses the impact of the current crisis on Malaysian capital flows followed by an examination of its impact on the real sector. The fourth section outlines policy responses to the crisis. The fifth section highlights the salient differences between the 2008 and 1997 crises. Finally, some concluding remarks are made.

7.2   BACKGROUND

The United States (US) experienced an economic downturn with the 'dotcom' bubble of 2000. This was followed by the 9/11 attack in 2001. Both crises had a big impact on the US economy and, as a consequence, necessitated expansionary economic policies to keep the economy buoyant. At the policy level, this resulted in a regime of low interest rates, and a rapid growth in credit supported by rapidly rising housing prices.

It is against this backdrop that the growth of credit instruments spelt the destruction of the financial system in the US (Barth, 2008). The emergence and proliferation of subprime market mortgage lending took on unprecedented dimensions (Bicksler, 2008). Mortgage lenders securitized subprime loans (loans that were made to people with inadequate means to pay their loans) and sold them as assets. The subprime loans were securitized by institutions such as Fannie Mae and Freddie Mac.

Although the credit instruments had a high level of risk, they were sold on false pretences, having been promoted as ways of spreading risk and offering opportunities for safer investment (Diamond and Rajan, 2009). Several factors contributed to the lack of caution in the purchase of subprime loans. First, rating agencies did not exercise adequate caution in awarding their ratings. Second, asset managers did not employ stringent guidelines as far as risk management was concerned due to the upswing in the global economy prior to the meltdown. Third, a climate of poor corporate governance prevailed, indicated, among other things, by the overpayment of chief executive officers.

At any rate, by mid-2007 the US saw defaults on mortgages and foreclosures. With the collapse of the subprime market and the nose dive in housing and stock prices, it was clear that the economy was on its way to a crisis. In September 2008 Fannie Mae and Freddie Mac were nationalized, followed by Lehman Brothers filing for bankruptcy. In September 2008, the US House of Representatives rejected a US$700 billion bailout proposal for financial firms affected by the credit crunch. This prompted panic in the financial markets in the US. What soon followed was the adverse impact of the crisis on banks in Europe due to their exposure to the markets in the US.

The impact of the 2008 financial crisis on the US economy need not be detailed; suffice it to say that the repercussions were immense (Taylor, 2009). The effects on the rest of the world depended on two primary factors: (a) exposure to US financial markets and investments within the US financial system, and (b) effects through the trade channel (Cali et al., 2008). In the case of Malaysia, since it had negligible direct investments in US financial markets, the brunt of the assault from the crisis was largely through the trade channel, mainly triggered by the plummeting consumer demand in the US and the EU. This is similar to the Indian experience where Indian financial markets were insulated from those in the US (Gupta, 2010).

In the Malaysian case, GDP growth over the period spanning 2002 to 2007 was at an average of 5.9 percent. This took a plunge in 2008 when it dropped to 4.8 percent and sank to −1.5 percent in 2009. Clearly, the drop in growth was felt most acutely in 2009. Indeed, growth was satisfactory in 2007, rising from 5.4 percent in the first quarter of 2007 and reaching an enviable 7.2 percent in the fourth quarter of 2007. Growth was at 7.4 percent in the first quarter of 2008 before tumbling to 0.1 percent in the fourth quarter of 2008. The impact of the crisis was not seriously felt in Malaysia until the first quarter of 2009, when growth contracted by 6.2 percent. It is to the effects via the trade channel and its subsequent transmission that we turn in the following sections.

7.3   IMPACTS OF THE CRISIS

7.3.1   Impacts on Trade and Capital Flows

The impact of crises tends to be felt most significantly by developing economies through the reduction in export earnings. In many developing countries this is realized through the decline in commodity prices (Te Velde, 2008 and Naude, 2009). In Malaysia's case it was slightly different in that the crisis in the West was transmitted to Malaysia through the trade and financial channels.

The sensitivity of the trade channel is understandable given the extent of openness in the economy. This can be judged from the extent of total exports and imports which, at the time of the crisis, was RM1.110 billion, or roughly twice the national gross domestic product (GDP). This gives some indication of Malaysia's dependence on the external sector. Being a small, open economy, the crisis had immediate consequences on trade. The decline in external demand from the country's dominant trade partners gave rise to repercussions that were felt throughout the economy.

An examination of the structure of exports clearly indicates the dominant position occupied by manufactured goods, which accounted for 82 percent of total exports. Other commodities accounted for less. Minerals contributed about 8 percent of exports and the share of agricultural commodities was about 7 percent of total exports. This reflects Malaysia's heavy reliance on export oriented manufacturing.

Within the category of manufactured goods, electronics, electrical machinery and appliances contributed about 53 percent of the share of exports. Again, as a component of this broad category, electronics goods were the most dominant. Exports of electronic products can be subdivided into semiconductors, and electrical equipment and appliances, both of which were equally important as export items. The importance of this sector in terms of its contribution to trade and hence to GDP growth has been acknowledged (Athukorala, 2001).

Since the demand for electronic goods largely emanates from developed countries, the decline in consumption in the US, EU and Japan negatively affected the export of Malaysian manufactured goods. The share of semiconductors as a percentage of total exports fell by 2.4 percent in 2008 compared to 2007 and by 3.3 percent for electronic equipment. The export of electronics, electrical machinery and appliances fell by 5.8 percent in 2008 against 2007. While manufactured goods accounted for 78.4 percent of total exports in 2007, it contributed 74.1 percent in 2008. Other items such as chemicals and chemical products; textiles, clothing and footwear; manufactures of metals; and optical and scientific equipment do not constitute a large share of Malaysia's exports. Neither were exports of these goods affected by the crisis.

The vulnerability of Malaysian exports is reconfirmed from an examination of trends in exports by Malaysia to its major trading partners. The US used to be the largest single destination for exports in the mid-1990s. However, it seems to have lost its favored position as other countries have come to take a place of roughly equal standing. In 1995, about 21 percent of exports were directed to the US, with a gentle decrease to about 18 percent in more recent years.

The EU stood next in importance as a destination for Malaysia's exports in 1995, claiming 14 percent of exports. The share of exports heading for the EU hovered around 12.5 percent after 2007. Japan, to which about 13 percent of Malaysia's exports went, witnessed a decrease to about 9 percent in 2007. The biggest decline has been noted in the case of Singapore. In the late 1990s, about 20 percent of exports went to the city state. Since 2006, the figure came down to about 15 percent. China, on the other hand, has been assuming a place of greater significance as a source for Malaysia's exports. About 3 percent of exports went to China in the late 1990s, but in the years leading up to the crisis it had almost tripled. The five most important economies to which Malaysia's exports went were to the US, Singapore, the EU, Japan and China, more or less in that order of importance, until 2007. In 2008, Singapore assumed a position of greater importance than the US. At any rate, export figures, which were doing well in the first three quarters of 2008, took a downturn toward the end of that year. A significant contraction in exports was registered in December 2008

(−14.9 percent), which worsened in January 2009 (−27.8 percent). What is perhaps most striking is the fact that the decline persisted even until the end of 2009, illustrating the depth of the impact of the crisis.

There is a strong relationship in Malaysia between exports and imports, in that the goods produced for export have substantial import content. Imports, which tend to follow export trends rather closely in Malaysia, reported a similar pattern of decline. Again, the change in imports dived into negative territory from October 2008, falling from −5.3 percent in that month to −32 percent in January 2009.

As with exports, the decline in imports extended into 2009. It is understandable that imports should fall along with decreases in exports because the import of intermediate goods is required to meet the production of exports. This was the case with imports from all countries, with the exception of China. In the case of China this was probably so because of the low technology nature of imports from China as well as the cheaper goods required by the light manufacturing industries. Also, the import of goods from China, which would be cheaper than those from other developed countries, would have increased in order to support consumer demand in Malaysia.

There is a close relationship between changes in total exports and the Industrial Production Index (IPI). As seen in Figure 7.1, the IPI dropped

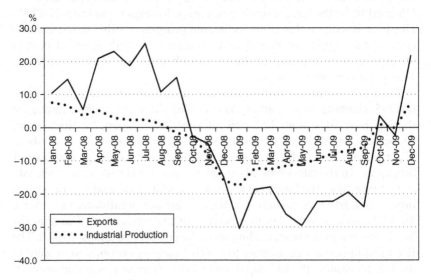

Source: Department of Statistics.

Figure 7.1 Percentage change in total exports and industrial production index

along with the decline in total exports. By October 2009, both total exports and the IPI were falling together. Through most of 2009 the IPI was in a state of contraction when the change in exports was also shrinking. This can be explained as a contraction in production that arose because of the decline in exports.

The capital outflows from Malaysia increased with the onset of the crisis. The capital outflows can be divided into those resulting from the outflows of foreign direct investments (otherwise known as overseas FDI, that is, OFDI) and those due to portfolio funds. Malaysian investments abroad in the form of outward FDI decreased (from about US$3 billion to US$2.2 billion in the last quarter of 2008 (Figure 7.2)). The outflows of portfolio funds were striking. The surge of portfolio flows into the country in the first quarter of 2008 (about US$7 billion) was completely negated by portfolio outflows amounting to US$18.6 billion in the third quarter of 2008.

Foreign direct investments (FDI) did not in any way compensate for portfolio outflows following the crisis, nor could they be expected to. With the crisis, and with Malaysia's traditional FDI sources being hit, FDI inflows were affected. This was seen distinctly in the third quarter of 2008 when FDI worth about US$0.3 billion was all that flowed into the country. FDI commitments are made on a longer time scale and, typically, are tied down to the host country. Thus, any loss in confidence would take

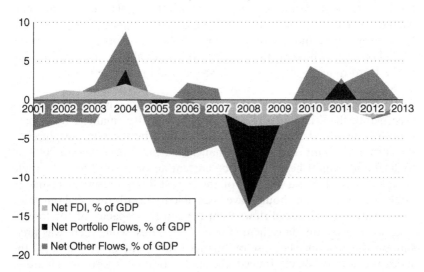

Source: IMF, IFS statistics.

Figure 7.2 Composition of financial flows to Malaysia

a longer period of time to produce a withdrawal of FDI. However, the loss in confidence as well as the lack of funds in the more developed economies led to a situation where FDI inflows were stymied. Portfolio funds, on the other hand, expect bigger returns in a shorter period of time and are more fluid in their movement, and that explains the sharp downturn in portfolio outflows.

Measured against GDP, OFDI sharply declined to −0.01 percent of GDP (as measured in US$ million) at the peak of the crisis in the third quarter of 2008. At the same time in 2008, portfolio flows contracted by almost −0.03 percent of GDP and FDIs were 0 percent of GDP. Although in 2007 FDIs were about 0.5 percent of GDP, they amounted to less than 0.25 percent in the latter part of 2008.

Malaysia held large reserves subsequent to the 1997 crisis, but the 2008 crisis took its toll on these reserves. The economy held foreign reserves valued at US$314 billion in 2006, but by the last quarter of 2008 reserves amounted to a mere US$91.5 billion. The shrinking of foreign reserves goes against the lesson that Malaysia had learnt during the 1997 Asian crisis. The 1997 crisis embedded in the minds of policymakers that abundant foreign reserves were necessary to defend the ringgit. The severity of the 2008 crisis necessitated the contraction of foreign reserves.

Nevertheless, the declines in FDI, foreign reserves and portfolio funds were well cushioned by the relatively stable current account balance. The current account balance did drop by about US$2.9 billion between the third and fourth quarters of 2008, but more striking was the overall balance, which declined drastically (from about −US$10.5 billion in the third quarter of 2008 to −US$20.6 million in the last quarter of 2008).

Closer examination reveals that there were negative net financial flows even before the crisis (Figure 7.3). In fact, negative financial flows have persisted since mid-2004 and can be explained by the huge surpluses in the current account. But the net financial outflows deepened in 2008 up to 2009 and cannot be explained by current account surpluses. It should be noted that Malaysia had one of the largest foreign reserves relative to GDP at that time and should have been able to absorb financial outflows. The negative net financial flows went beyond the capacity of the foreign reserves to accommodate them (Figure 7.4). Thus, while there was pressure on the economy because of financial flows, the main source of the shock was a trade shock. Indeed, the contraction in exports, which are so important to an export oriented economy, coupled with shrinking portfolio inflows and a decline in FDI had its impact on the real sector, as can certainly be expected.

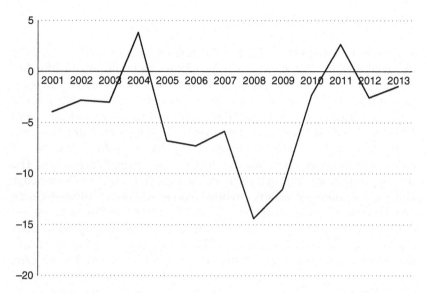

Source: IMF, IFS statistics.

Figure 7.3   Net financial flows, % of GDP

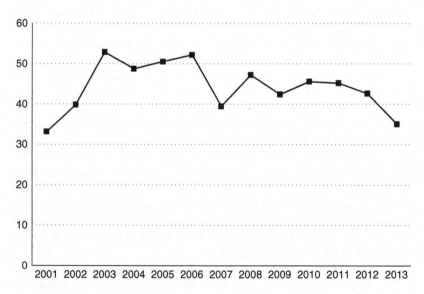

Source: IMF, IFS statistics.

Figure 7.4   Foreign reserves, % of GDP

7.3.2   Impact on the Real Sector

The impact of the crisis affected the real sector as much as it hit the financial sector. The manufacturing sector, naturally, was badly hit. China and India offer relevant comparisons because both, like Malaysia, were hit by the 2008 crisis. They differ from Malaysia in specific ways; India because it is not as export dependent as Malaysia and China, and China invites an interesting comparison because it had to introduce deep fiscal measures to counteract the impacts of the crisis. In China, the real sector was affected via challenges to the state owned enterprises. The primary impact was through the trade channel. The export of knowledge and capital intensive export oriented goods was most affected (Yang and Huizenga, 2010). This meant that the corresponding state owned enterprises were adversely hit. Private enterprises dealing with labor intensive goods were less affected. China, too, because of a downward dive in trade, suffered losses in the labor market. In the Malaysian case, the brunt of the crisis was borne by the E&E sector (as was earlier discussed) and the construction and property sectors. This was reflected in the fall in the industrial production index (IPI) and, very concretely, in the level of retrenchments. The IPI reflected the damp export conditions imposed by the global environment. The IPI contracted in September 2008 (−1.7 percent year on year) and reached its worst in January 2009 (−20.2 percent) (Figure 7.1).

The construction sector was adversely affected by the crisis. The number of new sales permits fell in mid-2008, indicating pessimism in the industry (Figure 7.5). The change in the production of construction related products index also reflected the negative sentiments of the construction industry for all of 2008. Although the production of construction products was negative in early 2009, housing approvals and new sales permits started to recover in January 2009.

The effects of the crisis were reflected in the GDP numbers by the third quarter of 2008. In no sector was this clearer than the manufacturing sector (Figure 7.6). The manufacturing sector had a 5.6 percent increase year on year in the second quarter of 2008, but it was negative (−8.8 percent) by the fourth quarter of 2008. The construction sector also showed negative growth in the fourth quarter of 2008. Clearly, the effect of the crisis was felt right through 2009 for all sectors.

In terms of real GDP by demand expenditure, gross investment (−10.2 percent), exports (−13.4 percent) and imports (−10.1 percent) all recorded decreases (Figure 7.7). Private consumption also fell, but remained at a rate of 5.3 percent, although in the first quarter of 2008 private consumption had increased by 11.7 percent. The net effect of all

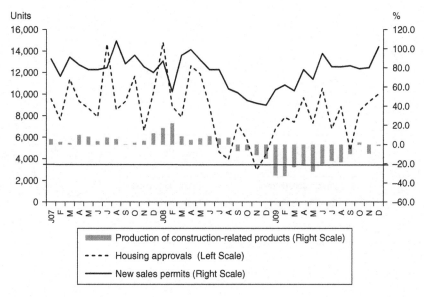

Source: Department of Statistics.

Figure 7.5 **Production of construction related products index, housing approvals and new sales permits**

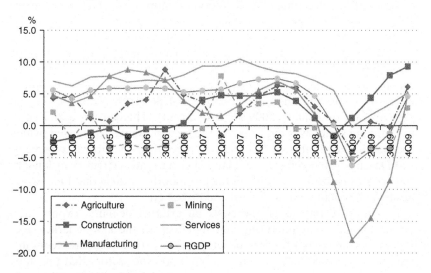

Source: Department of Statistics.

Figure 7.6 **GDP by sectors (% change)**

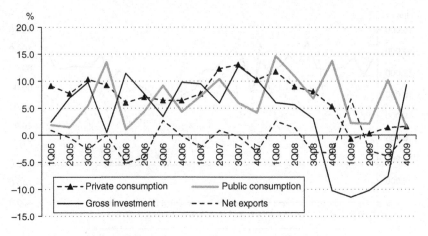

Source: Department of Statistics.

Figure 7.7   Real GDP by demand expenditure (% change)

the decreases in the various components of real GDP was a decline in real GDP growth to 0.1 percent for the last quarter of 2008 as opposed to about 7 percent in the first half of the same year.

The outflow of capital and the mood of caution triggered by developments in the US affected the Malaysian financial sector, despite limited direct exposure to the subprime crisis. The mood of uncertainty resulted in a contraction in local credit markets. Consequently, the number of loans approved slipped down (Figure 7.8). The growth in loans approved was in the negative region in September 2008. Loans approved shrank markedly in the months of October (−14.4 percent), November (−44.0 percent) and in January 2009 (−35.6 percent). The caution exercised in the banking sector was indicated by the growth in loans disbursed, which declined in the months of October (8.2 percent), November (7.6 percent) and December (0.6 percent), and landed into negative territory in January 2009 (−10.0 percent). It is only in the last months of 2009 that there was a positive growth in loans approved and disbursed.

The negative impact of the crisis on external demand, exports and export oriented manufacturing had its effect on the labor market, too. Indeed, the impacts of crises depend on the structure of an economy, leading to negative outcomes depending upon the sectors that are most prominent. Here there are parallels with events in China, where the crisis triggered declines in employment, particularly among urban workers and migrant workers employed in export oriented factories (Yang and

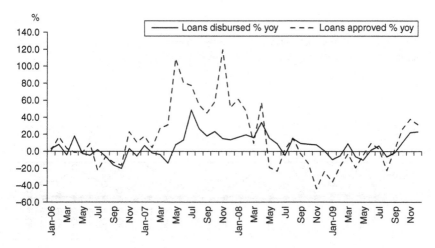

Source: Bank Negara Malaysia.

Figure 7.8   Loans approved and disbursed

Huizenga, 2010). In India, too, the job losses were in the manufacturing sector, particularly labor intensive industries, and some of the subsectors in services were also affected (Gupta, 2010). There was a greater degree of resilience in the services sector, but that did not stop the export of software services growing by less than 1 percent in the second half of 2008 to 2009 (Borchert and Mattoo, 2009).

In Malaysia, the manufacturing sector suffered the most from the crisis in terms of retrenchments. Two points deserved to be highlighted. First, the manufacturing sector is highly export oriented and, secondly, the electronics and electrical subsector is a key component of the manufacturing sector. Thus, retrenchments were significant in the second half of 2008 (Figure 7.9). Retrenchments were also high in the services sector in the third and fourth quarters of 2008. The agriculture sector was largely exempt, but about 20,000 workers were retrenched in the second half of 2008. In fact, retrenchments were high even in 2009 and moderated only toward the end of 2009.

7.4   POLICY RESPONSES TO THE CRISIS

Malaysia responded to the crisis with a combination of monetary and fiscal policies. China's approach to managing the 2008 global crisis was by

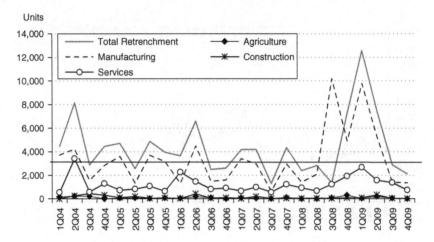

Source: Ministry of Human Resources.

Figure 7.9   Total retrenchment by sector

predominantly using fiscal measures, spearheaded by stimulus packages (Yang and Huizenga, 2010; Zhang and Yu, 2012), and that is very much what Malaysia did. The Indian scenario was slightly different in two ways. First, the Indian economy was slowing down when the crisis hit India (and in this sense there was a crucial difference compared to China or Malaysia). Second, India, although integrated within the global economy, was not (and is not) as export dependent as China and Malaysia. The latter is a difference that puts the Indian experience apart. In any case, India used a policy mix that favored monetary measures (Kumar and Vashisht, 2012).

Malaysia used a mix of monetary and fiscal policies. Athukorala (2010) notes that Malaysia was the first country in the region to put in place expansionary monetary policies. Bank Negara Malaysia (BNM), Malaysia's central bank, announced monetary policy responses to the crisis by cutting the overnight policy rate from 3.5 percent to 3.25 percent in November 2008. On February 24, 2009, BNM announced an even lower rate of 2 percent and this was maintained until January 2010. The loose interest rate policy was to facilitate bank lending and to boost investment. Bank Negara Malaysia reduced the statutory reserve requirement from 4 percent to 3.5 percent effective December 1, 2008. Furthermore, there was also a change of policy in the banking sector, specifically upon the law of the Central Bank. The Central Bank of Malaysia Act 2009 came into force on November 25, 2009, giving BNM a more effective role in managing risks and challenges.

In addition, several measures were also introduced to ensure continued access to credit. New financing facilities were set up to increase access to financing by small, medium and micro enterprises. Loan restructuring was also undertaken by the financial institutions to lessen the burden on the affected groups.

As the global slowdown continued and its impact on the Malaysian economy was felt, the Malaysian government launched policy measures to mitigate the effects of the crisis. The government introduced the first stimulus package (SP1) of about US$2.3 billion in November 2008. This was followed by a second stimulus package (SP2) of US$20 billion in March 2009. On the monetary side, interest rate cuts were initiated by Bank Negara Malaysia (BNM) and the Central Bank of Malaysia.

The introduction of these measures indicates that the government realized the seriousness of the problem and, recognizing that there was no way out, decided to use the full array of fiscal and monetary measures to mitigate the effects of the crisis. It was necessary to support the economy against declining aggregate demand and to ensure that domestic spending did not recede. Further, there was an urgent demand to support the economy against any erosion of confidence. No less crucial was the recognition that social wellbeing could not be sacrificed should the crisis strike with all its fury.

The two principle objectives of the First Stimulus Package (SP1) were to: (a) reinforce and stimulate the economy and (b) to improve the wellbeing of the people, particularly the disadvantaged. The principle allocations under SP1 were to build infrastructure and thereby boost the building and construction sector. The focus was to build affordable houses, schools and hospitals, and to construct roads, especially in rural areas. Import duties on cement and iron and steel products were also abolished to encourage these activities.

The government offered incentives that had the effect of both stimulating the economy and relieving the burden of the disadvantaged. Among these initiatives was the provision offered to government servants to extend the period over which housing loans could be paid. Employment Provident Fund members were given the option to reduce their contributions by 3 percent for two years. The last two measures were designed to reduce the immediate burden of targeted groups and to increase their disposable income. It should be noted that up to 25 percent of the population in Malaysia are in the public service. This is indicative of the reach of the policy. In order to increase consumption, hypermarkets were allowed to extend their business operations beyond normal working hours and even to work on a 24 hour basis in shopping complexes.

The Second Stimulus Package (SP2) was more ambitious in as much as it covered a broader range of issues. The SP2 had four objectives: (a) reduce unemployment and increase job opportunities, (b) ease the economic burden of the people, particularly those belonging to vulnerable sections of society, (c) support the private sector and d) undertake capacity building for the future. The SP2 also provided targeted support for a number of sectors.[2]

The SP2 was meant to provide the necessary support for the private sector to tide itself through the crisis. This included direct financial assistance, incentive packages and mega projects that drew upon private sector participation. The focus of these initiatives was the small and medium enterprises (SMEs) as SMEs comprise 99 percent of total registered businesses in Malaysia, account for 56 percent of total employment and contribute to almost 32 percent of GDP. The government extended several guarantee schemes that were specifically directed at SMEs. Through these schemes the government provided guarantees to assist SMEs in raising funds for working capital and industry restructuring, and to raise loans in the bond market. Most of these guarantee schemes were meant for companies with shareholder equity below RM20 million.

The SP2 also attempted to reduce the cost of doing business. It sought to achieve this by exempting and reducing levy payments that companies had to pay to the government. Under the SP2, companies in the E&E sector did not have to make levy payments to the Human Resource Development Fund for a period of six months. Further, levy payments were reduced from 1 percent to 5 percent for a period of two years for all employers.

Several notable fiscal measures were created in stimulus packages for the resuscitation of the private sector. The accelerated capital allowance was proposed. This deduction is applicable to investments incurred on plant and machinery as well as expenses incurred on renovation and refurbishment of business premises. Another tax instrument that was created was the scheme to allow companies to set losses made in the current year against any profits that had been made in the preceding year (2008). This arrangement allowed companies to pay a lower tax on the profits made in 2008, or to enjoy a tax refund should they have made losses in that year.

Several measures were undertaken with a view to building the future capacity of the economy. These included investments that were supposed to be made by Khazanah Nasional Berhad (KNB), the government's investment arm, in sectors such as telecommunications, technology, tourism, agriculture and the life sciences. A sum of about US$1 billion was allocated for the development of the telecommunications sector, particularly for the improvement of the country's broadband infrastructure. Several off budget projects were listed under the SP2 and these included:

(a) the building and expansion of airports (US$0.4 billion), (b) projects to improve the telecommunications infrastructure (US$0.8 billion) and (c) the construction of sky bridges and covered walkways (US$33 million).

A crucial aspect of the government's policy included measures centered on relieving the burden of the people.[3] A further US$276 million was allocated to implementing social safety net programs for the elderly, disabled and single mothers. In particular an attempt was made to address the concerns of vulnerable groups.[4]

The policy measures that were announced by the government did not completely recognize that part of the problem was structural in nature. To begin with, the federal government had been running a deficit in its fiscal balance since the 1977 Asian financial crisis. With the 2008 financial crisis deepening, the government adopted a countercyclical fiscal policy. The large stimulus packages resulted in the fiscal deficits widening, amounting to a fiscal deficit that was 7.6 percent of GDP, opening up the problem of fiscal profligacy as has been a longstanding issue (Athukorala, 2010).

Of the US$20 billion that had been allocated, only US$5 billion was direct expenditure, with about US$3 billion being allocated for the first year (2009) and the remaining US$1.5 billion for the following year (2010). Much of the second stimulus package consisted of government guarantees. The guarantees were meant to take the burden of failed loans from banks. Given the climate of pessimism prevailing at the time, one cannot expect the government guarantees to have been successfully used. Neither has any evidence supporting the use of these guarantees been revealed. It is difficult to assess whether the banks would be encouraged to be less risk averse with the guarantees being put in place by the government.

Some of the measures that were designed were of uncertain value. The heavy emphasis on providing huge funds through the GLCs (Government-linked Companies) would have worked against the private sector's participation in the economy through the crisis and after. The measures that were instituted to assist the GLCs in stimulating investments would have crowded out the private sector's share of investments. In any case, with a global slowdown the rationale of attracting FDI was questionable.

The government did take other useful measures, including the efforts made to improve the position of SMEs and the development of infrastructure projects to stimulate the economy. However, the manner in which the government set out to accomplish the task of developing the SMEs is questionable since it relied on providing guarantees to raise loans. Clearly, this did not address the issue of building a robust SME sector. Indeed, a more comprehensive plan was necessary to reshift the focus to domestic investors and to create vibrant domestic consumption. The concern for social protection, an issue which was long evaded by policymakers, should have been seriously revisited as part of a long term plan rather than as a tool to recover from the crisis.

The industrial policy over the last 20 years had centered on increasing export growth. It is through the channel of export-led economic growth that the government has tackled employment generation and poverty eradication. The government's five year plans and industrial policy have been largely premised on this phenomenon. This approach should have been questioned and alternative scenarios devised, both to plan a recovery from the crisis (which was due to a period of softened demand for Malaysia's exports) and also to reorient the economy so as to avoid future fluctuations arising due to a sudden collapse in external demand.

Even though, with the 2008 crisis, a rethinking of Malaysia's strategy for growth was in order, this opportunity was not seized upon. Instead, the government chose to take a closer look at short term strategies and not at systemic issues. The main challenge was whether Malaysia should repair the damage caused by the crisis and return to its usual state of affairs, or whether there should be shift away from its preponderant emphasis on export oriented growth. This is not to suggest that Malaysia should not pursue export oriented manufacturing, something that Malaysia cannot afford to stop doing given the small size of its domestic market. Rather, it is suggested that Malaysia should have taken the 2008 crisis as an opportunity to pursue a more balanced approach, where export oriented growth policies are retained but with a concomitant emphasis on grounding it within a structural change to the economy.

A rebalancing strategy would function along two lines. First, resources would be shifted from manufacturing industries that are concentrated on exports to developed countries, to industries and services that serve the domestic market. Second, strategies would have to be designed to improve the disposable income of individuals. Third, the government would strengthen the provision of public goods, particularly those affecting the wellbeing of individuals. These policies, if successful, would imply a rebalancing of growth in the economy. Along with these rebalancing strategies, the government should spread its export oriented policies to cover a wider range of countries, including those in Asia, not to mention increasing trade with ASEAN member countries. A fifth strand would be to cover more comprehensive regional integration policies.

Growth rebalancing, when pursued, would definitely have an impact on the economy's macroeconomic variables. The consequences of growth rebalancing, generally speaking, would be targeted at achieving: (a) reduction in savings rate, (b) increase in domestic consumption and (c) increase in domestic investment. While a reduction in savings and an increase in domestic consumption might be goals that need to be achieved for other

Asian countries, this is not the case for Malaysia, which has extraordinary levels of household debt amounting to close to 80 percent of GDP in 2013.

Health care and education are areas where, with the privatization wave of the 1980s, there has been a feeling that the government cannot bear the burden of making these services available to individuals (Nambiar, 2009). In the case of health care, there was an added dimension since it was argued that with escalating health care costs the government could not afford to fund health care in the manner that it had previously committed itself. These rising costs were associated with the rising cost of pharmaceutical products, medical equipment and investigative procedures. Higher standards of living and education also led to a higher demand for specialized treatment. Furthermore, the cost of retaining medical personnel within government employment was rising. The government reasoned that, with greater demands on its expenditure for health care, there was a need for the private sector to play a more active role in the market for health care.

The government has also been reluctant to create social safety nets and to ensure adequate social protection for the disadvantaged on a sustained basis. There have been complaints from nongovernmental organizations, activists and citizen's groups that social safety nets have to be given more consideration and have to be implemented, but the response from the government has been lukewarm if not poor (Lee, Mat Zin and Abdul-Rahman, 2002). Similarly, the government has shown no interest in introducing unemployment benefits, nor has it introduced any scheme that supports workers who lose their jobs in times of economic downturn.

The argument that public spending on education, health care, pensions and social safety nets does not foster growth and would encourage a welfare state is flawed. Well-designed social safety nets would minimize the disincentive effects that have been wrongly attributed to social safety nets. In any case, there is evidence that the disincentive effect is not as severe as it is made out to be in public debates (Coady, Grosh and Hoddinott, 2004 and Grosh et al., 2008). More importantly, socially oriented programs have the capacity to generate multiplier effects due to the investments they can generate. This is obvious in the construction of schools, the improvement of public transport and the building of health care centers. These activities will generate growth.

Primarily, the 2008 crisis was caused by a sudden contraction in external demand. This has been explained as being caused by excessive savings by households in developing economies. This does not apply to Malaysia at the present juncture where the evidence points in the opposite direction. However, there are elements that are nevertheless relevant in the present context in so far as there is a higher risk that individuals and households have to manage in the face of global uncertainties.

Finding solutions to the issues that have been suggested would require a shift in developmental emphasis. In the first instance this would mean a shift in emphasis to small and medium enterprises that produce for the domestic and ASEAN market. This in no way implies that the markets of developed economies should be excluded from consideration. Second, the government should favor improving infrastructure facilities. Many aspects of transportation that have been ignored in the last decade or so should have been revisited, and this includes improving urban transportation and rapid travel between cities. Third, the government should reinvolve itself in education and training, as well as the provision of health care and low cost housing. Besides, the connection between the crisis and the revised developmental strategy has not really been highlighted.

7.5 WAS THE 2008 CRISIS DIFFERENT?

The immediate factor that triggered the 1997 crisis in Malaysia was the negative perceptions of foreign investors regarding the Malaysia economy following the dramatic collapse of the Thai economy. Foreign investors and international rating agencies had failed to consider the underlying real risks that were seething beneath the economy in Thailand. In a preemptive move, and spurred by the fear that the Thai baht debacle would occur in the region, foreign portfolio investors sought to withdraw from markets that could possibly have underlying fragilities. This influenced their assessment of Malaysia, leading to the fall of the ringgit exchange rate (Ariff and Yap, 2001).

From RM2.48 against the US dollar in March 1997, the exchange rate went down to RM2.57 in July. By the end of 1997 the exchange rate had gone down to RM3.77 against the US dollar. Bank Negara Malaysia (BNM) tried to defend the ringgit by raising short term interest rates, but this did nothing to halt the slide of the ringgit and BNM thought it prudent to discontinue this policy of attempting to maintain the ringgit (Ariff et al., 1998). In early 1998, the ringgit had hit a low of RM4.88 against US$1.

Along with the dive in the ringgit, the Kuala Lumpur Composite Index (KLCI) went into a tumble. The KLCI, which was at 1,216 points at the end of January 1997, went down to 594 points in December 1997. Market capitalization contracted from about US$60 billion in August 1998 compared to about US$92 billion in January 1997. The twin events of a slide in the exchange rate and a dive in the KLCI caused alarm in the markets. This led to a sell down of stocks and there was a rush to sell the ringgit.

The policy responses that were elicited by the crisis could be divided into two phases: (a) the initial phase, and (b) the second phase. The initial policy response to the 1997 crisis was to raise interest rates. The three month interbank rate was raised to 8.7 percent by the end of 1997 from 7.6 percent in September 1997. The three month interbank rate rose to 11 percent in February 1998. These efforts did little to control the ringgit. The contagion effect, spearheaded by the depreciation of the Korean won and the Indonesian rupiah, took effect, leaving the ringgit volatile against major currencies. Some of the early monetary policy measures included limits on loans to the property sector and for the purchase of stock and shares by commercial banks and finance companies. There was also reduction of financing on hire purchase loans for noncommercial vehicles. Attempts were made to reduce the supply of offshore ringgit to stem the attacks that were made on the ringgit. There were also changes made to disclosure requirements on nonperforming loans (reduced from six month arrears to three month arrears) for the early detection of problem loans.

The 1998 Budget that was proposed in October 1997 was based on a policy of pursuing fiscal restraint. In line with this approach a fiscal surplus of 2 percent of GNP was proposed. The measures introduced in immediate response to the crisis were not found to be effective. The unfavorable outcomes that emerged in response to the first phase of policy measures called for a reversal in strategy. There was an urgent need to boost the economy and at the same time to bring some stability to the ringgit, which was still subject to volatility (Athukorala, 1998). The solution that was ultimately taken was in complete variance with the measures taken in the first phase. The second phase of policy measures was based on the twin objectives of: (a) reducing interest rates to boost the economy, and (b) imposing selective capital controls to mitigate market forces that would contribute to the further fall of the ringgit (Athukorala, 2001).

The second phase of economic measures to curb the impact of the crisis was punctuated by a set of selective capital controls that were implemented on September 1, 1998. The following day the ringgit exchange rate was fixed at RM3.80 to US$1. The capital controls helped insulate the economy from the volatile external environment and the threat of further pressure on the ringgit. This also created some room for the use of monetary policy to respond to the declining GDP.

Other policies were also undertaken under the second phase of measures, that is, after the introduction of the capital controls. These included an expansionary fiscal policy, with a fiscal deficit in October 1998 that was 6 percent of GNP. In the first half of 1998, government expenditure fell by 34.4 percent, but in the second half of the same year, government expenditure rose by 56.6 percent. The government undertook substantial institutional restructuring during the second phase of policy measures. A crucial part of this exercise consisted of establishing a number of institutions to deal with the crisis, such as Danaharta, Danamodal and the Corporate Debt Restructuring Committee (CDRC). Danaharta was an institution established with the aim of removing nonperforming loans from the banking sector. Danamodal was formed to recapitalize sick banks, and CDRC's objective was to enable borrowers and creditors to find amicable solutions to debt problems without resorting to legal wrangles. CDRC was also meant to enable companies to obtain credit lines during the crisis. The process of institutional restructuring was extended to the merger program for banking institutions. It was thought that there were too many banks (21 domestic commercial banks, 25 finance companies and 12 merchant banks) in existence at the time and that they should be merged into six core banks.

Institutions such as Danaharta, Danamodal and the National Economic Action Council (NEAC) that were founded to serve immediate needs were dismantled once the economy recovered. This crisis may have emphasized the importance of a strong position of reserves to defend the ringgit, but that is not a lesson that could be carried to excess. The ample stock of reserves possibly came to be seen as a source of strength, overlooking the costs connecting with holding them (Nambiar, 2003). The increase in current account surpluses would have played its role in encouraging the accumulation of reserves.

The threat of a decreased demand for exports was not imminent at that time, and it may well have been relevant to attract FDIs soon after the crisis, but the present crisis demanded an altogether different approach. The 1997 crisis had a different set of causes than the 2008 crisis that hit Malaysia. Athukorala (2010) argues that, more than external triggers, it was Malaysia's fiscal profligacy that was the root cause of Malaysia's vulnerability to the Asian financial crisis (1997 to 2008). While the 1997 crisis put Malaysia in an insecure position by virtue of its imprudent fiscal policies, the 2008 crisis saw a response that resorted to fiscal excess. Furthermore, the 1997 crisis pointed out the need for strong banking and financial regulatory frameworks and the necessity of adequate foreign reserves. These institutional lessons were well learnt from the 1997 crisis.

The 2008 crisis revealed Malaysia's weakness in several areas. The obvious source of susceptibility was Malaysia's dependence on external markets. But more than that, Malaysia had neglected production for the domestic market and increased domestic consumption. The 2008 crisis would have suggested that Malaysia undertake a rebalancing exercise, focus more on the domestic markets and less on export oriented manufacturing, and subsidies and incentives for these activities. A reconfiguration of rebalancing policies was called for, with a need to address social safety nets and fluctuations in employment (Nambiar, 2012). Primarily, the 2008 crisis was a signal for structural transformation on the production side, and a call for relieving consumers of the burden of paying for education, health care and housing. It also pointed to the need for devising mechanisms to support cyclical unemployment and social safety nets.

7.6 CONCLUSION

Malaysia's response to the economic and financial crisis of 1997 was a set of unorthodox policy measures, highlighted by the use of capital controls. This was complemented by institutional measures, some of which were temporary, as was the establishment of organizations to restructure debt, while others were more of a long term nature. Among those in the latter category were actions taken to strengthen the banking sector through the merger of banks and the initiatives for the phased liberalization of the financial sector.

The 2008 crisis was different in nature; having been triggered by the subprime crisis in the US, it spilled to the other developed economies. The crisis resulted in the collapse of financial markets in the US and it spread to financial markets elsewhere. There was a decline in output in the US and the EU and, with it, a drop in consumer spending in these economies. The total effect for developing economies such as Malaysia was a contraction in trade, which led to the transmission of other negative outcomes in other markets within the country. The real sector was affected, but the lesson to be learnt from the crisis was Malaysia's vulnerability to external shocks and the ensuing consequences. The crisis points to a need to devise development strategies that keep in mind the reoccurrence of similar episodes.

At the center of Malaysia's development plans stands its export-oriented growth strategy. This includes measures encouraging and providing incentives for export oriented manufacturing industries. Closely related are efforts to attract FDIs and support the location of MNCs in Malaysia. In view of the nature of the 2008 crisis and the economies involved, the bases for these policies must be reconsidered. In fact, the crisis calls for rebalancing strategies and a consideration of policies that will spell a structural change in the economy. The 2008 crisis required adjustments in view of decreased demand for exports, but in the long term it suggests new strategies to enhance human security and upgrade human capital for Malaysia's passage into a more knowledge intensive era of economic development in times when export demand may weaken.

NOTES

1. The useful comments of the editors and anonymous referees in the preparation of this chapter are gratefully acknowledged. The usual disclaimer applies.
2. One of the sectors that received special attention was the transportation sector. In particular, the automotive and aviation industries were selected. The tourism sector was also a beneficiary, being allocated US$66.6 billion to upgrade and develop. The Low Cost Carrier Terminal was built at the existing Kuala Lumpur International Airport for an estimated cost of US$0.6 billion.
3. The specific forms that this concern took related to: (a) poverty eradication, (b) a social safety net scheme to protect oil palm and rubber smallholders who may be affected in the event of a fall in the prices of these commodities, (c) subsidies and assistance for fuel consumption, food security and educational assistance, (d) the provision of microcredit programs for small businesses and (e) a fisherman's welfare fund.
4. The attempt to address the needs of the vulnerable groups included projects such as: (a) repairing and maintaining drains and roads, (b) improving the living conditions of those in public flats, (c) maintaining and repairing welfare homes, fire stations and their quarters, as well as public toilets, (d) improving school facilities by building and repairing schools, and (e) improving basic amenities in rural areas (especially public utilities and roads).

REFERENCES

Ariff, M., M.H. Piei, W. Azidin, G.E. Ong and E.L. Tan (1998), *Currency Turmoil and the Malaysian Economy: Genesis, Prognosis and Response*, Kuala Lumpur: Malaysian Institute of Economic Research, Kuala Lumpur.

Ariff, M. and M.M. Yap (2001), 'Financial crisis in Malaysia', in T. Yu and D. Xu (eds), *From Crisis to Recovery: East Asia Rising Again?*, Singapore: World Scientific, 305–346.

Athukorala, P. (1998), 'Swimming against the tide: crisis management in Malaysia', *ASEAN Economic Bulletin*, 15 (3), December, 281–289.

Athukorala, P. (2001), *Crisis and Recovery in Malaysia: The Role of Capital Controls*, Cheltenham, UK and Northampton, MA, USA: Edward Elgar Publishing.

Athukorala, P. (2010), 'Malaysian economy in three crises', Working Paper 2010/12, Crawford School of Economics and Government, Canberra: Australian National University.

Asian Development Bank (2009), *Asian Development Outlook 2009: Rebalancing Asia's Growth*, Manila: Asian Development Bank.

Bank Negara Malaysia (2009a), *Annual Report 2008*, Kuala Lumpur: Bank Negara Malaysia.

Bank Negara Malaysia (2009b), *Financial Stability and Payment Systems Report*, Kuala Lumpur: Bank Negara Malaysia.

Barth, J.R. (2008), 'US subprime mortgage meltdown', Paper presented at the 14th Dubrovnik Economic Conference, June 25, Dubrovnik. Retrieved on March 3, 2016 from www.hnb.hr/dub-konf/14-konferencija/barth.ppt.

Bicksler, J.L. (2008), 'The subprime mortgage debacle and its linkages to corporate governance', *International Journal of Disclosure and Governance*, 5 (4), 295–300.

Borchert, I. and A. Mattoo (2009), 'The crisis resilience of services trade', *Policy Research Working Paper Series* No. 4917, Washington, DC: World Bank.

Cali, M., I. Massa and D.W. Te Velde (2008), 'The global financial crisis: financial flows to developing countries set to fall by one quarter', ODI Report, London: Overseas Development Institute.

Coady, D., M. Grosh and J. Hoddinott (2004), *Targeting of Transfers in Developing Countries: Review of Lessons and Experience*, Washington, DC: World Bank and International Food Policy Research Institute (IFPRI).

Diamond, D.W.D. and R. Rajan (2009), 'The credit crisis: conjectures about causes and remedies', Working Paper 14739, National Bureau of Economic Research, Cambridge.

Grosh, M., C. del Ninno, E. Tesliuc and A. Ouerghi (2008), *For Protection and Promotion: The Design and Implementation of Effective Safety Nets for Protection*, Washington, DC: The International Bank for Reconstruction and Development/World Bank.

Gupta, A.S. (2010), 'Sustaining growth in a period of global downturn: the case of India', in S. Dullien, D.J. Kotte, A. Marquez and J. Priewe (eds), *The Financial and Economic Crisis of 2008–2009 and Developing Countries*, UNCTAD and Hochschule Fur Technik und Wirtschaft, Berlin, 149–170.

James, W., D. Park, S. Jha, J. Jongwanich, A. Terada-Hagiwara and L. Sumulong (2008), 'The US financial crisis, global turmoil, and developing Asia: is the era of high growth at an end?', ADB Economics Working Paper Series No. 139, Asian Development Bank, Manila.

Kumar, R. and P. Vashisht (2012), 'The global economic crisis: impact on India and policy responses', in M. Kawai, M.B. Lamberte and Y.C. Park (eds), *The Global Financial Crisis and Asia: Implications and Challenges*, Oxford: Oxford University Press, 162–181.

Lee, H.A., R. Mat Zin and S. Abdul Rahman (2002), 'Malaysia', in Adam Erfried et al. (eds), *Social Protection in Southeast and East Asia*, Singapore: Friedrich Ebert Stiftung, 119–169.

Nambiar, S. (2003), 'Malaysia's response to the financial crisis: reconsidering the viability of unorthodox policy', *Asia-Pacific Development Journal*, 10 (1), June, 1–23.

Nambiar, S. (2009), 'Revisiting privatisation in Malaysia: the importance of institutional process', *Asian Academy of Management Journal*, 14 (2), 21–40.

Nambiar, S. (2012), 'Malaysia and the global crisis: impact, response, and rebalancing strategies', in M. Kawai, M.B. Lamberte and Y.C. Park (eds), *The Global Financial Crisis and Asia: Implications and Challenges*, Oxford: Oxford University Press, 218–246.

Naude, W. (2009), 'The financial crisis of 2008 and the developing countries', UNU Discussion Paper 2009/01, Helsinki: United Nations University.

Taylor, J.B. (2009), 'The financial crisis and the policy responses: an empirical analysis of what went wrong', *NBER Working Paper 14631*, Cambridge, MA: National Bureau of Economic Research.

Te Velde, D.W. (2008), 'The global financial crisis and the developing countries', ODI Background Note, London: Overseas Development Institute.

Yang, L. and C. Huizenga (2010), 'China's economy in the global economic crisis: impact and policy responses', in S. Dullien, D.J. Kotte, A. Marquez and J. Priewe (eds), *The Financial and Economic Crisis of 2008–2009 and Developing Countries*, UNCTAD and Hochschule Fur Technik und Wirtschaft, Berlin, 119–148.

Zhang, B. and Y. Yu (2012), 'The global financial crisis: impact on the economy, policy responses and rebalancing approach', in M. Kawai, M.B. Lamberte and Y.C. Park (eds), *The Global Financial Crisis and Asia: Implications and Challenges*, Oxford: Oxford University Press, 140–161.

8. The impacts of the global crisis on the Turkish economy, and policy responses[1]

Hasan Cömert and Mehmet Selman Çolak

8.1 INTRODUCTION

The liberalization of the domestic economy and the balance of payment transactions began after the 1980s in Turkey. Parallel to these liberalization attempts, the Turkish economy has had many fluctuations since the 1980s. The frequency and magnitude of the fluctuations in the Turkish real GDP growth have been higher relative to the previous period before the 1980s. The performance of the Turkish economy has become more and more dependent on the movements of international finance, as in the case of many developing countries. The periods of high financial inflows have coincided with high credit and high overall economic growth. Whenever the Turkish economy experienced reversals in its financial account, the credit boom and economic growth faded away. Indeed, since 1990 the Turkish economy has experienced four big crises (Figure 8.1) which were mainly related to reversals of financial flows.[2] The last crisis to hit the Turkish economy began in the third quarter of 2008 and inflicted a heavy toll on the economy until the last quarter of 2009. The crisis stemmed mainly from the shock waves of the global crisis that originated in the US.

This chapter focuses on the impacts of the recent global crisis on the Turkish economy and the policy measures taken in response to the crisis. The Turkish economy was adversely affected by the crisis through three main channels, namely the expectations, the trade and the finance channels. The distinctive characteristic of the crisis was a severe export shock, which can account for an important part of the decline in production in Turkey. Besides this, a sudden stop in financial flows worsened the credit conditions in the economy. As a result, the Turkish economy witnessed one of its worst economic downturns since the Second World War. In fact, the Turkish growth performance was one of the worst among developing countries. However, unlike previous crises, the financial markets in Turkey and many other developing countries did not experience a collapse. We argue that this is mainly related to the small magnitude and short duration of the financial shocks hitting Turkey and other developing countries relative to the ones in previous decades. In this sense, the Turkish economy might not have been fully tested during the last global crisis. How the economy will behave in the face of a larger financial shock is still unknown.

The outline of the chapter is as follows. Section 8.2, focusing on the period after the 1980s, gives a brief account of important macroeconomic developments in the Turkish economy. The channels through which the recent global crisis has hit the Turkish economy are also discussed. For the purpose of comparison, the cases of some other developing countries are also investigated in this section. Section 8.3 examines fiscal and monetary policies implemented by the government and the Turkish Central Bank in response to the crisis. Section 8.4 concludes.

8.2   THE TURKISH ECONOMY 1980 TO 2008[3]

As in the case of many developing countries, the growth rate of the Turkish economy slowed from an average of 5.2 percent in the period of 1961 to 1979, to 4.2 percent in the succeeding period (1980 to 2014). Furthermore, as an indication of a more erratic growth performance, the standard deviation of the growth increased from 3 percent to 4.4 percent after the 1980s. In this vein, as shown in Figure 8.1, the Turkish economy has experienced several crises since the 1980s. The first major crisis to hit the Turkish economy after the 1980s was the crisis of 1994. An unsustainable budget deficit with very high interest rates and very high inflation led to a sudden financial reversal resulting in the collapse of the lira. The contagion impacts of the Asian and the Russian crises of 1999 also affected the Turkish economy adversely. The devastating earthquake of August 1999 worsened the situation. As a result the Turkish GDP fell by 3.4 percent in that year.

The 1999 crisis pushed the Turkish coalition government into implementing a structural reform package under the auspices of the IMF. The program was mainly based on pegging Turkish currency to a basket of foreign currencies, which was supposed to curb very high inflation by reducing tradable goods prices. Although the exchange rate peg policy reduced the inflation rate from high to moderate, it also caused the over appreciation of the Turkish lira vis-à-vis foreign currencies, which contributed to the widening of the Turkish current account deficit. As a result of sudden reversals of financial flows, the pressure on the exchange rate increased significantly in the late 2000s and the beginning of 2001. The

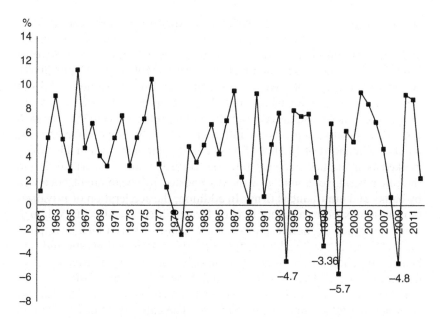

Source: World Development Indicators.

Figure 8.1   Turkish annual real GDP growth

Turkish Central Bank's foreign exchange rate interventions and high inter-est rate policy did not produce desired outcomes. After losing almost half of its reserves the bank had to leave the currency to float in February 2001. The balance sheets of the fragile banking system deteriorated due to high interest rates and a high rate of depreciation of the currency. Many banks went bankrupt and the Turkish economy experienced its worst downturn in its history since the Second World War.

After the crisis of 2001 a new program, again under the auspices of the IMF, was put into practice. This new program included many struc-tural changes in financial markets and the governance of the economy. Privatization attempts were accelerated, new financial regulatory bodies were introduced and some regulations in the banking sector were tight-ened. Significantly, the independence of the Central Bank was granted. After 2002, the Central Bank began implementing an implicit inflationary targeting regime, which became an explicit one in 2006. In this monetary policy regime, short term interest rates became the main policy instrument accompanied by a relatively flexible exchange rate system.[4]

In the international arena, the change in the institutional structure of advanced financial markets together with expansionary monetary policies led to an increase in the credit generation capacity of financial institutions and a decrease in interest rates. The higher interest rates redirected global funds to emerging market countries like Turkey (Mohan and Kapur, 2009). Along with the 'global great moderation', the Turkish economy did not experience a large financial account shock in the period 2002 to 2008. In fact, in the same period the economy benefited from financial flows through both their positive impacts on inflation and credit growth. On the one hand, the bonanza of financial flows caused an appreciation in TL, which worked as an implicit exchange rate peg (Benlialper and Cömert, 2013). On the other hand, economic growth was boosted by cheap credit borrowed by banks and nonfinancial firms. In addition, the acceleration of privatization programs led to a higher level of foreign direct investment. Although many important economic and social problems, such as a high unemployment rate, could not be addressed, as a result of positive domestic and very benign international conditions, the Turkish economy experienced its 'great moderation' from 2002 to 2008 with high growth and low inflation.

However, the global financial crisis ended this honeymoon. The Turkish economy fell into a significant recession. The capacity utilization rate in the manufacturing sector declined from 80 percent to about 60 percent.[5] Overall, Turkish economic growth significantly deteriorated and the economy experienced one of its worst recessions after the Second World War. As will be elaborated below, in line with deterioration in expectations, investment expenditures started to decline as early as the second quarter of 2008 (Table 8.1). Likewise, the fall in consumption expenditures began in the third quarter of 2008, and negative export growth was first observed in the third quarter in the same year. As a result of the massive decline in consumption, investments and exports, a steep decline in imports expenditures was experienced.[6]

The government expenditure figures demonstrate that the Turkish government was hesitant about its responses to the crisis. Overall, as will be discussed in the third section of this chapter, government expenditures were not used effectively to insulate the economy against the impacts of the global crisis.[7]

Although the crisis began in advanced economies, it quickly spread all over the world, causing negative GDP growth and significant increases in the unemployment rate in Turkey and in many other developing countries. Turkish GDP growth began to decline in the third quarter of 2008. The fall in GDP continued until the third quarter of 2009. The Turkish economy experienced 0.7 percent annual real GDP growth in 2008 and it shrank by −4.8 percent in 2009. Indeed, as the first chapter of this book on the worst affected developing countries demonstrates, the Turkish economic

Table 8.1 Growth of gross domestic products and its components (%)

	2008Q1	2008Q2	2008Q3	2008Q4	2009Q1	2009Q2	2009Q3	2009Q4	2010Q1
GDP	7.01	2.63	0.86	−6.97	−14.74	−7.77	−2.77	5.86	12.59
Consumption Expenditures Growth	5.72	0.62	−0.35	−6.67	−10.23	−1.75	−1.91	4.98	7.92
Share in GDP	71.6	68.8	65.7	69.9	75.3	73.3	66.3	69.3	72.2
Government Expenditure Growth	5.52	−3.44	2.65	2.83	5.26	−0.14	5.11	18.20	0.52
Share in GDP	9.1	9.9	9.0	12.7	11.2	10.7	9.7	14.2	10.0
Gross Fixed Capital Formation Growth	7.33	−2.04	−8.66	−18.75	−27.86	−24.46	−18.21	−4.23	17.21
Share in GDP	24.9	25.1	21.1	23.1	21.0	20.5	17.8	20.9	21.9
Change in Stocks Growth	−95.48	−140.88	18.73	149.50	1790.91	−517.15	1.76	−32.94	−94.85
Share in GDP	−0.1	0.7	5.3	−6.0	−9.2	−3.4	5.6	−3.8	−0.4

227

Table 8.1 (continued)

	2008Q1	2008Q2	2008Q3	2008Q4	2009Q1	2009Q2	2009Q3	2009Q4	2010Q1
Exports of Goods and Services Growth	12.95	4.26	3.85	**–8.16**	**–11.06**	**–10.78**	**–5.22**	7.24	–0.85
Share in GDP	25.5	25.5	**25.6**	**25.4**	**26.6**	**24.6**	**24.9**	25.8	23.4
Imports of Goods and Services Growth	14.03	2.01	**–3.84**	**–24.89**	**–30.99**	**–20.60**	**–11.66**	11.02	21.99
Share in GDP	30.9	29.9	**26.7**	**25.1**	**25.0**	**25.8**	**24.3**	26.3	27.1

Note: Growth rates represent percentage changes in real GDP relative to the same quarter in previous year. Share in GDP represents the percentage share of the level of each variable in GDP.

Source: CBRT.

228

performance was one of the worst in the world during this period. Apart from very small countries from the sample, the Turkish economic performance was only better than a few ex-Eastern Bloc countries and raw material exporters. The negative growth performance of the economy deteriorated the already weakened employment conditions further. In this sense, the unemployment rate rose to record levels of 15 percent in April 2009.

The global crisis has affected the Turkish economy through three main channels, namely the expectation, the trade and the finance channels. We will discuss each channel separately below.

8.2.1   Expectations Channel

In Turkey the initial impact of the crisis was felt as falls in consumption and investment spending due to the worsening expectations of investors and consumers. It is very difficult to measure the exact influence of the turmoil in the US financial markets on the expectations of Turkish investors and consumers. Although there are some problems with the existing data, the fact that the expectations quickly started to decline in Turkey just after the emergence of crisis in the US can be considered as an indicator (Figure 8.2). Negative developments in consumer confidence about the future of the economy adversely influenced consumption expenditures. In turn, total

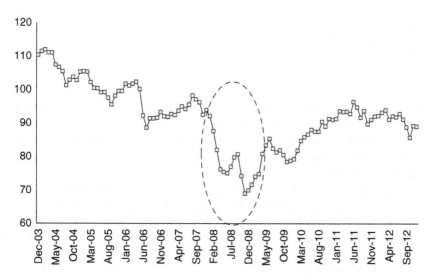

Source: CBRT.

Figure 8.2   Consumer confidence index (2005=100)

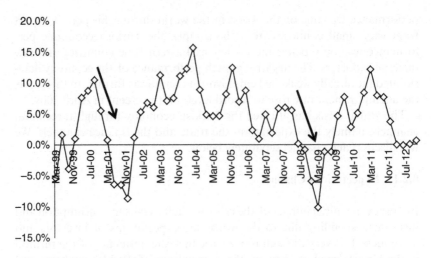

Note: This figure shows the percentage change in consumption expenditures relative to corresponding quarter of the previous year.

Source: CBRT.

Figure 8.3   Quarterly annual consumption expenditures (constant 1998 Prices)

consumption declined significantly (Figure 8.3). The dramatic decline in consumption was even larger than the decline during the 2001 crisis.

In addition to the consumers, the confidence of producers sharply deteriorated in response to the global developments. The real sector confidence index, which reflects the expectations of producers, had a declining trend from December 2007 to November 2008 and remained low for a while (Figure 8.4). Similar to the picture in consumer expectations, this development demonstrates that rising risks in the global markets seemed to influence producer expectations negatively before the crisis was fully felt in the Turkish economy.

As Figure 8.5 suggests, the negative growth in investments was maintained for seven consecutive quarters. This investment shock was as large as the shock during the 2001 crisis. This sizeable contraction in investment expenditures inevitably played a significant role in the recession of 2009 in Turkey.

8.2.2   Trade Channel

Another channel through which the Turkish economy was hit by the global crisis was exports. Even though the crises of 1994 and 2001 increased

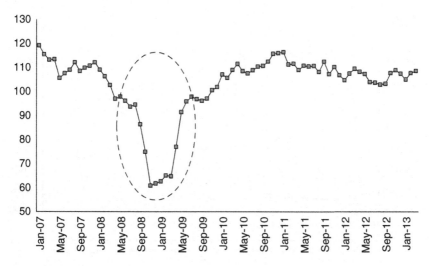

Source: CBRT.

Figure 8.4   Real sector confidence index (2010=100)

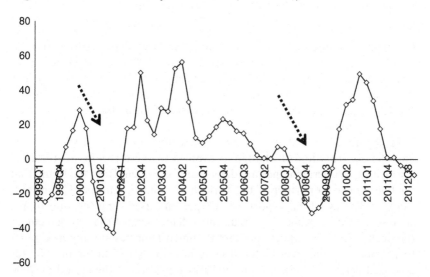

Note: This figure shows the percentage change in total investment expenditures relative to corresponding quarter of the previous year.

Source: CBRT.

Figure 8.5   Change in total fixed private investment spending (%, 1998 prices)

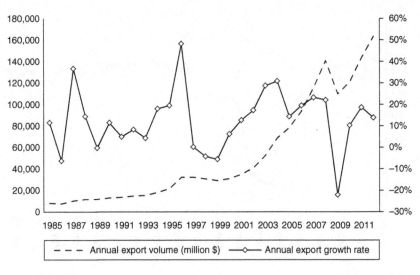

Source: IMF.

Figure 8.6   Export performance of the Turkish economy

the export volume of Turkey due mainly to large depreciations in TRY, we observed a substantial fall in export earnings during the global crisis. Export earnings halted by more than 20 percent in 2009 (Figure 8.6). The main reason for this shock was that the biggest export partner of Turkey, the EU, was in a deep crisis and the demand from the European area slowed significantly.

In Figure 8.7, the shares of different regions in total Turkish exports and the contribution of change in exports to these regions to the total Turkish export performance are depicted. It is evident from the figure that the biggest export partner of the Turkish economy is Europe. The average share in Turkey's total export was 63 percent, exceeding the sum of the shares of other regions. The figure also demonstrates that 70 percent of the decline in total exports in 2009 stemmed from the decline in exports to Europe. In other words, the decline in exports to Europe in 2009 far exceeded Europe's average share in Turkish exports in the period of 2006 to 2008. This was caused by the fact that although overall Turkish export growth decreased by 22 percent, Turkish exports to Europe declined by 26 percent.[8] The contribution of the fall in exports to the negative GDP growth of 2009 was around 25 percent. By analogy, the fall in exports to Europe directly explains about 20 percent of the recession in 2009.[9] Considering the contagion impact of export reduction to other items of

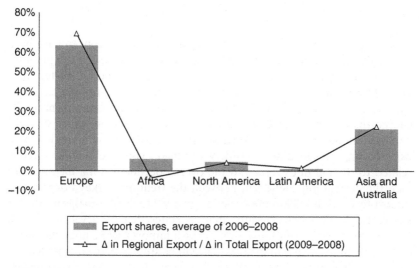

Source: Turkstat.

Figure 8.7   Turkish exports by regional classification

GDP (multiplier effect), the fall in exports, specifically to Europe, may account for a large part of the recession in 2009 in Turkey.

The literature tells us that the contagion effects of change in exports take place mainly via two channels. The first is the Keynesian multiplier mechanism. In developing countries, which, in general, have idle capital and high unemployment, export variations have a large impact on growth (Bilgin and Şahbaz, 2009). In other words, a reduction in exports may bring about a large GDP decline due to multiplier effects. The second important channel implies that developing economies are in need of imported intermediate goods for their production sector, and these developing economies often need export incomes in foreign currency in order to import these vital intermediate goods. Moreover, countries like Turkey are always in need of intermediate goods imports for their exports since their exports are mainly in the form of final goods. Hence, a fall in exports leads to a contraction in import demands. In some cases this would prevent developing countries from importing very crucial inter-mediate goods that would improve their production capacity. In Turkey's case, a third channel can be considered in relation to the second channel. Export oriented firms will have serious balance sheet problems when their foreign currency earnings decrease because many of these firms borrow heavily from the rest of the world. Therefore, an export shock can directly deteriorate the financial health of export oriented firms, bringing about lower investment levels.

During the global crisis, the first and third channels seem to have been especially influential in the Turkish case. As we presented in the previous section, the drop in consumption and investment spending started after 2008. During the slowdown, the export channel was as influential as the expectations channel. The 20 percent fall in export revenues naturally caused the income of investors and consumers to decline, which brought about a dramatic decline in Turkish GDP in 2009. In conjunction with exports, import spending in Turkey declined. This decline was directly related to the fall in exports and the overall decline in total income.[10] In fact, the correlation coefficient between the trend in Turkey's export and import revenues is 0.99 in the period from 1989 to 2012. Furthermore, our simple Engle–Granger causality analysis states that the level of Turkish exports has a significant impact on Turkish imports, while imports do not explain the movements in exports. The other studies that investigated the export GDP growth relation in Turkey show us there is a close relationship between growth and exports revenues.[11]

The trade channel was also effective in many other developing countries in the global crisis and the trend observed in their exports was similar to that of Turkish exports. Figure 8.8 demonstrates that, with the exception

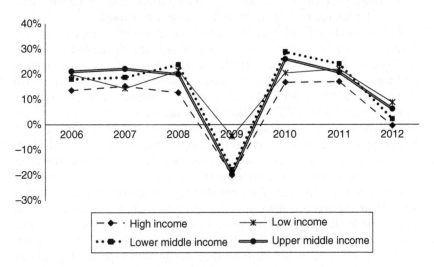

Source: IMF.

Figure 8.8   Change in exports in different income groups (% change, goods and services)

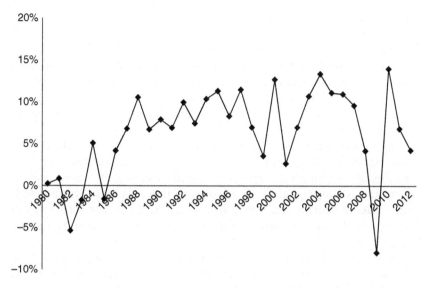

Source: IMF.

Figure 8.9 *Exports of goods and services (all developing countries, %*
change)

of the lowest income group countries, all other groups of countries experienced a fall in their export levels by more than 20 percent in 2009. The
drop in the export growth rates in these groups was as high as the drop of
exports in the north, which was at the center of the crisis.

The best way to interpret the magnitude of this decline properly is to
compare the level of this shock with the trade shocks observed in the past
crises on a global scale. It is obvious that the export shock in the recent
crisis was much greater than in past shocks (Figure 8.9). For example, a
similar export squeeze was observed in 1982 when the developed countries
experienced a slowdown; however, the magnitude of this export decline
was much lower than the one in 2009. Similarly, during the Asian financial
crisis, the export growth rate of developing countries declined but never
became negative. In this vein, the recent crisis should be treated as different
to the ones in the 1980s and 1990s, which were mainly triggered by financial reversals and brought about financial market collapses.

8.2.3 Financial Channel

Another channel through which the crisis spread into developing countries
is the financial channel. This channel works as the liquidity or exchange

rate shocks destabilizing financial markets. In general, the majority of developing countries including Turkey did not experience a financial system collapse in the recent crisis. Relative to the 1994 and 2001 crises, Turkey's financial system displayed a rapid recovery. While 18 banks were bankrupted in the crisis of 2001, not a single bank collapsed in the global crisis. Moreover, the profitability of the banking sector did not decline, and their capital to asset ratios further increased during the global crisis (Uygur, 2010).

The literature ties the resilience of the financial system of developing countries during the crisis to a lot of factors. Large accumulated reserves and flexible exchange rate regimes are the most significant factors according to the existing literature. In addition to these, financial stability policies, banking reforms and strong balance of payments are considered to be responsible for the better performance of developing countries in the recent crisis.

We believe that all the factors mentioned in the literature might have played some role in mitigating the impact of the crisis on developing countries. However, there is another important factor that has been mostly ignored by the literature. We believe that the Turkish financial system was not substantially tested by the global crisis. The shock that the Turkish economy was exposed to in the global crisis was actually smaller than the shocks observed in both the 1994 and 2001 crises. Similarly, as will be shown below, the magnitude of the financial shocks that the Turkish economy and the majority of developing countries faced in the recent crisis was much smaller than the shocks observed in previous developing country crises.

Financial shocks can basically be assessed by looking at the magnitude of sudden stops or capital reversals. As a first approximation, analyzing the trend in the net financial flows can provide us with very useful information about the magnitude of the shock a country encounters through its financial account.[12] According to Figure 8.10, net financial flows as a percentage of GDP were 7.2 percent in Turkey in 2007, and in the third quarter of 2008 it started to decline due to the turmoil in the financial markets in the US. In 2009 the net flows slowed significantly to 1.7 percent of GDP. This clearly indicates that the Turkish financial system faced an extensive sudden stop but not a reversal.

In terms of the financial shocks, the picture in Turkey during the global crisis was different from that of previous crises. In 2001 the net reversals of flows scaled by GDP were 7.5 percent, meaning that global funds left the Turkish economy in substantial amounts. Likewise, in 1994 the annual exit of funds was nearly 3 percent of GDP. All of this means that there were large financial account reversals during these two crises, which were

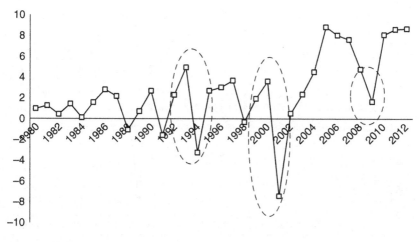

Source: CBRT.

Figure 8.10   Net financial flows to the Turkish economy, % of GDP

much harsher than the sudden stop observed during the global crisis. This can be verified by investigating the composition of net financial flows relative to GDP. As can be seen in Figure 8.11, although net portfolio flows became negative in 2008, the other flows and net foreign direct investment did not show any sign of reversal during this year. Furthermore, overall, all three types of financial flows were low but positive in 2009. This can be considered as a sudden stop rather than a reversal. The reversals would have qualitatively different implications than sudden stops, particularly in an emerging market country. Reversals put a great strain on the central bank reserves and foreign exchange markets. The need for foreign currency increases because of the existence of current account deficits. A massive financial reversal brings about a financial collapse by causing sudden depletion of foreign exchange reserves and unsustainable depreciations in the domestic currency that can weaken balance sheets of domestic agents. Although a sudden stop may also bring about similar problems, if the central bank reserves are not low enough to trigger a panic, most likely a sudden stop would bring about credit restraints rather than a financial collapse. Furthermore, the impacts of sudden stops or reversals do not only depend on the magnitude of the shocks but also their duration.

Quarterly net flows data can be used to explain both magnitude and duration of the shocks during different crises. Figure 8.12 shows the quarterly trend of net financial flows as a share of annual GDP in the corresponding quarter in the Turkish economy during the last three big crises.

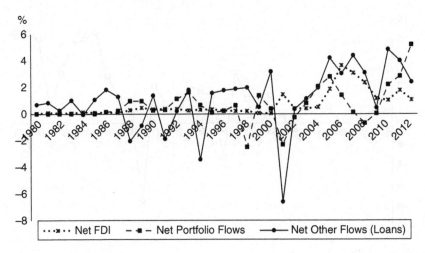

Source: CBRT, World Bank.

Figure 8.11   *Composition of capital flows to the Turkish economy, net (% of GDP)*

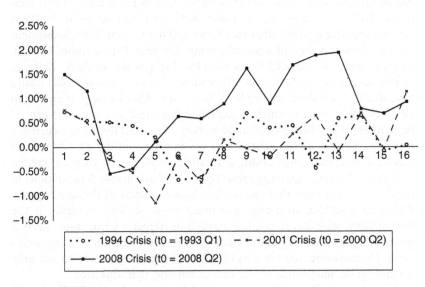

Source: CBRT.

Figure 8.12   *Quarterly net financial flows to the Turkish economy during crisis periods (% of GDP)*

It starts from the quarter when the share of flows initially began to decline. t0 shows the quarter just before the flows started to fall. In the 1994 crisis sudden stops first appeared in the first quarter of 1993, and reversals occurred during the following fifth and eighth quarters, which indicate that the financial shock was influential for 8 quarters. In the 2001 crisis, just after three quarters from t0, financial account reversals took place and lasted until the 10th quarter, meaning that the duration of the shock was 10 quarters. For the global crisis, in the third quarter of 2008, net flows started to decline, and after the third and the fourth quarters we observed a net reversal. Following the fifth quarter the share of net flows started to rise. This shows that the duration of the shock was about five quarters, which was much shorter than the other two crises. Even though the financial reversal in Turkey during the global crisis was two quarters long, as indicated above, annually there was not a financial reversal in 2009. In 2009 both the duration and magnitude of financial shocks in the global crisis were shorter and weaker than the other two earlier crises in Turkey.

The net flow, relative to total stock of foreign funds in an economy, is another indicator of the magnitude of the shocks the economy faced during crises.[13] This indicator shows the size of net financial flows relative to accumulated foreign liabilities. On an annual basis, large portions of foreign investment stock left the Turkish economy in the earlier crises, while during the global crisis foreign investment continued to flow in, albeit in small proportions. On a quarterly basis, the shock scaled by the total foreign liabilities in the global crisis was shorter in duration and smaller in magnitude compared to previous crises (Figure 8.13).

Since some of the pressure related to financial flows can be absorbed by exchange rate movements, exchange rates can also be utilized to examine the magnitude of pressure related to financial shocks. Figure 8.14 shows that the depreciation pressure was much milder during the global crisis than during previous crises. Here, it could be argued that reserve operations that mitigated exchange rate pressures might have decreased pressure in the Turkish financial markets. In Table 8.2 we give the ratio of quarterly net financial flows in quarter *t* to the existing international reserves amounts in the quarter *t2*. The shaded areas in the table depict that the pressure on central bank reserves in the last crisis was shorter and the magnitude of the pressure was lower. In other words, the reserve depletion during the global crisis was also less severe than the depletion during previous crises.[14] In the third quarter of 2008 the reserves of the central bank amounted to $76 billion and reached their lowest value of $63 billion in 2009. The reserve loss was 17 percent of total reserves. Nevertheless, reserve depletion in the 2001 crisis was 36 percent, and in 1994 it was more than 50 percent.

Similar to the case of Turkey, developing countries in general did

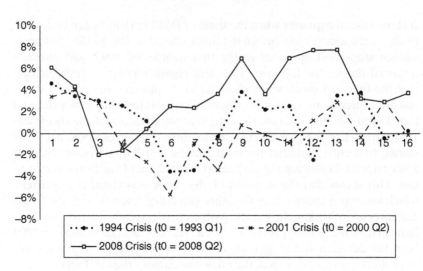

Source: CBRT.

Figure 8.13   *Quarterly net financial flows to the Turkish economy during crisis periods (% of total foreign liabilities)*

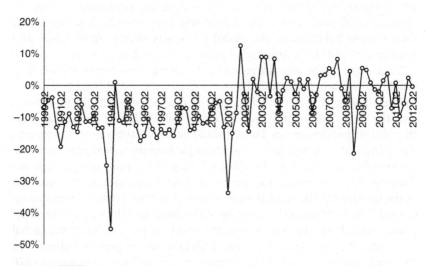

Source: CBRT.

Figure 8.14   *Quarterly change in the value of TL against USD (%)*

Table 8.2   Net flows at time t / foreign reserves at t2

t	Net financial flows / reserves		
	1994 Crisis (t0=1993 Q1)	2001 Crisis (t0=2000 Q2)	2008 Crisis (t0=2008 Q2)
0	50%	19%	22%
1	36%	13%	17%
2	29%	−6%	−7%
3	27%	−13%	−5%
4	12%	−29%	2%
5	−40%	−6%	10%
6	−73%	−23%	10%
7	−5%	5%	14%
8	42%	−1%	26%
9	24%	−5%	15%
10	17%	7%	29%
11	−14%	15%	30%

Source: Authors' calculations based on CBRT data.

not experience a destructive financial account shock in the global crisis (Cömert and Çolak, 2013 and 2014). For example, if we compare the magnitude of the financial shock in the recent crisis with the 1998 Asian crisis, the shock to net financial account was shorter and smaller during the global crisis compared to the Asian crisis. The comparison between the magnitudes of the Latin American crisis in the 1980s and the recent global crisis yields more striking results.[15] The net private flows amounted to 3 percent of GDP in all developing countries in 1981. Starting from the debt crisis in 1982, net private flows began to fall. And for three years we observe negative net private flows, indicating that private investors left these economies in the middle of the 80s. This shock is clearly much larger than the shock that occurred in 2008. Overall, all indicators demonstrate developing countries in general and not just Turkey experienced a relatively milder shock during the recent crisis.

Among other reasons, such as the contribution of some policy reforms put into practice in the previous period, there are three distinct reasons behind the mild shocks the Turkish economy experienced in the recent crisis. First, financial markets in developed countries could not fully serve their safe haven roles in the recent crisis as they did in the crisis in emerging markets in the 1980s and the 1990s. Second, the massive quantitative easing accompanied by very low interest rates in developed countries rapidly rejuvenated financial flows to developing countries. Third, given the turmoil in the US and prolonged instability in the euro area, developing countries enjoyed greater legitimacy and autonomy in implementing expansionary monetary and fiscal policies, which partially offset the inadequate aggregate demand problems in developing countries for a while.[16]

8.3 POLICY RESPONSES TO THE CRISIS

The authorities adopted a wide range of policy measures in order to mitigate the impact of the financial crisis, despite criticisms that they were too late to respond. These measures might be grouped into three categories: fiscal policy measures, monetary responses and financial sector measures. Initially, starting from the beginning of 2008, monetary measures were adopted. Later, in March 2009, the first fiscal package was introduced. Additionally, the Banking Regulation and Supervision Agency (BRSA), in coordination with the Central Bank, implemented several measures in order to control the possible risks that might have occurred in the banking sector during the crisis. We will not go into every detail of these policies here, but we will broadly explain them.

8.3.1 Fiscal Policies

Fiscal responses to the crisis came with the announcement of the first comprehensive fiscal measure package in March 2009, when the crisis had already taken hold in Turkey (Uygur, 2010).[17] Table 8.3 depicts the types of fiscal measures, their targets and general characteristics. Fiscal measures were taken in large part to recover main macroeconomic fundamentals (Table 8.3). In general, changes in tax regulations and tax reductions were aimed at lowering the tax burden on consumers and firms, and at stimulating consumption and investment.[18] By offering incentives specifically for firms, the government attempted to cushion the revenue losses of firms resulting from the export squeeze and financing constraints that prevailed. The government tried to directly create employment opportunities through various expenditure programs to address sharp increases in unemployment. And, as stated earlier, the sudden stop in capital inflows resulted in credit shortages and financing issues for investment projects. In order to tackle this challenge, the government enacted several policies to keep global savings in Turkey and called for residents' investments abroad.

Compared to advanced countries and many other emerging market countries, the Turkish government was slow and reluctant in its fiscal response to the crisis. For example, while the advanced countries decided to implement huge stimulation packages in the second quarter of 2008, the first directly significant fiscal measures to be adopted by the Turkish

Table 8.3   Fiscal policy responses

Types of Fiscal Measures	Characteristics	Target
Tax Policies	• VAT and Special Consumption Tax reductions • Cuts in corporate tax rates varying to the regions and sectors	Encouraging consumption and investment
Private sector incentives	• Interest rate subsidies • The payment of employers' share in employees' social security payments by Treasury	Protecting firms against bankruptcy and promoting them to invest
Employment support	• Exemptions in the social security payments of workers • Employing part-time workers whose allowances were paid by Turkish Employment Organization • Hiring nearly 200,000 people as temporary workers or interns in public sector	To counteract against rising unemployment and its social costs
Access to global capital	• Tax amnesty for all unrecorded assets if they are declared • Tax relief on credits obtained from foreign sources • Tax exemptions on foreign assets held by residents provided that these assets were transferred to Turkey	Softening the impact of sudden stops in capital account

Source: Authors' compilation based on various reports.

government only took place in the first quarter of 2009, when the crisis had already affected the Turkish economy. Figure 8.15 depicts the year on year change in quarterly noninterest government expenditure from the same quarter of the previous year.[19] The beginning of the subprime mortgage crisis is dated back to the third quarter of 2007 and the slowdown in economic activity in Turkey started in the second quarter of 2008 with a GDP growth rate decreased from about 7 percent to 2.7 percent. In the subsequent quarters up to the fourth quarter of 2009, GDP growth remained negative in Turkey (Table 8.1). Nevertheless, despite low growth, the Turkish government remained inactive and the scale of government spending was unchanged. The year on year growth rate of quarterly

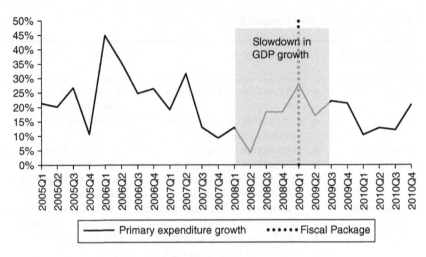

Source: Undersecretariat of Treasury (2014).

Figure 8.15   Quarterly government primary expenditures (growth rate from the same quarter in previous year)

primary expenditure plummeted until the third quarter of 2008, with the first substantial increase in the expenditure growth rate being observed in the first quarter of 2009 (Figure 8.15). With the comprehensive stimulus package in the first quarter of 2009, primary government expenditures were increased by nearly 15 percent. Taking the implementation and response lags of these stimulus measures into account, the fiscal response of government spending seems to be quite delayed in Turkey.

Several reports by the OECD and the IMF reveal that Turkey was among the slowest respondents in terms of fiscal stimulus compared to other countries. Besides the delayed response, the costs of adopted fiscal measures as a ratio of GDP were among the lowest considering other advanced and developing economies. An OECD report (2009) identifies Turkey and Greece as the only two OECD economies having no fiscal stimulus package until March 2009. An IMF report (2009) on G20 economies' fiscal measures in the crisis demonstrates that, while the average cost of fiscal measures already amounted to 0.5 percent of G20 GDP, Turkey did not announce any measure in 2008. And the costs of discretionary fiscal measures enacted in 2009 in Turkey were among the lowest in G20 economies and far below the G20 emerging markets average[20] (IMF, 2010). In Turkey, the average annual growth rate of the real government primary expenditures during the crisis (2008 to 2010) was also significantly below the same ratio in the

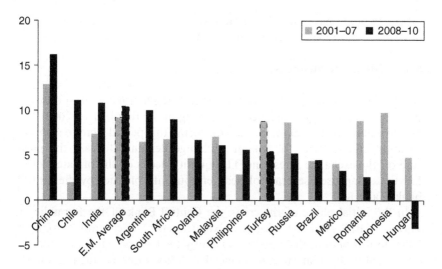

Note: The numbers in the figure were collected from the report, 'From stimulus to consolidation: revenue and expenditure policies in advanced and emerging economies' prepared by the IMF (2010).

Source: IMF (2010).

Figure 8.16   *Primary government expenditures in selected countries (% average annual real growth)*

2001 to 2007 period. Figure 8.16 demonstrates the averages of annual real growth rates of primary spending in 2001 to 2007 and 2008 to 2010 periods in several emerging markets. In many emerging markets, as expected, this growth rate was larger in the crisis years than the prior to crisis average. However, in Turkey this ratio declined unexpectedly from 8.8 percent in 2001 to 2007, to 5.4 percent in 2008 to 2010. Besides, the primary government expenditure growth in Turkey was significantly lower than the emerging market average of 9.2 percent during the crisis years.

Overall, the fiscal response to the global crisis was relatively weaker and delayed in Turkey compared to many other countries. This resulted in a rise in general government budget deficit by 4.2 percent of GDP, which was smaller than that of the OECD average of 6.3 percent (Rawdanowicz, 2010).[21] Those countries that were unwilling to use active fiscal measures and/or did not have enough fiscal space witnessed deeper declines in their GDP. Turkey can be considered as one of them. In the Turkish case, although the government had enough fiscal space for an expansionary policy, its reluctance in conducting expansionary fiscal measures might have played an important role in the severity of the crisis in terms of both magnitude and duration.

8.3.2 Monetary Measures

As in the case of many other countries, the Turkish monetary responses to the crisis preceded the fiscal actions starting in the first half of 2008. The primary objectives of monetary policy during this period were to stabilize inflation and to meet the foreign exchange demand (to ease the pressure on the exchange rates) and TL liquidity needs of the private sector. For these purposes, several policies were put into practice by the central bank (Table 8.4).

In the initial phase of the crisis, the Central Bank of the Republic of Turkey (CBRT) did not adopt an expansionary stance until November 2008. In this period, the measures taken by the Central Bank were mostly concerned with inflation and financial stability without much emphasis on growth and unemployment issues. When financial systems in advanced countries started to give very bad signals at the end of 2007, it was apparent that both a plunge in aggregate demand and recession were looming for advanced countries. Hence these countries significantly cut their policy rates. However, the CBRT took a tightening stance in this period and did not cut its rates. Indeed, it even increased the policy rates further in the second quarter of 2008 (Figure 8.17). According to the authorities, the reason behind this stance was a higher level of exchange rate pass through, a low output gap and a resulting rise in inflation expectations.[22]

As Figure 8.17 demonstrates, after the onset of the crisis in the US there was a rising tendency in CPI inflation. Nevertheless, when the inflation pressure abated in the last quarter of 2008, the CBRT started to take an expansionary stance. As the former president of the bank, Durmuş Yılmaz (2009), stated in a speech:

> the rather low exchange rate pass through under deficient domestic and foreign demand conditions coupled with the tightness of financing conditions for the corporate sector, the downward trend in import prices, accompanied by improving inflation expectations not only necessitated, but also made possible, a 'controlled but rather rapid rate cut cycle'.

Hence, as inflation was no longer a concern due to slowing aggregate demand, monetary policy was relaxed significantly with a cutting of policy rates by 10.5 basis points in the 11 months from November 2008. Figure 8.17 shows that the policy rate cuts after November 2008 perfectly coincide with the falling inflation rates.

The expansionary stance of the Central Bank is evidenced by its liquidity

Table 8.4   Monetary policy responses

Types of Monetary Measures	Characteristics	Targets
Interest rate adjustments	• Policy rates were increased from first half of 2007 till July 2008 to stabilize rising inflation • The rates sharply declined by 11 times after November 2008 from 16.75 percent to 7.25 percent till September 2009	To meet the inflation target, spur domestic demand and meet the liquidity needs of private sector.
FX interventions	• FX purchase auctions nearly stopped in the second half of 2008 • FX selling auctions took place 20 times from late 2008 till mid-2009 • The maturity of FX lending to banks was extended from one week to three months • The interest rate on FX lending was significantly reduced • The FX required reserve ratio was reduced from 11 percent to 9 percent	To meet the FX demand of private sector and lessen the volatility in the exchange rate.
Other liquidity policies	• Liquidity started to be provided via 1-week repo auctions • Interest payments on TL required reserves were increased • Export rediscount credits were issued to more exporting firms • The upper limit of export rediscount credits was increased from $500 million to $2.5 billion • TL required reserve ratio dropped	To ease the conditions of banks and firms in reaching liquidity.

Source: Authors' compilation based on various reports.

and FX market interventions (see Table 8.4). The Central Bank even added new policy instruments to its arsenal. The CBRT stopped FX buying auctions in late 2008 and started to use its FX reserves in auctions and through direct FX interventions until the second half of 2009 (Figure 8.18). Nearly

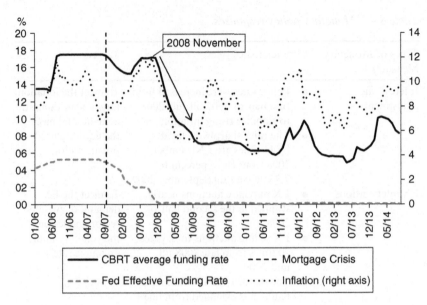

Source: CBRT and FED.

Figure 8.17   CBRT, Fed average funding rates (%) and Turkish inflation (%)

Source: CBRT.

Figure 8.18   CBRT FX reserves, million $

Table 8.5   Measures related to the banking sector

Types of Financial Sector Measures	Characteristics	Targets
Banking Sector Liquidity	• Provision rules loosened • Adjustments made in the liquidity adequacy ratio	To mitigate the impacts of liquidity tightness in global economy on Turkish banking sector
Banking Sector Capital Adequacy	• Restrictions on profit distribution of banks • Risk weights of credit card credits were raised	To strengthen the capital structure of Turkish banks
Debt Relief	• The records of bad cheques, protested bills and dead loans by legal entities and households erased provided that they are paid in six months • Debts of credit card holders rescheduled	To eliminate the systemic risk that may arise from the liquidity problem in real sector

Source: Authors' compilation based on various reports.

US$15 billion worth of reserves were sold in this period. In addition to FX interventions, the monetary authorities lowered the FX reserve requirement ratio and extended the maturity of FX lending. Furthermore, some policies aiming at helping institutions reach TRY liquidity were put into practice. The amount of export rediscount credits widened, the TRY reserve requirement ratio was lowered and interest paid for required reserves increased.

After the initial shock of the crisis, advanced countries began implementing extreme monetary easing with efforts to recapitalize their financial markets. This led to cross border short term liquidity bonanzas for emerging market countries. The illiquidity problem in the early phase of the crisis was replaced by short term volatile capital flows. Considering the threat of short term volatile cross border flows, the Turkish monetary authorities started implementing a nonconventional monetary policy in 2009. In addition to the conventional inflation targeting regime, the CBRT targeted financial stability as another objective and utilized nonconventional policy instruments with a particular emphasis on credit expansion and exchange rate volatility (Kara, 2012). Several macro prudential measures have been taken since then.[23]

8.3.3   Financial Sector Measures

Besides fiscal and monetary authorities, the BRSA adopted measures specifically geared toward financial sector stability and the health of bank balance sheets (Table 8.5). In order to tighten liquidity conditions, some balance sheet adjustments were made. In particular, the amount of provisions set aside for loans was reduced and the calculation of liquidity adequacy ratio was adjusted downward. In order to strengthen the capital structure of the banking sector, profit distributions to shareholders were limited and only allowed under the control of the BRSA. To decrease the amount of risky assets, the risk weights on credit card usage were raised. Furthermore, in coordination with the Central Bank, a wide range of debt relief regulations were put into practice.

8.4   CONCLUSION

The financial systems in Turkey and in many developing countries were stable in the 2000s. They were not hit by destructive financial crises as in the 1980s and the 1990s. As explained in Chapter 1, even though domestic factors might have played a role in this stability, external factors and policies in the North would account for much of the success in developing countries in the 2000s. The recent crisis ended this honeymoon. It has inflicted a heavy toll on Turkey and many other developing cou
ntries through different channels, namely the expectation, trade and financial channels. Although there are many similarities between the recent crisis and the crises after the 1980s (the crisis of 1994 and the crisis of 2001) with regard to the Turkish economy, there are some important differences as well. First, unlike the 2007/2008 crisis, the large decline in the demand for Turkish goods amid a considerable depreciation of the TRY never occurred in the previous crises. In this sense, the Turkish economy was mostly affected by very large exports shocks. Second, unlike previous crises, there was no significant financial reversal during the last crisis. In this sense, the financial shocks hitting the economy in the recent crisis were very small in magnitude and short in duration relative to the shocks in earlier crises. As a result, the Turkish financial system proved to be very resilient and GDP growth did not decline as much as in the case of 2001. However the financial markets in Turkey might not have been tested enough during the last crisis. It is very difficult to know how the Turkish economy would behave under a severe financial reversal.

NOTES

1. This research is conducted as a part of the FESSUD project. We are grateful to the comments of FESSUD-Turkish team members, especially Oktar Türel, Ebru Voyvoda and Gökçer Özgür, on the previous version of this chapter.
2. The years of the crises are determined by annual negative real GDP growth rates.
3. Here, we briefly summarize important developments in the Turkish economy after the 1980s especially by focusing on the crises hitting the economy. For a comprehensive discussion on the evolution of several macroeconomic developments in Turkey after the 1980s, see FESSUD report called 'Perspective on Financial System in the EU: Country Report on Turkey'. Here, we will briefly summarize important developments in the Turkish economy especially, by focusing on the crises hitting the economy.
4. The Turkish Central Bank has frequently intervened in foreign exchange markets. Indeed, as pointed out in the next subsections, the Central Bank seems to have tolerated the appreciation of the currency whereas it tried to decrease the amount of depreciation in order to use the exchange rate as an implicit anchor during this period.
5. Although the quarterly capacity utilization in the manufacturing sector data set shows some seasonality, it does not affect the overall conclusion much.
6. As discussed in the text, the decline in exports also brought about a decline in imports due to reliance on imports goods in order to produce exports goods.
7. For example, while the advanced countries decided to implement huge stimulation packages in the second quarter of 2008, the Turkish government cut its expenditures by about 3.5 percent.
8. There was an increase in exports to African countries in 2009. This is an indication that the Turkish economy tried to widen its export market in order to compensate for its loss through the falling demand from Europe. However, in general, there was also a significant reduction in exports to all other regions.
9. Considering the −4.5 percent real GDP growth rate at the time, the depression in Europe cost Turkey nearly 0.9 percent of its GDP.
10. Historically, a reduction in Turkish GDP often coincides with an improvement in its current account.
11. For instance, Karahasan (2009) analyzes the causality between exports and GDP growth in Turkey for the years 1950 to 2008 and concludes that there is bidirectional causality between them. The causality analyses conducted by Halıcıoğlu (2007) for the years 1980 to 2005 and Bilgin and Şahbaz (2009) for the years 1987 to 2007 conclude that changes in exports have a unidirectional impact on industrial production and GDP growth.
12. There are different approaches about which indicator would best describe the impact of financial flows on economies. Borio and Disyatat (2011) argue that gross flows are much more important indicators for this purpose. However, as Cömert and Düzçay (2014) argue, although gross flows would be a much more meaningful indicator for developed countries, net flows are still crucial to understand the pressure on exchange rates which are the most important factors for asset prices and reserves in developing countries. Moreover, the difference between net flows and gross flows are not very significant in many developing countries. Therefore, we will focus on net financial flows in our discussion on developing countries whereas gross flows will be emphasized more in our discussion on the advanced economies. The trends in gross and net private flows will be discussed in some cases for the purpose of highlighting different risk perceptions of private players in different periods.
13. Total stock of foreign funds is the existing foreign investment in Turkish assets in a given quarter. It is represented by the foreign liabilities in the international investment position data.
14. By depletion, we mean the reserve loss occurred from the beginning of the crisis until the reserves reached minimum levels in the crisis period. It is the difference between maximum amounts and minimum amounts of reserves achieved in the course of a crisis.
15. Due to data constraints, this comparison is made through the net private financial flows.

16. The details of this discussion can be found in Cömert and Çolak (2013) and Cömert and Çolak (2014).
17. Many blamed the government for being very late in comprehending the severity of the crisis and in its response to the crisis (Uygur, 2010; Öniş and Güven, 2011).
18. Besides expanding expenditures, Turkish government enacted several tax reforms as demonstrated in Table 8.3 above. These reforms resulted in a decline in the growth rate of tax revenues in 2009 compared to 2008. However, despite a decline in growth rate, tax revenues continued increasing in 2009 by 3 percent. Considering the income effect of falling GDP in 2009 by 4.9 percent, the Turkish government did not seem to face a tax income shock in the recent global crisis.
19. Real primary expenditure is calculated as the nominal expenditure over CPI taking 2003 as the base year. Since there is a high seasonality in government expenditures, the growth rate was calculated not from the previous quarter but the same quarter of the previous year in order to deal with the seasonality problem. Government spending usually tends to increase as the year ends.
20. The emerging markets in the G20 group on average spent 2.4 percent of their GDP on fiscal measures in 2009, and Turkey's fiscal spending amounted to only 1.2 percent of GDP.
21. This might be explained by the fact that the Turkish government did not need to bail its financial market out as in the case of 2001 crisis, because Turkey did not experience a financial collapse in the global crisis as presented in detail in the sections above. Another factor might be that the government size became significantly smaller after the huge privatization efforts in the 2004 to 2006 period.
22. Furthermore, the confidence of the Turkish government that the Turkish economy was strong enough to alleviate the crisis might have caused the CBRT to wait longer for policy rate cuts.
23. Since the policy shift in central banking is a significant issue all by itself, we will not go into detail about the new monetary framework in this chapter.

REFERENCES

Benlialper, A. and H. Cömert (2013), 'Implicit asymmetric exchange rate peg under inflation targeting regimes: the case of Turkey' (No. wp333), ERC-Economic Research Center, Middle East Technical University.

Bilgin, C. and A. Şahbaz (2009), 'Causality relations between growth and export in Turkey', *Gaziantep University Journal of Social Sciences*, 8 (1), 177–197.

Borio, Claudio, and Piti Disyatat (2011), 'Global imbalances and the financial crisis: link or no link?' (No. 346), Bank for International Settlements.

CBRT (2014), 'Markets data', retrieved on March 4, 2015 from www.tcmb.gov.tr/.

Cömert, H. and S. Çolak (2013), 'Gelişmekte Olan Ülkelerdeki Kriz Sırası ve Sonrasındaki Trendleri Açıklamakta "Güvenli Liman Faktörü" ve Finansal Şokların Boyutunun Önemi: Türkiye Örneği' (No. 2013/10), ERC-Economic Research Center, Middle East Technical University.

Cömert, H. and S. Çolak (2014), *Can Financial Stability be Maintained in Developing Countries after the Global Crisis: The Role of External Financial Shocks?* (No. 1411), ERC-Economic Research Center, Middle East Technical University.

Cömert, H. and Düzçay. U. (2014), 'Küresel Dengesizlikler ve Kriz Tartışması Işığında Cari Hesapları Yorumlamak' (No. 2014/16), ERC-Economic Research Center, Middle East Technical University.

FED (2014), *Federal Funds Data*, retrieved on March 4, 2016 from www.newyork fed.org/.

Halıcıoglu, F. (2007), 'A multivariate causality analysis of export and growth for Turkey', *Munich Personal RePEc Archive*. No. 3565.

IMF (2009), *The State of Public Finances: Outlook and Medium-Term Policies After the 2008 Crisis*. Washington, DC: IMF.

IMF (2010), *From Stimulus to Consolidation: Revenue and Expenditure Policies in Advanced and Emerging Economies*, Washington, DC: IMF.

Kara, H. (2012), 'Monetary policy in Turkey after the global crisis', CBRT Working Paper, No. 12/17.

Karahasan, B.C. (2009), 'Financial liberalization and regional impacts on entrepreneurial behavior in Turkey', *Munich Personal RePEc Archive*, No. 29814.

Mohan, R. and M. Kapur (2009), *Liberalisation and Regulation of Capital Flows: Lessons for Emerging Market Economies*, Stanford, CA: Center for International Development, Stanford University.

OECD (2009), *Fiscal Packages across OECD Countries: Overview and Country Details*. Paris: OECD.

Öniş, Z. and A.B. Güven (2011), 'Global crisis, national responses: the political economy of Turkish exceptionalism', *New Political Economy*, 16 (5), 585–608.

Rawdanowicz, Ł. (2010), 'The 2008–09 crisis in Turkey: performance, policy responses and challenges for sustaining the recovery' (No. 819), OECD Publishing.

Undersecretariat of Treasury (2014), Public finance statistics, retrieved on March 4, 2016 from http://www.treasury.gov.tr.

Uygur, Ercan (2010), *The Global Crisis and the Turkish Economy*, Third World Network (TWN).

World Bank (2013), 'World Development Indicators', retrieved on March 4, 2016 from http://data.worldbank.org/data-catalog/world-development-indicators.

Yılmaz, Durmuş (2009), *Global Crisis, Effects and Monetary Policy*, Istanbul: Boğaziçi University.

Index